A BOOK OF HAPPINESS

A

Book

of

Happiness

Compiled by Gilbert Harding

London
MICHAEL JOSEPH

First published by
MICHAEL JOSEPH LTD
*26 Bloomsbury Street
London, W.C.1*
1959

© *copyright* 1959 *by Gilbert Harding*

*Set and printed in Great Britain by Unwin Brothers
Limited at the Gresham Press, Woking, in Imprint type,
eleven point, leaded, on paper made by Henry Bruce at
Currie, Midlothian, and bound by James Burn at Esher*

O Happiness! our being's end and aim!
Good, pleasure, ease, content! whate'er thy name:
That something still which prompts the eternal sigh,
For which we bear to live, or dare to die,
Which still so near us, yet beyond us lies,
O'erlook'd, seen double, by the fool, and wise.
Plant of celestial seed! if dropp'd below,
Say, in what mortal soil thou deign'st to grow?
Fair opening to some court's propitious shrine,
Or deep with diamonds in the flaming mine?
Twined with the wreaths Parnassian laurels yield,
Or reap'd in iron harvests of the field?
Where grows?—where grows it not? If vain our toil,
We ought to blame the culture, not the soil:
Fix'd to no spot is happiness sincere,
'Tis no where to be found, or every where:
'Tis never to be bought, but always free,
And fled from monarchs, St. John! dwells with thee.

ALEXANDER POPE
From *An Essay on Man*

INTRODUCTION

This is a book of many happinesses, because happiness has many moods. The poets have revealed for us the happiness of remembrance of things past, and the happiness of future delights; and of grasping and clasping the day. They have shown us how to be happy in many ways: in freedom and service, in enjoyment of nature and art, in going out and staying at home, doing something and doing nothing, in great occasions and simple things. Happiness is fun and friendship, merry-making and mirth; it is also compassion, and victory over adversity. Happiness can be ecstatic or poignant, spiritual or sensuous, light-hearted or passionate. It is the love of man, and the knowledge and love of God.

Happiness is all round us if only we can see it, but unfortunately most of us either cannot or will not look hard enough; so it is fortunate that there have always been a few persons who not only looked and saw, but found their own greatest happiness in passing their visions on to us. Hence Shakespeare's delight in the last two lines of his loveliest and happiest sonnet:

> So long as men can breathe, or eyes can see,
> So long lives this, and this gives life to thee.

As a little boy I was often unhappy and nearly always without reason or excuse. My paternal grandfather used to tell me that happiness is what you make it, and my invariable reply was that I needed help—nearly always of some material kind. Many years later, after an unhappy love affair, I was given a 'slim volume' called *The Book of Sorrow*. Ever since then I have thought that there should be a book of happiness but I have had to reach late middle-age for the chance to present it.

7

Happiness is for everyone but the great difficulty in achieving and understanding it lies in the fact that the word means so many things to so many different people. It was Herodotus who said 'Call no man happy 'til he is dead.' That I do not believe, but one sure thing that I have learnt is that the deliberate pursuit of happiness for its own sake and for one's own self is bound to fail. The smile of happiness is more often seen on the face of another than in the looking-glass. It is so elusive. The more urgently we chase it, the quicker it runs away and it is hard to say which is the more disappointing—the failure to catch it up or, when we have it, to find out how different it is from what we had hoped and expected.

Do any of us deserve it? And, what is so much more important, what have we done to earn it?

This book can offer no material aid to happiness. It isn't a memorable meal of exquisite flavours: it isn't a bottle of fine wine or a scented garden on a summer night. But it is a kind of treasury on which you can often draw without fear of overdraft and perhaps with a little happiness from time to time. That is its only purpose—and I can think of no better.

GILBERT HARDING

ACKNOWLEDGEMENTS

Acknowledgement is gratefully made for permission to include the following works or extracts from them:

Adam, Karl: *The Spirit of Catholicism* (Sheed & Ward Ltd.). Barrie, J. M.: *The Admirable Crichton* (Hodder & Stoughton Ltd.). Belloc, Hilaire: *The Winged Horse* and *West Sussex Drinking Song* (from *Sonnets and Verse*, published by Gerald Duckworth & Co. Ltd.). *The Yak* (from *The Bad Child's Book of Beasts*, published by Gerald Duckworth & Co. Ltd.). Betjeman, John: *In the Licorice Fields at Pontefract* (from *Collected Poems*, published by John Murray Publishers Ltd.). Blunden, Edmund: *The Survival*. Bridges, Robert: *I love all beauteous things* and *The Downs* (from *The Shorter Poems of Robert Bridges*, by permission of The Clarendon Press, Oxford). *Nightingales* (The Clarendon Press, Oxford). Brooke, Rupert: *The Great Lover* (from *The Collected Poems*, published by Sidgwick & Jackson Ltd.). Campbell, Roy: *Choosing a Mast* (from *Collected Poems*, Volume I, published by The Bodley Head). *Horses on the Camargue*. Chesterton, G. K.: *The Donkey* (from *The Wild Knight and Other Poems*, published by J. M. Dent & Sons Ltd.). *Wine and Water* (from *Collected Poems*, by permission of Miss Collins and Methuen & Co. Ltd.). Cripps, A. S.: *The Death of St. Francis* (published by George Allen & Unwin Ltd.). Curtis, Basil; Bader, Douglas; Morena, Frederic: *Conquest of Disability* (published by Odhams Press Ltd.). Davies, W. H.: *Leisure* (from *The Collected Poems of W. H. Davies*, by permission of Mrs. H. M. Davies and Jonathan Cape Ltd.). Dobson, Austin: *Fame is a food that dead men eat* (Oxford University Press). Eliot, T. S.: *Journey of the Magi* (Faber and Faber Ltd.). Fraser, Lord: *Whereas I was Blind* (Hodder & Stoughton Ltd.). Graves,

9

Robert: *Quayside* and *Flying Crooked* (from *Collected Poems 1959*, by permission of Mr. Robert Graves). Hallack, Cecily R.: *The Divine Office of the Kitchen* (by permission of Mrs. J. Anne Vennor Bright). Hardy, Thomas: *The Darkling Thrush* and *The Oxen* (from *Collected Poems*, published by Macmillan & Co. Ltd., by permission of the Trustees of the Hardy Estate and the publishers). Herbert, A. P.: *Let's Stop Somebody From Doing Something* and *Start Her on Champagne, Boy* (both from *A Book of Ballads*, published by Ernest Benn Ltd., by permission of the Author, the Proprietors of *Punch* and Messrs. Ernest Benn Ltd.). Housman, A. E.: *Loveliest of Trees* (permission granted by The Society of Authors as the literary representative of the Trustees of the Estate of the late A. E. Housman, and Messrs. Jonathan Cape, Ltd., publishers of A. E. Housman's *Collected Poems*). Keller, Helen: *The World I Live In* (published by Hodder & Stoughton Ltd.). Lawrence, D. H.: *Don'ts* (The Estate of the late Mrs. Frieda Lawrence, and Messrs. William Heinemann, Ltd.). Lucas, E. V.: *Oh England, Country of My Heart's Desire* (Wells Gardner, Darton & Co. Ltd.). Masefield, John: *Tewkesbury Road*, *Sea Fever* and *Laugh and be Merry* (by permission of The Society of Authors and Dr. John Masefield, O.M., and The Macmillan Company of New York). Meynell, Alice: *To A Daisy* (from *The Poems of Alice Meynell*, published by the Oxford University Press and by permission of Mrs. S. Mulvey). Monro, Harold: *Milk for the Cat* (by permission of Mrs. A. Monro). Nicolson, Harold: *King George the Fifth*. Noyes, Alfred: *The Barrel Organ* (by permission of the late Dr. Alfred Noyes and Wm. Blackwood & Sons Ltd.). *A Song of England* (Wm. Blackwood & Sons Ltd.). Pearson, Sir Arthur: *Victory over Blindness* (Hodder & Stoughton Ltd.). Russell, Bertrand: *The Conquest of Happiness* (George Allen & Unwin Ltd.). Shaw, Bernard: *Saint Joan* (by permission of the Public Trustee and The Society of Authors). Simpson, William: *I Burned My Fingers* (Putnam & Co. Ltd.). Sitwell, Dame Edith: *Scotch Rhapsody* (from *Façade and Other Poems 1910–1935*, Gerald Duckworth & Co. Ltd.). Spring-Rice, Cecil: *I vow to thee, my country* . . .

(from *Poems*, published by Longmans, Green & Co. Ltd.).
Turner, W. J.: *Ecstasy* (from *The Hunter and Other Poems*, published by Sidgwick & Jackson Ltd.). Underhill, Evelyn: *Immanence* (from *Immanence: A Book of Verses*, published by J. M. Dent & Sons Ltd.).

CONTENTS

Looking Back

WHEN TO THE SESSIONS OF SWEET
SILENT THOUGHT

When to the Sessions of sweet silent thought
I summon up remembrance of things past,
I sigh the lack of many a thing I sought,
And with old woes new wail my dear time's waste:
Then can I drown an eye, unused to flow,
For precious friends hid in death's dateless night,
And weep afresh love's long since cancelled woe,
And moan the expense of many a vanished sight:
Then can I grieve at grievances foregone,
And heavily from woe to woe tell o'er
The sad account of fore-bemoaned moan,
Which I new pay as if not paid before.
But if the while I think on thee, dear friend,
All losses are restored and sorrows end.

WILLIAM SHAKESPEARE

SWEET WAS THE SONG THAT
YOUTH SANG ONCE

Sweet was the song that Youth sang once,
And passing sweet was the response;
But there are accents sweeter far
When Love leaps down our evening star,
Holds back the blighting wings of Time,
Melts with his breath the crusty rime,

15

And looks into our eyes, and says,
'Come, let us talk of former days.'

WALTER SAVAGE LANDOR

THE RECOLLECTION

Now the last day of many days,
All beautiful and bright as thou,
The loveliest and the last, is dead:
Rise, Memory, and write its praise!
Up—to thy wonted work! come, trace
The epitaph of glory fled,
For now the earth has changed its face,
A frown is on the heaven's brow.

We wander'd to the Pine Forest
    That skirts the Ocean's foam.
The lightest wind was in its nest,
    The tempest in its home;
The whispering waves were half asleep,
    The clouds were gone to play,
And on the bosom of the deep
    The smile of Heaven lay:
It seem'd as if the hour were one
    Sent from beyond the skies
Which scatter'd from above the sun
    A light of Paradise!

We paused amid the pines that stood
    The giants of the waste,
Tortured by storms to shapes as rude
    As serpents interlaced,—
And soothed by every azure breath
    That under Heaven is blown,

To harmonies and hues beneath,
   As tender as its own.
Now all the tree-tops lay asleep
   Like green waves on the sea,
As still as in the silent deep
   The ocean woods may be.

How calm it was!—the silence there
   By such a chain was bound,
That even the busy woodpecker
   Made stiller by her sound
The inviolable quietness;
   The breath of peace we drew
With its soft motion made not less
   The calm that round us grew.
There seem'd, from the remotest seat
   Of the wide mountain waste
To the soft flower beneath our feet,
   A magic circle traced,—
A spirit interfused around
   A thrilling silent life;
To momentary peace it bound
   Our mortal nature's strife;—
And still I felt the centre of
   The magic circle there
Was one fair form that fill'd with love
   The lifeless atmosphere.

We paused beside the pools that lie
   Under the forest bough;
Each seem'd as 'twere a little sky
   Gulf'd in a world below—
A firmament of purple light
   Which in the dark earth lay,
More boundless than the depth of night
   And purer than the day—

In which the lovely forests grew
  As in the upper air,
More perfect both in shape and hue
  Than any spreading there.
There lay the glade and neighbouring lawn,
  And through the dark-green wood
The white sun twinkling like the dawn
  Out of a speckled cloud.
Sweet views which in our world above
  Can never well be seen
Were imaged in the water's love
  Of that fair forest green;
And all was interfused beneath
  With an Elysian glow,
An atmosphere without a breath,
  A softer day below.

Like one beloved, the scene had lent
  To the dark water's breast
Its every leaf and lineament
  With more than truth exprest;
Until an envious wind crept by,
  Like an unwelcome thought
Which from the mind's too faithful eye
  Blots one dear image out.
—Though thou art ever fair and kind,
  The forests ever green,
Less oft is peace in Shelley's mind
  Than calm in waters seen!

PERCY BYSSHE SHELLEY

TIME OF ROSES

It was not in the Winter
  Our loving lot was cast;
It was the time of roses—
  We pluck'd them as we pass'd!

That churlish season never frown'd
  On early lovers yet:
O no—the world was newly crown'd
  With flowers when first we met!

'Twas twilight, and I bade you go,
  But still you held me fast;
It was the time of roses—
  We pluck'd them as we pass'd!

THOMAS HOOD

RECOLLECTION

Having emerged from the poverty and obscurity in which I was born and bred, to a state of affluence and some degree of reputation in the world, and having gone so far through life with a considerable share of felicity, the conducing means I made use of, which with the blessing of God so well succeeded, my posterity may like to know, as they may find some of them suitable to their own situations, and therefore fit to be imitated.

That felicity, when I reflected on it, has induced me sometimes to say, that were it offered to my choice, I should have no objection to a repetition of the same life from its beginning, only asking the advantages authors have in a second edition to correct some faults of the first. So I might, besides correcting the faults, change some sinister accidents and events of it for others more favourable. But though this were denied, I should still accept the offer. Since such a repetition is not to be expected, the next thing most

19

like living one's life over again seems to be a recollection of that life, and to make that recollection as durable as possible by putting it down in writing.

Hereby, too, I shall indulge the inclination so natural in old men, to be talking of themselves and their own past actions; and I shall indulge it without being tiresome to others, who, through respect to age, might conceive themselves obliged to give me a hearing, since this may be read or not as any one pleases. And, lastly (I may as well confess it since my denial of it will be believed by nobody), perhaps I shall a good deal gratify my own *vanity*. Indeed, I scarce ever heard or saw the introductory words, '*Without vanity I may say*,' etc., but some vain thing immediately followed. Most people dislike vanity in others, whatever share they have of it themselves; but I give it fair quarter wherever I meet with it, being persuaded that it is often productive of good to the possessor, and to others that are within his sphere of action; and therefore, in many cases, it would not be altogether absurd if a man were to thank God for his vanity among the other comforts of life.

And now I speak of thanking God, I desire with all humility to acknowledge that I owe the mentioned happiness of my past life to His kind providence, which lead me to the means I used and gave them success. My belief of this induces me to *hope*, though I must not *presume*, that the same goodness will still be exercised toward me, in continuing that happiness, or enabling me to bear a fatal reverse, which I may experience as others have done; the complexion of my future fortune being known to Him only in whose power it is to bless to us even our afflictions.

BENJAMIN FRANKLIN
From *Autobiography*

SWEET AUBURN! LOVELIEST VILLAGE
OF THE PLAIN

Sweet Auburn! loveliest village of the plain,
Where health and plenty cheered the labouring swain,
Where smiling spring its earliest visit paid,
And parting summer's lingering blooms delayed:
Dear lovely bowers of innocence and ease,
Seats of my youth, when every sport could please;
How often have I loitered o'er thy green,
Where humble happiness endeared each scene!
How often have I paused on every charm,
The sheltered cot, the cultivated farm,
The never-failing brook, the busy mill,
The decent church that topped the neighbouring hill,
The hawthorn-bush, with seats beneath the shade,
For talking age and whispering lovers made!
How often have I blessed the coming day,
When toil remitting lent its turn to play,
And all the village train, from labour free,
Led up their sports beneath the spreading tree:
While many a pastime circled in the shade,
The young contending as the old surveyed;
And many a gambol frolicked o'er the ground,
And sleights of art and feats of strength went round:
And still, as each repeated pleasure tired,
Succeeding sports the mirthful band inspired;
The dancing pair that simply sought renown,
By holding out, to tire each other down;
The swain mistrustless of his smutted face,
While secret laughter tittered round the place;
The bashful virgin's sidelong looks of love,
The matron's glance that would those looks reprove,—
These were thy charms, sweet village! sports like these,
With sweet succession, taught e'en toil to please;

These, round thy bowers their cheerful influence shed,
These were thy charms,—but all these charms are fled!

OLIVER GOLDSMITH
From The Deserted Village

THE RETREAT

Happy those early days, when I
Shin'd in my Angel-infancy!
Before I understood this place
Appointed for my second race,
Or taught my soul to fancy aught
But a white celestial thought:
When yet I had not walk'd above
A mile or two from my first Love,
And looking back—at that short space—
Could see a glimpse of His bright face;
When on some gilded cloud, or flow'r,
My gazing soul would dwell an hour,
And in those weaker glories spy
Some shadows of eternity:
Before I taught my tongue to wound
My Conscience with a sinful sound,
Or had the black art to dispense
A several sin to ev'ry sense,
But felt through all this fleshly dress
Bright shoots of everlastingness.

O how I long to travel back,
And tread again that ancient track!
That I might once more reach that plain
Where first I left my glorious train;
From whence th' enlightened spirit sees
That shady City of Palm-trees.

But ah! my soul with too much stay
Is drunk, and staggers in the way!
Some men a forward motion love,
But I by backward steps would move;
And when this dust falls to the urn,
In that state I came, return.

HENRY VAUGHAN

IN GLENCULLEN

Thrush, linnet, stare and wren,
Brown lark beside the sun,
Take thought of kestrel, sparrow-hawk,
Birdlime and roving gun.

You great-great-grand-children
Of birds I've listened to,
I think I robbed your ancestors
When I was young as you.

J. M. SYNGE

THE VOYAGE

As slow our ship her foamy track
    Against the wind was cleaving,
Her trembling pennant still look'd back
    To that dear isle 'twas leaving.
So loth we part from all we love,
    From all the links that bind us;
So turn our hearts, as on we rove,
    To those we've left behind us!

When, round the bowl, of vanish'd years
    We talk with joyous seeming—
With smiles that might as well be tears,
    So faint, so sad their beaming;
While memory brings us back again
    Each early tie that twined us,
Oh, sweet's the cup that circles then
    To those we've left behind us!

And when, in other climes, we meet
    Some isle or vale enchanting,
Where all looks flowery, wild, and sweet,
    And nought but love is wanting;
We think how great had been our bliss
    If Heaven had but assign'd us
To live and die in scenes like this,
    With some we've left behind us!

As travellers oft look back at eve
    When eastward darkly going,
To gaze upon that light they leave
    Still faint behind them glowing—
So, when the close of pleasure's day
    To gloom hath near consign'd us,
We turn to catch one fading ray
    Of joy that's left behind us.

THOMAS MOORE

AMORET

If rightly tuneful bards decide,
    If it be fix'd in Love's decrees,
That Beauty ought not to be tried
    But by its native power to please,

Then tell me, youths and lovers, tell—
What fair can Amoret excel?

Behold that bright unsullied smile,
   And wisdom speaking in her mien:
Yet—she so artless all the while,
   So little studious to be seen—
We naught but instant gladness know,
Nor think to whom the gift we owe.

But neither music, nor the powers
   Of youth and mirth and frolic cheer,
Add half the sunshine to the hours,
   Or make life's prospect half so clear,
As memory brings it to the eye
From scenes where Amoret was by.

This, sure, is Beauty's happiest part;
   This gives the most unbounded sway;
This shall enchant the subject heart
   When rose and lily fade away;
And she be still in spite of Time,
Sweet Amoret in all her prime.

MARK AKENSIDE

LOVE AND AGE

I played with you 'mid cowslips blowing,
When I was six and you were four;
When garlands weaving, flower-balls throwing,
Were pleasures soon to please no more.
Through groves and meads, o'er grass and heather,
With little playmates, to and fro,
We wandered hand in hand together;
But that was sixty years ago.

You grew a lovely roseate maiden,
And still our early love was strong;
Still with no care our days were laden,
They glided joyously along;
Then I did love you, very dearly,
How dearly words want power to show;
I thought your heart was touched as nearly;
But that was fifty years ago.

Then other lovers came around you,
Your beauty grew from year to year,
And many a splendid circle found you
The centre of its glittering sphere.
I saw you then, first vows forsaking,
On rank and wealth your hand bestow;
Oh, then I thought my heart was breaking,—
But that was forty years ago.

And I lived on, to wed another;
No cause she gave me to repine;
And when I heard you were a mother,
I did not wish the children mine.
My own young flock, in fair progression,
Made up a pleasant Christmas row:
My joy in them was past expression;—
But that was thirty years ago.

You grew a matron plump and comely,
You dwelt in fashion's brightest blaze;
My earthly lot was far more homely;
But I too had my festal days.
No merrier eyes have ever glistened
Around the hearth-stone's wintry glow,
Than when my youngest child was christened—
But that was twenty years ago.

Time passed. My eldest girl was married,
And I am now a grandsire grey;
One pet of four years old I've carried
Among the wild-flowered meads to play.
In our old fields of childish pleasure,
Where now, as then, the cowslips blow,
She fills her basket's ample measure,—
And that is not ten years ago.

But though first love's impassioned blindness
Has passed away in colder light,
I still have thought of you with kindness,
And shall do, till our last good-night.
The ever-rolling silent hours
Will bring a time we shall not know,
When our young days of gathering flowers
Will be an hundred years ago.

THOMAS LOVE PEACOCK
From *Gryll Grange*

SONG

False though she be to me and love,
    I'll ne'er pursue revenge;
For still the charmer I approve,
    Though I deplore her change.

In hours of bliss we oft have met;
    They could not always last;
And though the present I regret,
    I'm grateful for the past.

WILLIAM CONGREVE

THE HAPPINESS OF THE ROMANS

If a man were called to fix the period in the history of the world during which the condition of the human race was most happy and prosperous, he would, without hesitation, name that which elapsed from the death of Domitian to the accession of Commodus. The vast extent of the Roman empire was governed by absolute power, under the guidance of virtue and wisdom. The armies were restrained by the firm but gentle hand of four successive emperors whose characters and authority commanded involuntary respect. The forms of the civil administration were carefully preserved by Nerva, Trajan, Hadrian, and the Antonines, who delighted in the image of liberty, and were pleased with considering themselves as the accountable ministers of the laws. Such princes deserved the honour of restoring the republic, had the Romans of their days been capable of enjoying a rational freedom.

The labours of these monarchs were overpaid by the immense reward that inseparably waited on their success; by the honest pride of virtue, and by the exquisite delight of beholding the general happiness of which they were the authors. A just but melancholy reflection embittered, however, the noblest of human enjoyments. They must often have recollected the instability of a happiness which depended on the character of a single man.

EDWARD GIBBON

From *The History of the Decline and Fall of the Roman Empire*

AT THE MID HOUR OF NIGHT

At the mid hour of night, when stars are weeping, I fly
To the lone vale we loved, when life shone warm in thine eye;
And I think oft, if spirits can steal from the regions of air
To revisit past scenes of delight, thou wilt come to me there
And tell me our love is remember'd, even in the sky!

Then I sing the wild song it once was rapture to hear
When our voices, commingling, breathed like one on the ear;
And as Echo far off through the vale my sad orison rolls,
I think, O my Love! 'tis thy voice, from the Kingdom of Souls
Faintly answering still the notes that once were so dear.

THOMAS MOORE

Looking Forward

SAY NOT THE STRUGGLE
NOUGHT AVAILETH

Say not the struggle nought availeth,
   The labour and the wounds are vain,
The enemy faints not, nor faileth,
   And as things have been they remain.

If hopes were dupes, fears may be liars;
   It may be, in yon smoke conceal'd,
Your comrades chase e'en now the fliers,
   And, but for you, possess the field.

For while the tired waves, vainly breaking,
   Seem here no painful inch to gain,
Far back, through creeks and inlets making,
   Comes silent, flooding in, the main.

And not by eastern windows only,
   When daylight comes, comes in the light;
In front, the sun climbs slow, how slowly,
   But westward, look, the land is bright.

ARTHUR HUGH CLOUGH

UP-HILL

Does the road wind up-hill all the way?
   Yes, to the very end.
Will the day's journey take the whole long day?
   From morn to night, my friend.

But is there for the night a resting place?
  A roof for when the slow dark hours begin.
May not the darkness hide it from my face?
  You cannot miss that inn.

Shall I meet other wayfarers at night?
  Those who have gone before.
Then must I knock, or call when just in sight?
  They will not keep you standing at that door.

Shall I find comfort, travel-sore and weak?
  Of labour you shall find the sum.
Will there be beds for me and all who seek?
  Yea, beds for all who come.

CHRISTINA GEORGINA ROSSETTI

ONE DAY I WROTE HER NAME

One day I wrote her name upon the strand;
But came the waves and washed it away;
Again I wrote it with a second hand;
But came the tide, and made my pains his prey.
'Vain man,' said she, 'that dost in vain essay
A mortal thing so to immortalise,
For I myself shall like to this decay,
And eke my name be wiped out likewise.'
'Not so,' quoth I, 'let baser things devise
To die in dust, but you shall live by fame;
My verse your virtues rare shall eternise,
And in the heavens write your glorious name.
Where, whenas death shall all the world subdue,
Our love shall live, and later life renew.'

EDMUND SPENSER

THE GOOD-MORROW

I wonder by my troth what thou and I
Did till we loved? were we not weaned till then?
But sucked on country pleasures childishly?
Or snorted we in the seven sleepers' den?
'Twas so; but this, all pleasures fancies be.
If ever any beauty I did see,
Which I desired and got, 'twas but a dream of thee.

And now good morrow to our waking souls,
Which watch not one another out of fear;
For love all love of other sights controls,
And makes one little room an everywhere.
Let sea-discoverers to new worlds have gone,
Let maps to other worlds on worlds have shown,
Let us possess one world, each hath one, and is one.

My face in thine eye, thine in mine appears,
And true plain hearts do in the faces rest;
Where can we find two better hemispheres
Without sharp North, without declining West?
Whatever dies was not mixt equally;
If our two loves be one, or thou and I
Love so alike that none do slacken, none can die.

JOHN DONNE

HOPE

Hope like the gleaming taper's light
  Adorns and cheers our way,
And still as darker grows the night
  Emits a brighter ray.

OLIVER GOLDSMITH
From *The Captivity*

NOW THE GOLDEN MORN

Now the golden Morn aloft
  Waves her dew-bespangled wing;
With vermeil cheek and whisper soft
  She woos the tardy spring:
Till April starts, and calls around
The sleeping fragrance from the ground;
And lightly o'er the living scene
Scatters his freshest, tenderest green.

New-born flocks in rustic dance
  Frisking ply their feeble feet.
Forgetful of their wintry trance
  The birds his presence greet.
But chief the sky-lark warbles high
His trembling thrilling ecstasy
And, less'ning from the dazzled sight,
Melts into air and liquid light.

Yesterday the sullen year
  Saw the snowy whirlwind fly;
Mute was the musick of the air,
  The herd stood drooping by:
Their raptures now that wildly flow,
No yesterday, nor morrow know;
'Tis Man alone that joy descries
With forward and reverted eyes.

Smiles on past Misfortune's brow
  Soft Reflection's hand can trace;
And o'er the cheek of Sorrow throw
  A melancholy grace;
While Hope prolongs our happier hour,
Or deepest shades, that dimly lour

34

And blacken round our weary way,
Gilds with a gleam of distant day.

Still, where rosy Pleasure leads,
    See a kindred Grief pursue;
Behind the steps that Misery treads,
    Approaching Comfort view:
The hues of bliss more brightly glow,
Chastised by sabler tints of woe;
And blended form, with artful strife,
The strength and harmony of life.

See the Wretch, that long has tost
    On the thorny bed of pain,
At length repair his vigour lost,
    And breathe and walk again:
The meanest flowret of the vale,
The simplest note that swells the gale,
The common sun, the air, and skies,
To him are opening Paradise.

THOMAS GRAY

THE RAINBOW

My heart leaps up when I behold
    A rainbow in the sky:
So was it when my life began,
So is it now I am a man,
So be it when I shall grow old,
    Or let me die!
The Child is father of the Man:
And I could wish my days to be
Bound each to each by natural piety.

WILLIAM WORDSWORTH

JERUSALEM

Jerusalem, my happy home,
  When shall I come to thee?
When shall my sorrows have an end,
  Thy joys when shall I see?

O happy harbour of the saints,
  O sweet and pleasant soil,
In thee no sorrow may be found,
  No grief, no care, no toil.

There lust and lucre cannot dwell,
  There envy bears no sway;
There is no hunger, heat nor cold,
  But pleasure every way.

Thy walls are made of precious stones,
  Thy bulwarks diamonds square;
Thy gates are of right orient pearl,
  Exceeding rich and rare.

Thy turrets and thy pinnacles
  With carbuncles do shine;
Thy very streets are paved with gold,
  Surpassing clear and fine.

Ah, my sweet home Jerusalem,
  Would God I were in thee!
Would God my woes were at an end,
  Thy joys that I might see!

Thy gardens and thy gallant walks
  Continually are green;
There grows such sweet and pleasant flowers
  As nowhere else are seen.

Quite through the streets, with silver sound,
    The flood of life doth flow;
Upon whose banks on every side
    The wood of life doth grow.

There trees for evermore bear fruit,
    And evermore do spring;
There evermore the angels sit,
    And evermore do sing.

Our Lady sings *Magnificat*
    With tune surpassing sweet;
And all the virgins bear their part,
    Sitting about her feet.

Jerusalem, my happy home,
    Would God I were in thee!
Would God my woes were at an end,
    Thy joys that I might see!

UNKNOWN

TO-MORROW

In the downhill of life, when I find I'm declining,
    May my lot no less fortunate be
Than a snug elbow-chair can afford for reclining,
    And a cot that o'erlooks the wide sea;
With an ambling pad-pony to pace o'er the lawn,
    While I carol away idle sorrow,
And blithe as the lark that each day hails the dawn
    Look forward with hope for to-morrow.

With a porch at my door both for shelter and shade too,
    As the sunshine or rain may prevail;
And a small spot of ground for the use of the spade too,
    With a barn for the use of the flail;

A cow for my dairy, a dog for my game,
  And a purse when a friend wants to borrow,—
I'll envy no nabob his riches or fame,
  Or what honours await him to-morrow.

From the bleak northern blast may my cot be completely
  Secured by a neighbouring hill;
And at night may repose steal upon me more sweetly
  By the sound of a murmuring rill;
And while peace and plenty I find at my board,
  With a heart free from sickness and sorrow,
With my friends may I share what to-day may afford,
  And let them spread the table to-morrow.

And when I at last must throw off this frail cov'ring
  Which I've worn for threescore years and ten,
On the brink of the grave I'll not seek to keep hov'ring,
  Nor my thread wish to spin o'er again;
But my face in the glass I'll serenely survey,
  And with smiles count each wrinkle and furrow,
As this old worn-out stuff, which is threadbare to-day,
  May become everlasting to-morrow.

                                        J. COLLINS

TO LUCASTA, GOING BEYOND
THE SEAS

If to be absent were to be
    Away from thee;
  Or that when I am gone
  You or I were alone;
Then, my Lucasta, might I crave
Pity from blustering wind, or swallowing wave.

But I'll not sigh one blast or gale
    To swell my sail,
  Or pay a tear t' assuage
  The foaming blue god's rage;
For whether he will let me pass
Or no, I'm still as happy as I was.

Though seas and land betwixt us both,
    Our faith and troth,
  Like separated souls,
  All time and space controls;
Above the highest sphere we meet
Unseen, unknown, and greet as Angels greet.

So then we do anticipate
    Our after-fate,
  And are alive i' the skies,
  If thus our lips and eyes
Can speak like spirits unconfined
In Heaven, their earthly bodies left behind.

RICHARD LOVELACE

MAN'S MEDLEY

Hark, how the birds do sing,
    And woods do ring!
All creatures have their joy, and man hath his.
  Yet if we rightly measure,
  Man's joy and pleasure
Rather hereafter than in present is.

To this life things of sense
    Make their pretence;

In th' other angels have a right by birth.
    Man ties them both alone,
    And makes them one,
With th' one hand touching heav'n, with th' other earth.

    In soul he mounts and flies,
        In flesh he dies.
He wears a stuff whose thread is coarse and round,
    But trimmed with curious lace,
    And should take place
After the trimming, not the stuff and ground.

    Not that he may not here
        Taste of the cheer;
But as birds drink and straight lift up their head,
    So must he sip and think
    Of better drink
He may attain to after he is dead.

    But as his joys are double,
        So is his trouble.
He hath two winters, other things but one.
    Both frosts and thoughts do nip
    And bite his lip,
And he of all things fears two deaths alone.

    Yet ev'n the greatest griefs
        May be reliefs,
Could he but take them right and in their ways.
    Happy is he whose heart
    Hath found the art
To turn his double pains to double praise.

GEORGE HERBERT

EUTHANASIA

Wouldst see blithe looks, fresh cheeks beguile
Age? wouldst see December smile?
Wouldst see nests of new roses grow
In a bed of reverend snow?
Warm thoughts, free spirits, flattering
Winter's self into a spring?
In sum wouldst see a man that can
Live to be old, and still a man?
Whose latest and most leaden hours,
Fall with soft wings stuck with soft flowers;
And, when life's sweet fable ends,
Soul and body part like friends;
No quarrels, murmurs, no delay—
A kiss, a sigh, and so away.
This rare one, reader, wouldst thou see?
Hark hither!—and thyself be he.

RICHARD CRASHAW

SONG OF THE SIRENS

Steer hither, steer, your winged pines,
    All beaten mariners,
Here lie Love's undiscovered mines
    A prey to passengers;
    Perfumes far sweeter than the best
Which make the Phoenix urn and nest.
    Fear not your ships,
Nor any to oppose you save our lips,
    But come on shore,
Where no joy dies till Love hath gotten more.

41

For swelling waves, our panting breasts,
  Where never storms arise,
Exchange; and be awhile our guests;
  For stars gaze on our eyes.
The compass Love shall hourly sing,
And as he goes about the ring,
  We will not miss
To tell each point he nameth with a kiss.

WILLIAM BROWNE
From *The Inner Temple Masque*

EL DORADO

It seems as if a great deal were attainable in a world where there
are so many marriages and decisive battles, and where we all,
at certain hours of the day, and with great gusto and despatch,
stow a portion of victuals finally and irretrievably into the bag
which contains us. And it would seem also, on a hasty view, that
the attainment of as much as possible was the one goal of man's
contentious life. And yet, as regards the spirit, this is but a sem-
blance. We live in an ascending scale when we live happily, one
thing leading to another in an endless series. There is always a
new horizon for onward-looking men, and although we dwell
on a small planet, immersed in petty business and not enduring
beyond a brief period of years, we are so constituted that our
hopes are inaccessible, like stars, and the term of hoping is pro-
longed until the term of life. To be truly happy is a question of
how we begin and not of how we end, of what we want and not
of what we have. An aspiration is a joy for ever, a possession as
solid as a landed estate, a fortune which we can never exhaust
and which gives us year by year a revenue of pleasurable activity.
To have many of these is to be spiritually rich. Life is only a
very dull and ill-directed theatre unless we have some interests
in the piece; and to those who have neither art nor science, the
world is a mere arrangement of colours, or a rough footway where

they may very well break their shins. It is in virtue of his own desires and curiosities that any man continues to exist with even patience, that he is charmed by the look of things and people, and that he wakens every morning with a renewed appetite for work and pleasure. Desire and curiosity are the two eyes through which he sees the world in the most enchanted colours: it is they that make women beautiful or fossils interesting: and the man may squander his estate and come to beggary, but if he keeps these two amulets he is still rich in the possibilities of pleasure. Suppose he could take one meal so compact and comprehensive that he should never hunger any more; suppose him, at a glance, to take in all the features of the world and allay the desire for knowledge; suppose him to do the like in any province of experience—would not that man be in a poor way for amusement ever after?

One who goes touring on foot with a single volume in his knapsack reads with circumspection, pausing often to reflect, and often laying the book down to contemplate the landscape or the prints in the inn parlour; for he fears to come to an end of his entertainment, and be left companionless on the last stages of his journey. A young fellow recently finished the works of Thomas Carlyle, winding up, if we remember aright, with the ten note books upon Frederick the Great. 'What!' cried the young fellow, in consternation, 'is there no more Carlyle? Am I left to the daily papers?' A more celebrated instance is that of Alexander, who wept bitterly because he had no more worlds to subdue. And when Gibbon had finished the *Decline and Fall*, he had only a few moments of joy; and it was with a 'sober melancholy' that he parted from his labours.

Happily we all shoot at the moon with ineffectual arrows; our hopes are set on inaccessible El Dorado; we come to an end of nothing here below. Interests are only plucked up to sow themselves again, like mustard. You would think, when the child was born, there would be an end to trouble; and yet it is only the beginning of fresh anxieties; and when you have seen it through its teething and its education, and at last its marriage alas! it is only to have new fears, new quivering sensibilities, with every day, and the health of your children's children grows as touching a concern as that of your own. Again, when you have married your wife, you would think you were got upon a hilltop, and might begin to go downward by an easy slope. But you have only ended courting to begin marriage. Falling in love and winning love are often difficult tasks to overbearing and rebellious spirits; but to keep in love is also a business of some importance, to which both man and wife must bring kindness and goodwill. The true love story commences at the altar, when there lies before the married pair a most beautiful contest of wisdom and generosity, and a life-long struggle towards an unattainable ideal. Unattainable? Ay, surely unattainable, from the very fact that they are two instead of one.

'Of making books there is no end,' complained the Preacher; and did not perceive how highly he was praising letters as an occupation. There is no end, indeed, to making books or experiments, or to travel, or to gathering wealth. Problem gives rise to problem. We may study for ever, and we are never as learned as we would. We have never made a statue worthy of our dreams. And when we have discovered a continent, or crossed a chain of mountains, it is only to find another ocean or another plain upon the further side. In the infinite universe there is room for our swiftest diligence and to spare. It is not like the works of Carlyle, which can be read to an end. Even in a corner of it, in a private park, or in the neighbourhood of a single hamlet, the weather and the seasons keep so deftly changing that although we walk there for a lifetime there will be always something new to startle and delight us.

There is only one wish realisable on the earth; only one thing that can be perfectly attained: Death. And from a variety of circumstances we have no one to tell us whether it be worth attaining.

A strange picture we make on our way to our chimeras, ceaselessly marching, grudging ourselves the time for rest; indefatigable, adventurous pioneers. It is true that we shall never reach

44

the goal; it is even more than probable that there is no such place; and if we lived for centuries and were endowed with the powers of a god, we should find ourselves not much nearer what we wanted at the end. O toiling hands of mortals! O unwearied feet, travelling ye know not whither! Soon, soon, it seems to you, you must come forth on some conspicuous hilltop, and but a little way further, against the setting sun, descry the spires of El Dorado. Little do ye know your own blessedness; for to travel hopefully is a better thing than to arrive, and the true success is to labour.

ROBERT LOUIS STEVENSON
From *Virginibus Puerisque*

MILTON

And did those feet in ancient time
Walk upon England's mountains green?
And was the holy Lamb of God
On England's pleasant pastures seen?

And did the Countenance Divine
Shine forth upon our clouded hills?
And was Jerusalem builded here,
Among these dark Satanic Mills?

Bring me my Bow of burning gold;
Bring me my Arrows of desire:
Bring me my Spear: O clouds unfold:
Bring me my Chariot of fire!

I will not cease from Mental Fight,
Nor shall my Sword sleep in my hand:
Till we have built Jerusalem,
In England's green and pleasant Land.

WILLIAM BLAKE

PRELUDE

The north-east spends his rage; and now, shut up
Within his iron caves, the effusive south
Warms the wide air, and o'er the void of heaven
Breathes the big clouds with vernal showers distent . . .
At first a dusky wreath they seem to rise,
Scarce staining ether; but by fast degrees,
In heaps on heaps, the doubling vapour sails
Along the loaded sky, and, mingling deep,
Sits on the horizon round a settled gloom:
Not such as wintry storms on mortals shed,
Oppressing life; but lovely, gentle, kind,
And full of every hope and every joy;
The wish of Nature. Gradual sinks the breeze
Into a perfect calm; that not a breath
Is heard to quiver through the closing woods,
Or rustling turn the many-twinkling leaves
Of aspen tall. The uncurling floods, diffused
In Glassy breadth, seem through delusive lapse
Forgetful of their course. 'Tis silence all,
And pleasing expectation.

JAMES THOMSON

SALLY IN OUR ALLEY

Of all the girls that are so smart
    There's none like pretty Sally,
She is the darling of my heart,
    And she lives in our alley.
There is no lady in the land,
    Is half so sweet as Sally,
She is the darling of my heart,
    And she lives in our alley.

46

Her father he makes cabbage-nets,
  And through the streets does cry 'em;
Her mother she sells laces long,
  To such as please to buy 'em:
But sure such folks could ne'er beget
  So sweet a girl as Sally!
She is the darling of my heart,
  And she lives in our alley.

When she is by I leave my work,
  (I love her so sincerely)
My master comes like any Turk,
  And bangs me most severely;
But, let him bang his belly-full,
  I'll bear it all for Sally;
She is the darling of my heart,
  And she lives in our alley.

Of all the days that's in the week,
  I dearly love but one day,
And that's the day that comes betwixt
  A Saturday and Monday;
For then I'm dress'd, all in my best,
  To walk abroad with Sally;
She is the darling of my heart,
  And she lives in our alley.

My master carries me to church,
  And often am I blamed,
Because I leave him in the lurch,
  As soon as text is named:
I leave the church in sermon time,
  And slink away to Sally;
She is the darling of my heart,
  And she lives in our alley.

When Christmas comes about again,
   O then I shall have money;
I'll hoard it up, and box and all
   I'll give it to my honey:
And, would it were ten thousand pounds,
   I'd give it all to Sally;
She is the darling of my heart,
   And she lives in our alley.

My master and the neighbours all
   Make game of me and Sally;
And (but for her) I'd better be
   A slave and row a galley:
But when my seven long years are out,
   O then I'll marry Sally!
O then we'll wed and then we'll bed,
   But not in our alley.

HENRY CAREY

I.M.
MARGARITAE SORORIS
(1886)

A late lark twitters from the quiet skies;
And from the west,
Where the sun, his day's work ended,
Lingers as in content,
There falls on the old, gray city
An influence luminous and serene,
A shining peace.

The smoke ascends
In a rosy-and-golden haze. The spires
Shine, and are changed. In the valley
Shadows rise. The lark sings on. The sun,
Closing his benediction,

Sinks, and the darkening air
Thrills with a sense of the triumphing night—
Night with her train of stars
And her great gift of sleep.

So be my passing!
My task accomplished and the long day done,
My wages taken, and in my heart
Some late lark singing,
Let me be gathered to the quiet west,
The sundown splendid and serene,
Death.

WILLIAM ERNEST HENLEY

YE GOLDEN LAMPS OF HEAVEN

Ye golden Lamps of Heav'n, farewel
   With all your feeble Light;
Farewel, thou ever-changing Moon,
   Pale Empress of the Night.

And thou refulgent Orb of Day
   In brighter Flames array'd,
My Soul, that springs beyond thy Sphere,
   No more demands thine Aid.

Ye Stars are but the shining Dust
   Of my divine Abode,
The Pavement of those heav'nly Courts,
   Where I shall reign with God.

The Father of eternal Light
   Shall there his Beams display;
Nor shall one Moment's Darkness mix
   With that unvaried Day.

No more the Drops of piercing Grief
   Shall swell into mine Eyes;
Nor the Meridian Sun decline
   Amidst those brighter Skies.

There all the Millions of his Saints
   Shall in one Song unite,
And Each the Bliss of all shall view
   With infinite Delight.

PHILIP DODDRIDGE

THE SURVIVAL

To-day's house makes to-morrow's road;
   I knew these heaps of stone
When they were walls of grace and might,
The country's honour, art's delight
That over fountained silence showed
   Fame's final bastion.

Inheritance has found fresh work,
   Disunion union breeds;
Beauty the strong, its difference lost,
Has matter fit for flood and frost.
Here's the true blood that will not shirk
   Life's new-commanding needs.

With curious costly zeal, O man,
   Raise orrery and ode;
How shines your tower, the only one
Of that especial site and stone!
And even the dream's confusion can
   Sustain to-morrow's road.

EDMUND BLUNDEN

DEATH, BE NOT PROUD

Death, be not proud, though some have called thee
Mighty and dreadful, for thou art not so:
For those whom thou think'st thou dost overthrow
Die not, poor Death; nor yet canst thou kill me.
From Rest and Sleep, which but thy picture be,
Much pleasure, then from thee much more must flow;
And soonest our best men with thee do go—
Rest of their bones and souls' delivery!
Thou'rt slave to fate, chance, kings, and desperate men,
And dost with poison, war, and sickness dwell;
And poppy or charms can make us sleep as well
And better than thy stroke. Why swell'st thou then?
  One short sleep past, we wake eternally,
  And Death shall be no more: Death, thou shalt die!

JOHN DONNE

LAST LINES

  No coward soul is mine,
No trembler in the world's storm-troubled sphere:
  I see Heaven's glories shine,
And faith shines equal, arming me from fear.

  O God within my breast,
Almighty, ever-present Deity!
  Life—that in me has rest,
As I—undying Life—have power in Thee!

  Vain are the thousand creeds
That move men's hearts: unutterably vain;
  Worthless as withered weeds,
Or idle froth amid the boundless main,

51

To waken doubt in one
Holding so fast by Thine infinity;
   So surely anchored on
The steadfast rock of immortality.

   With wide-embracing love
Thy Spirit animates eternal years,
   Pervades and broods above,
Changes, sustains, dissolves, creates, and rears.

   Though earth and man were gone,
And suns and universes ceased to be,
   And Thou were left alone,
Every existence would exist in Thee.

   There is not room for Death,
Nor atom that his might could render void:
   Thou—Thou art Being and Breath,
And what thou art may never be destroyed.

EMILY BRONTË

I LOVE ALL BEAUTEOUS THINGS

   I love all beauteous things,
      I seek and adore them;
   God hath no better praise,
   And man in his hasty days
      Is honoured for them.

   I too will something make
      And joy in the making;
   Altho' to-morrow it seem
   Like the empty words of a dream
      Remembered on waking.

ROBERT BRIDGES

LEAD, KINDLY LIGHT

Lead, kindly Light, amid the encircling gloom,
  Lead thou me on;
The night is dark, and I am far from home,
  Lead thou me on.
Keep Thou my feet; I do not ask to see
The distant scene; one step enough for me.

JOHN HENRY, CARDINAL NEWMAN

ETERNITY

He who bends to himself a joy
Doth the winged life destroy;
But he who kisses the joy as it flies
Lives in eternity's sunrise.

WILLIAM BLAKE

Now is the Hour

TO THE VIRGINS, TO MAKE
MUCH OF TIME

Gather ye rose-buds while ye may,
  Old Time is still a-flying:
And this same flower that smiles to-day,
  To-morrow will be dying.

The glorious lamp of heaven, the sun,
  The higher he's a-getting;
The sooner will his race be run,
  And nearer he's to setting.

That age is best, which is the first,
  When youth and blood are warmer;
But being spent, the worse, and worst
  Times, still succeed the former.

Then be not coy, but use your time;
  And while ye may, go marry:
For having lost but once your prime,
  You may for ever tarry.

ROBERT HERRICK

HOLD BACK THY HOURS,
DARK NIGHT

Hold back thy hours, dark Night, till we have done;
  The Day will come too soon;

Young maids will curse thee, if thou steal'st away
And leav'st their losses open to the day:
   Stay, stay, and hide
   The blushes of the bride.

Stay, gentle Night, and with thy darkness cover
   The kisses of her lover;
Stay, and confound her tears and her shrill cryings,
Her weak denials, vows, and often-dyings;
   Stay, and hide all:
   But help not, though she call.

JOHN FLETCHER
From *The Maid's Tragedy*

O MISTRESS MINE

O Mistress mine, where are you roaming?
O stay and hear! your true love's coming
   That can sing both high and low;
Trip no further, pretty sweeting,
Journeys end in lovers meeting—
   Every wise man's son doth know.

What is love? 'tis not hereafter;
Present mirth hath present laughter;
   What's to come is still unsure:
In delay there lies no plenty,—
Then come kiss me, Sweet-and-twenty,
   Youth's a stuff will not endure.

WILLIAM SHAKESPEARE

IT WAS A LOVER AND HIS LASS

It was a lover and his lass,
  With a hey, and a ho, and a hey nonino,
That o'er the green corn-field did pass
  In the spring time, the only pretty ring time,
When birds do sing, hey ding a ding, ding:
Sweet lovers love the spring.

Between the acres of the rye,
  With a hey, and a ho, and a hey nonino,
These pretty country folk would lie,
  In the spring time, the only pretty ring time,
When birds do sing, hey ding a ding, ding:
Sweet lovers love the spring.

This carol they began that hour,
  With a hey, and a ho, and a hey nonino,
How that a life was but a flower
  In the spring time, the only pretty ring time,
When birds do sing, hey ding a ding, ding,
Sweet lovers love the spring.

And therefore take the present time,
  With a hey, and a ho, and a hey nonino,
For love is crowned with the prime
  In the spring time, the only pretty ring time,
When birds do sing, hey ding a ding, ding,
Sweet lovers love the spring.

WILLIAM SHAKESPEARE
From *As You Like It*

FOR THAT LOVELY FACE WILL FAIL

For that lovely face will fail,
Beauty's sweet, but beauty's frail;
'Tis sooner past, 'tis sooner done
Than summer's rain or winter's sun,
Most fleeting when it is most dear;
'Tis gone, while we but say 'tis here.
These curious locks so aptly twined,
Whose every hair a soul doth bind,
Will change their auburn hue and grow
White and cold as winter's snow.
That eye which now is Cupid's nest
Will prove his grave, and all the rest
Will follow; in the cheek, chin, nose,
Nor lily shall be found nor rose;
And what will then become of all
Those whom now you servants call?
Like swallows, when your summer's done
They'll fly and seek some warmer sun.
For when the storms of time have moved
Waves on that cheek that was beloved,
When a fair lady's face is pined
And yellow spread where red once shined,
When beauty, youth and all sweets leave her,
Love may return, but lovers never.
Oh, love me then, and now begin it,
Let us not lose this present minute.

THOMAS CAREW
From *Persuasions to Love*

LOVE IN THY YOUTH, FAIR MAID

Love in thy youth, fair maid; be wise,
　　Old Time will make thee colder,
And though each morning new arise
　　Yet we each day grow older.

Thou as heaven art fair and young,
　　Thine eyes like twin stars shining:
But ere another day be sprung,
　　All these will be declining.

Then winter comes with all his fears
　　And all thy sweets shall borrow;
Too late then wilt thou shower thy tears,
　　And I too late shall sorrow.

UNKNOWN

TO HIS COY MISTRESS

Had we but world enough, and time,
This coyness, Lady, were no crime.
We would sit down and think—which way
To walk and pass our long love's day.
Thou by the Indian Ganges' side
Shouldst rubies find: I by the tide
Of Humber would complain. I would
Love you ten years before the Flood,
And you should, if you please, refuse
Till the conversion of the Jews.
My vegetable love should grow
Vaster than empires, and more slow;
An hundred years should go to praise
Thine eyes and on thy forehead gaze;

Two hundred to adore each breast;
But thirty thousand to the rest;
An age at least to every part,
And the last age should show your heart;
For, Lady, you deserve this state,
Nor would I love at lower rate.
　　But at my back I always hear
Time's winged chariot hurrying near;
And yonder all before us lie
Deserts of vast eternity.
Thy beauty shall no more be found,
Nor, in thy marble vault, shall sound
My echoing song: then worms shall try
That long preserved virginity,
And your quaint honour turn to dust,
And into ashes all my lust:
The grave's a fine and private place,
But none, I think, do there embrace.
　　Now therefore, while the youthful hue
Sits on thy skin like morning dew,
And while thy willing soul transpires
At every pore with instant fires,
Now let us sport us while we may,
And now, like amorous birds of prey,
Rather at once our time devour
Than languish in his slow-chapt power,
Let us roll all our strength and all
Our sweetness up into one ball,
And tear our pleasures with rough strife
Thorough the iron gates of life:
Thus, though we cannot make our sun
Stand still, yet we will make him run.

ANDREW MARVELL

LOVE AND LIFE

All my past life is mine no more,
  The flying hours are gone;
Like transitory dreams given o'er,
Whose images are kept in store
  By memory alone.

The time that is to come is not;
  How can it then be mine?
The present moment's all my lot,
And that as fast as it is got,
  Phyllis, is only thine.

Then talk not of inconstancy,
  False hearts and broken vows;
If I by miracle can be
This live-long minute true to thee,
'Tis all that Heaven allows.

JOHN WILMOT, EARL OF ROCHESTER

USE THE TIME

Pleasures, beauty, youth attend ye,
  Whilst the Spring of nature lasteth;
Love and melting thoughts befriend ye,
  Use the time ere Winter hasteth.
    Active blood and free delight
    Place and privacy invite.
Do, do! be kind as fair,
Lose not opportunity for air.

She is cruel that denies it,
  Bounty best appears in granting,
Stealth of sport as soon supplies it,
  Whilst the dues of love are wanting.

61

Here's the sweet exchange of bliss
When each whisper proves a kiss.
In the game are felt no pains,
For in all the loser gains.

JOHN FORD
From *The Lady's Trial*

CARPE DIEM

Strive not, Leuconoë, to know what end
The gods above to me or thee will send;
Nor with astrologers consult at all,
That thou mayst better know what can befall;
Whether thou liv'st more winters, or thy last
Be this, which Tyrrhen waves 'gainst rocks do cast.
Be wise! drink free, and in so short a space
Do not protracted hopes of life embrace,
Whilst we are talking, envious time doth slide:
This day's thine own; the next may be denied.

HORACE
Translated by Sir Thomas Hawkins

GENTLE NYMPHS, BE NOT REFUSING

Gentle nymphs, be not refusing,
Love's neglect is time's abusing,
    They and beauty are but lent you,
Take the one and keep the other;
Love keeps fresh what age doth smother;
    Beauty gone, you will repent you.

'Twill be said when ye have proved,
Never swains more truly loved;

Oh then, fly all nice behaviour.
Pity fain would, as her duty,
Be attending still on beauty,
Let her not be out of favour.

WILLIAM BROWNE OF TAVISTOCK
From *Britannia's Pastorals*

YOUTH'S THE SEASON

Youth's the Season made for Joys,
Love is then our Duty,
She alone who that employs,
Well deserves her Beauty.
Let's be gay,
While we may,
Beauty's a Flower, despis'd in Decay.

Let us drink and sport to-day,
Ours is not to-morrow.
Love with Youth flies swift away,
Age is nought but Sorrow.
Dance and sing,
Time's on the Wing.
Life never knows the Return of Spring.

JOHN GAY
From *The Beggar's Opera*

LOVE NEW AND OLD

And were they not the happy days
When Love and I were young,
When earth was robed in heavenly light,
And all creation sung?

When gazing in my true love's face,
　　Through greenwood alleys lone,
I guessed the secrets of her heart,
　　By whispers of mine own.

And are they not the happy days
　　When Love and I are old,
And silver evening has replaced
　　A morn and noon of gold?
Love stood alone mid youthful joy,
　　But now by sorrow tried,
It sits and calmly looks to heaven
　　With angels at its side.

CHARLES MACKAY

Stanzas from
THE RUBÁ'IYÁT OF OMAR KHAYYÁM

Ah, my Beloved, fill the Cup that clears
To-day of past Regrets and future Fears—
　　To-morrow?—Why, To-morrow I may be
Myself with Yesterday's sev'n Thousand Years.

Ah, make the most of what we yet may spend.
Before we too into the Dust descend;
　　Dust into Dust, and under Dust, to lie,
Sans Wine, sans Song, sans Singer, and—sans End!

Ah, fill the Cup:—what boots it to repeat
How Time is slipping underneath our Feet:
　　Unborn *To-morrow*, and dead *Yesterday*,
Why fret about them if *To-day* be sweet!

Ah, Moon of my Delight who know'st no wane,
The Moon of Heav'n is rising once again:
   How oft hereafter rising shall she look
Through this same Garden after me—in vain!

And when Thyself with shining Foot shall pass
Among the Guests Star-scatter'd on the Grass,
   And in thy joyous Errand reach the Spot
Where I made one—turn down an empty Glass!

EDWARD FITZGERALD

LIVE WHILE YOU LIVE

Live while you live, the Epicure would say,
And seize the pleasures of the present day.
Live while you live, the sacred Preacher cries,
And give to God each moment as it flies.
Lord, in my view, let both united be,
I live in pleasure if I live to Thee.

PHILIP DODDRIDGE

Doing Something

THE HAPPY CRAFTSMAN

I believe the right question to ask, respecting all ornament, is simply this: Was it done with enjoyment—was the carver happy while he was about it? It may be the hardest work possible, and the harder because so much pleasure was taken in it; but it must have been happy too, or it will not be living.

JOHN RUSKIN
From *The Seven Lamps of Architecture*
(Chapter 5: 'The Lamp of Life')

DON'TS

Fight your little fight, my boy,
fight and be a man.
Don't be a good little, good little boy
being as good as you can
and agreeing with all the mealy-mouthed, mealy-mouthed
truths that the sly trot out
to protect themselves and their greedy-mouthed, greedy-
    mouthed
cowardice, every old lout.

Don't live up to the dear little girl who costs
you your manhood, and makes you pay.
Nor the dear old mater who so proudly boasts
that you'll make your way.

Don't earn golden opinions, opinions golden,
or at least worth Treasury notes,
from all sorts of men; don't be beholden
to the herd inside the pen.

Don't long to have dear little, dear little boys
whom you'll have to educate
to earn their living; nor yet girls, sweet joys
who will find it so hard to mate.

Nor a dear little home, with its cost, its cost
that you have to pay,
earning your living while your life is lost
and dull death comes in a day.

Don't be sucked in by the su-superior,
don't swallow the culture bait,
don't drink, don't drink and get beerier and beerier,
do learn to discriminate.

Do hold yourself together, and fight
with a hit-hit here and a hit-hit there,
and a comfortable feeling at night
that you've let in a little air.

A little fresh air in the money sty,
knocked a little hole in the holy prison,
done your own little bit, made your own little try
that the risen Christ should be risen.

D. H. LAWRENCE

THE EXERCISE OF SKILL

Every man who has acquired some unusual skill enjoys exercising
it until it has become a matter of course, or until he can no longer

improve himself. This motive to activity begins in early child-hood: a boy who can stand on his head becomes reluctant to stand on his feet. A great deal of work gives the same pleasure that is to be derived from games of skill. The work of a lawyer or a politician must contain in a more delectable form a great deal of the same pleasure that is to be derived from playing bridge. Here, of course, there is not only the exercise of skill but the outwitting of a skilled opponent. Even where this competitive element is absent, however, the performance of difficult feats is agreeable. A man who can do stunts in an aeroplane finds the pleasure so great that for the sake of it he is willing to risk his life. I imagine that an able surgeon, in spite of the painful cir-cumstances in which his work is done, derives satisfaction from the exquisite precision of his operations. The same kind of pleasure, though in a less intense form, is to be derived from a great deal of work of a humbler kind. I have even heard of plumbers who enjoyed their work, though I have never had the good fortune to meet one. All skilled work can be pleasurable, provided the skill required is either variable or capable of indefinite improvement.

BERTRAND RUSSELL

From *The Conquest of Happiness*

THE PLOUGH
A Landscape in Berkshire

Above yon sombre swell of land
    Thou see'st the dawn's grave orange hue,
With one pale streak like yellow sand,
    And over that a vein of blue.

The air is cold above the woods;
    All silent is the earth and sky,
Except with his own lonely moods
    The blackbird holds a colloquy.

Over the broad hill creeps a beam,
　　Like hope that gilds a good man's brow;
And now ascends the nostril-stream
　　Of stalwart horses come to plough.

Ye rigid Ploughmen, bear in mind
　　Your labour is for future hours:
Advance—spare not—nor look behind—
　　Plough deep and straight with all your powers!

RICHARD HENRY HORNE

THE COBBLER

Wandering up and down one day,
　　I peeped into a window over the way;
And putting his needle through and through,
There sat a cobbler making a shoe:
For the world he cares never the whisk of a broom—
All he wants is elbow-room.
　　Rap-a-tap-tap, tick-a-tack-too,
　　That is the way he makes a shoe!

Over laths of wood his bits of leather
He stretches and fits, then sews together;
He puts his wax ends through and through;
And still as he stitches, his body goes too:
For the world he cares never the whisk of a broom—
All he wants is elbow-room.
　　Rap-a-tap-tap, tick-a-tack-too,
　　This is the way he makes a shoe!

With his little sharp awl he makes a hole
Right through the upper and through the sole;
He puts in one peg, and he puts in two,
And chuckles and laughs as he hammers them through:

For the world he cares never the whisk of a broom—
    Rap-a-tap-tap, tick-a-tack-too,
    This is the way to make a shoe!

UNKNOWN

THE PRAISE OF INDUSTRY

It was not by vile Loitering in Ease,
That Greece obtain'd the brighter Palm of Art,
That soft, yet ardent, Athens learn'd to please,
To keen the Wit, and to sublime the Heart,
In all supreme! compleat in every Part!
It was not thence majestic Rome arose,
And o'er the Nations shook her conquering Dart:
For Sluggard's Brow the Laurel never grows;
Renown is not the Child of indolent Repose.

Had unambitious Mortals minded Nought
But in loose Joy their Time to wear away;
Had they alone the Lap of Dalliance sought,
Pleas'd on her Pillow their dull Heads to lay:
Rude Nature's State had been our State To-day;
No Cities e'er their towery Fronts had rais'd,
No Arts had made us opulent and gay;
With Brother-Brutes the Human Race had graz'd;
None e'er had soar'd to Fame, None honour'd been, None prais'd.

Great Homer's Song had never fir'd the Breast,
To Thirst of Glory, and heroic Deeds;
Sweet Maro's Muse, sunk in inglorious Rest,
Had silent slept amid the Mincian Reeds:
The Wits of modern Time had told their Beads,
And monkish Legends been their only Strains;
Our Milton's Eden had lain wrapt in Weeds,
Our Shakespear stroll'd and laugh'd with Warwick Swains,
Ne had my Master Spenser charm'd his Mulla's Plains.

71

Dumb too had been the sage Historic Muse,
And perish'd all the Sons of antient Fame;
Those starry Lights of Virtue, that diffuse
Through the dark Depth of Time their vivid Flame,
Had all been lost with Such as have no Name.
Who then had scorn'd his Ease for others' Good?
Who then had toil'd rapacious Men to tame?
Who in the Public Breach devoted stood,
And for his Country's Cause been prodigal of Blood?

But should to Fame your Hearts impervious be,
If right I read, you Pleasure All require:
Then hear how best may be obtain'd this Fee,
How best enjoy'd this Nature's wide Desire.
Toil, and be glad! Let Industry inspire
Into your quicken'd Limbs her buoyant Breath!
Who does not act is dead; absorpt intire
In miry Sloth, no Pride no Joy he hath:
O Leaden-hearted Men, to be in Love with Death!

Better the toiling Swain, oh happier far!
Perhaps the happiest of the Sons of Men!
Who vigorous plies the Plough, the Team, or Car;
Who houghs the Field, or ditches in the Glen,
Delves in his Garden, or secures his Pen;
The Tooth of Avarice poisons not his Peace;
He tosses not in Sloth's abhorred Den;
From Vanity he has a full Release;
And, rich in Nature's Wealth, he thinks not of Increase.

Good Lord! How keen are his Sensations all!
His Bread is sweeter than the Glutton's Cates;
The Wines of France upon the Palate pall,
Compar'd with What his simple Soul elates,
The native Cup whose Flavour Thirst creates;

At one deep Draught of Sleep he takes the Night;
And for that Heart-felt Joy which Nothing mates,
Of the pure nuptial Bed the chaste Delight,
The Losel is to him a miserable Wight.

But what avail the largest Gifts of Heaven,
When sickening Health and Spirits go amiss?
How tasteless then Whatever can be given?
Health is the vital Principle of Bliss,
And Exercise of Health. In Proof of This,
Behold the Wretch, who slugs his Life away,
Soon swallow'd in Disease's sad Abyss;
While he whom Toil has brac'd, or manly Play,
Has light as Air each Limb, each Thought as clear as Day.

JAMES THOMSON (the elder)
From *The Castle of Indolence*

THE BUSY BEE

How doth the little busy Bee
   Improve each shining Hour,
And gather Honey all the Day
   From ev'ry op'ning Flow'r!

How skilfully she builds her Cell!
   How neat she spreads the Wax!
And labours hard to store it well
   With the sweet Food she makes.

In Works of Labour or of Skill
   I would be busy too:
For Satan finds some Mischief still
   For idle Hands to do.

73

In Books, or Work, or healthful Play,
Let my first Years be past,
That I may give for every Day
Some good Account at last.

ISAAC WATTS

HAPPINESS BY THE WAY

Those only are happy (I thought) who have their minds fixed on some object other than their own happiness; on the happiness of others, on the improvement of mankind, even on some art or pursuit, followed not as a means, but as itself an ideal end. Aiming thus at something else, they find happiness by the way. The enjoyments of life (such was now my theory) are sufficient to make it a pleasant thing, when they are taken *en passant*, without being made a principal object. Once make them so, and they are immediately felt to be insufficient. They will not bear a scrutinizing examination. Ask yourself whether you are happy, and you cease to be so. The only chance is to treat, not happiness, but some end external to it, as the purpose of life. Let your self-consciousness, your scrutiny, your self-interrogation, exhaust themselves on that; and if otherwise fortunately circumstanced you will inhale happiness with the air you breathe, without dwelling on it or thinking about it, without either forestalling it in imagination, or putting it to flight by fatal questioning. This theory now became the basis of my philosophy of life. And I still hold to it as the best theory for all those who have but a moderate degree of sensibility and capacity for enjoyment, that is, for the great majority of mankind.

JOHN STUART MILL
From Autobiography

Doing Nothing

LEISURE

What is this life if, full of care,
We have no time to stand and stare.

No time to stand beneath the boughs
And stare as long as sheep or cows.

No time to see, when woods we pass,
Where squirrels hide their nuts in grass.

No time to see, in broad daylight,
Streams full of stars, like skies at night.

No time to turn at Beauty's glance,
And watch her feet, how they can dance.

No time to wait till her mouth can
Enrich that smile her eyes began.

A poor life this if, full of care,
We have no time to stand and stare.

WILLIAM HENRY DAVIES

INDOLENCE PREFERRED

Reuben Pettingill was extremely industrious.
He worked hard all the year round on his father's little farm.
Right he was!

75

Industry is a very fine thing.

It is one of the finest things of which we have any knowledge.

Yet do not frown, 'do not weep for me,' when I state that I don't like it.

It doesn't agree with me.

I prefer indolence.

I am happiest when I am idle.

I could live for months without performing any kind of labour, and at the expiration of that time I should feel fresh and vigorous enough to go right on in the same way for numerous more months.

This should not surprise you.

Nothing that a modern novelist does should excite astonishment in any well-regulated mind.

ARTEMUS WARD
From *Pyrotechny*

SLEEP

Come, Sleep, and with thy sweet deceiving
  Lock me in delight awhile;
  Let some pleasing dreams beguile
  All my fancies; that from thence
  I may feel an influence
All my powers of care bereaving!

Though but a shadow, but a sliding,
  Let me know some little joy!
  We that suffer long annoy
  Are contented with a thought
  Through an idle fancy wrought:
O let my joys have some abiding!

JOHN FLETCHER

TO SLEEP

O soft embalmer of the still midnight!
    Shutting with careful fingers and benign
Our gloom-pleased eyes, embower'd from the light,
    Enshaded in forgetfulness divine;
O soothest Sleep! if so it please thee, close,
    In midst of this thine hymn, my willing eyes,
Or wait the amen, ere thy poppy throws
    Around my bed its lulling charities;
    Then save me, or the passed day will shine
Upon my pillow, breeding many woes;
Save me from curious conscience, that still lords
    Its strength for darkness, burrowing like a mole;
Turn the key deftly in the oiled wards,
    And seal the hushed casket of my soul.

                          JOHN KEATS

THE GARDEN OF PROSERPINE

Here, where the world is quiet;
    Here, where all trouble seems
Dead winds' and spent waves' riot
    In doubtful dreams of dreams;
I watch the green field growing
For reaping folk and sowing,
For harvest-time and mowing,
    A sleepy world of streams.

I am tired of tears and laughter,
    And men that laugh and weep;
Of what may come hereafter
    For men that sow to reap:

I am weary of days and hours,
Blown buds of barren flowers,
Desires and dreams and powers
    And everything but sleep.

Here life has death for neighbour,
    And far from eye or ear
Wan waves and wet winds labour,
    Weak ships and spirits steer;
They drive adrift, and whither
They wot not who make thither;
But no such winds blow hither,
    And no such things grow here.

No growth of moor or coppice,
    No heather-flower or vine,
But bloomless buds of poppies,
    Green grapes of Proserpine,
Pale beds of blowing rushes
Where no leaf blooms or blushes
Save this whereout she crushes
    For dead men deadly wine.

Pale, without name or number,
    In fruitless fields of corn,
They bow themselves and slumber
    All night till light is born;
And like a soul belated,
In hell and heaven unmated,
By cloud and mist abated
    Comes out of darkness morn.

Though one were strong as seven,
    He too with death shall dwell,
Nor wake with wings in heaven,
    Nor weep for pains in hell;

Though one were fair as roses,
His beauty clouds and closes;
And well though love reposes,
   In the end it is not well.

Pale, beyond porch and portal,
   Crowned with calm leaves, she stands
Who gathers all things mortal
   With cold immortal hands;
Her languid lips are sweeter
Than love's who fears to greet her
To men that mix and meet her
   From many times and lands.

She waits for each and other,
   She waits for all men born;
Forgets the earth her mother,
   The life of fruits and corn;
And spring and seed and swallow
Take wing for her and follow
Where summer song rings hollow
   And flowers are put to scorn.

There go the loves that wither,
   The old loves with wearier wings;
And all dead years draw thither,
   And all disastrous things;
Dead dreams of days forsaken,
Blind buds that snows have shaken,
Wild leaves that winds have taken,
   Red strays of ruined springs.

We are not sure of sorrow,
   And joy was never sure;
To-day will die to-morrow;
   Time stoops to no man's lure;

And love, grown faint and fretful,
With lips but half regretful
Sighs, and with eyes forgetful
    Weeps that no loves endure.

From too much love of living,
    From hope and fear set free,
We thank with brief thanksgiving
    Whatever gods may be
That no life lives for ever;
That dead men rise up never;
That even the weariest river
    Winds somewhere safe to sea.

Then star nor sun shall waken,
    Nor any change of light:
Nor sound of waters shaken,
    Nor any sound or sight:
Not wintry leaves nor vernal,
Nor days nor things diurnal;
Only the sleep eternal
    In an eternal night.

ALGERNON CHARLES SWINBURNE

THE LAND OF INDOLENCE

In lowly Dale, fast by a River's Side,
With woody Hill o'er Hill encompass'd round,
A most enchanting Wizard did abide,
Than whom a Fiend more fell is nowhere found.
It was, I ween, a lovely Spot of Ground;
And there a Season atween June and May,
Half·prankt with Spring, with Summer half imbrown'd,
A listless Climate made, where, Sooth to say,
No living Wight could work, ne cared even for Play.

Was nought around but Images of Rest:
Sleep-soothing Groves, and quiet Lawns between;
And flowery Beds that slumbrous Influence kest,
From Poppies breath'd; and Beds of pleasant Green,
Where never yet was creeping Creature seen.
Mean time unnumber'd glittering Streamlets play'd,
And hurled every-where their Waters sheen;
That, as they bicker'd through the sunny Glade,
Though restless still themselves, a lulling Murmur made.

Join'd to the Prattle of the purling Rills,
Were heard the lowing Herds along the Vale,
And Flocks loud-bleating from the distant Hills,
And vacant Shepherds piping in the Dale;
And now and then sweet Philomel would wail,
Or Stock-Doves plain amid the Forest deep,
That drowsy rustled to the sighing Gale;
And still a Coil the Grasshopper did keep:
Yet all these Sounds yblent inclined all to Sleep.

Full in the Passage of the Vale, above,
A sable, silent, solemn Forest stood;
Where nought but shadowy Forms were seen to move,
As Idless fancy'd in her dreaming Mood.
And up the Hills, on either Side, a Wood
Of blackening Pines, ay waving to and fro,
Sent forth a sleepy Horror through the Blood;
And where this Valley winded out, below,
Then murmuring Main was heard, and scarcely heard, to flow.

A pleasing Land of Drowsy-hed it was:
Of Dreams that wave before the half-shut Eye;
And of gay Castles in the Clouds that pass,
For ever flushing round a Summer-Sky:
There eke the soft Delights, that witchingly

F   81

Instil a wanton Sweetness through the Breast,
And the calm Pleasures always hover'd nigh;
But whate'er smack'd of Noyance, or Unrest,
Was far, far off expell'd from this delicious Nest.

JAMES THOMSON (the elder)
From *The Castle of Indolence*

SONG OF THE LOTOS-EATERS

There is sweet music here that softer falls
Than petals from blown roses on the grass,
Or night-dews on still waters between walls
Of shadowy granite, in a gleaming pass;
Music that gentlier on the spirit lies,
Than tired eyelids upon tired eyes;
Music that brings sweet sleep down from the blissful skies.
Here are cool mosses deep,
And thro' the moss the ivies creep,
And in the stream the long-leaved flowers weep,
And from the craggy ledge the poppy hangs in sleep.

Why are we weigh'd upon with heaviness,
And utterly consumed with sharp distress,
While all things else have rest from weariness?
All things have rest: why should we toil alone,
We only toil, who are the first of things,
And make perpetual moan,
Still from one sorrow to another thrown:
Nor ever fold our wings,
And cease from wanderings,
Nor steep our brows in slumber's holy balm;
Nor harken what the inner spirit sings,
'There is no joy but calm!'—
Why should we only toil, the roof and crown of things?

Lo! in the middle of the wood,
The folded leaf is woo'd from out the bud
With winds upon the branch, and there
Grows green and broad, and takes no care,
Sun-steep'd at noon, and in the moon
Nightly dew-fed; and turning yellow
Falls, and floats adown the air.
Lo! sweeten'd with the summer light,
The full-juiced apple, waxing over-mellow,
Drops in a silent autumn night.
All its allotted length of days,
The flower ripens in its place,
Ripens and fades, and falls, and hath no toil,
Fast-rooted in the fruitful soil.

Hateful is the dark-blue sky,
Vaulted o'er the dark-blue sea.
Death is the end of life; ah, why
Should life all labour be?
Let us alone. Time driveth onward fast,
And in a little while our lips are dumb.
Let us alone. What is it that will last?
All things are taken from us, and become
Portions and parcels of the dreadful Past.
Let us alone. What pleasure can we have
To war with evil? Is there any peace
In ever climbing up the climbing wave?
All things have rest, and ripen toward the grave
In silence; ripen, fall and cease:
Give us long rest or death, dark death, or dreamful ease.

How sweet it were, hearing the downward stream,
With half-shut eyes ever to seem
Falling asleep in a half-dream!
To dream and dream, like yonder amber light,
Which will not leave the myrrh-bush on the height;

To hear each other's whisper'd speech;
Eating the Lotos day by day,
To watch the crisping ripples on the beach,
And tender curving lines of creamy spray;
To lend our hearts and spirits wholly
To the influence of mild-minded melancholy;
To muse and brood and live again in memory,
With those old faces of our infancy
Heap'd over with a mound of grass,
Two handfuls of white dust, shut in an urn of brass!

Dear is the memory of our wedded lives,
And dear the last embraces of our wives
And their warm tears; but all hath suffer'd change;
For surely now our household hearths are cold:
Our sons inherit us: our looks are strange:
And we should come like ghosts to trouble joy.
Or else the island princes over-bold
Have eat our substance, and the minstrel sings
Before them of the ten years' war in Troy,
And our great deeds, as half-forgotten things,
Is there confusion in the little isle?
Let what is broken so remain,
The Gods are hard to reconcile:
'Tis hard to settle order once again.
There *is* confusion worse than death,
Trouble on trouble, pain on pain,
Long labour unto aged breath,
Sore task to hearts worn out with many wars
And eyes grown dim with gazing on the pilot-stars.

But propt on beds of amaranth and moly,
How sweet (while warm airs lull us, blowing lowly)
With half-dropt eyelids still,
Beneath a heaven dark and holy,
To watch the long bright river drawing slowly

His waters from the purple hill—
To hear the dewy echoes calling
From cave to cave thro' the thick-twined vine—
To watch the emerald-colour'd water falling
Thro' many a wov'n acanthus-wreath divine!
Only to hear and see the far-off sparkling brine,
Only to hear were sweet, stretch'd out beneath the pine.

The Lotos blooms below the barren peak:
The Lotos blows by every winding creek:
All day the wind breathes low with mellower tone:
Thro' every hollow cave and alley lone
Round and round the spicy downs the yellow Lotos-dust is
    blown.
We have had enough of action, and of motion we,
Roll'd to starboard, roll'd to larboard, when the surge was
    seething free,
Where the wallowing monster spouted his foam-fountains in
    the sea,
Let us swear an oath, and keep it with an equal mind,
In the hollow Lotos-land to live and lie reclined
On the hills like Gods together, careless of mankind.
For they lie beside their nectar, and the bolts are hurl'd
Far below them in the valleys, and the clouds are lightly curl'd
Round their golden houses, girdled with the gleaming world:
Where they smile in secret, looking over wasted lands,
Blight and famine, plague and earthquake, roaring deeps and
    fiery sands,
Clanging fights, and flaming towns, and sinking ships, and
    praying hands.
But they smile, they find a music centred in a doleful song
Steaming up, a lamentation and an ancient tale of wrong,
Like a tale of little meaning tho' the words are strong;
Chanted from an ill-used race of men that cleave the soil,
Sow the seed, and reap the harvest with enduring toil,
Storing yearly little dues of wheat, and wine and oil;

Till they perish and they suffer—some, 'tis whisper'd—down
  in hell
Suffer endless anguish, others in Elysian valleys dwell,
Resting weary limbs at last on beds of asphodel.
Surely, surely slumber is more sweet than toil, the shore
Than labour in the deep mid-ocean, wind and wave and oar;
O rest ye, brother mariners, we will not wander more.

LORD TENNYSON

COME, SLEEP, O SLEEP

Come, Sleep, O Sleep, the certain knot of peace,
  The baiting place of wit, the balm of woe,
The poor man's wealth, the prisoner's release,
  Th' indifferent judge between the high and low;
With shield of proof shield me from out the prease
  Of those fierce darts Despair at me doth throw;
O make me in those civil wars to cease;
  I will good tribute pay, if thou do so.
Take thou of me smooth pillows, sweetest bed,
  A chamber deaf to noise and blind to light,
A rosy garland and a weary head;
  And if these things, as being thine by right,
    Move not thy heavy grace, thou shalt in me,
    Livelier than elsewhere, Stella's image see.

SIR PHILIP SIDNEY

Going Out and About

TEWKESBURY ROAD

It is good to be out on the road, and going one knows not where,
  Going through meadow and village, one knows not whither nor
    why;
Through the grey light drift of the dust, in the keen cool rush of
    the air,
  Under the flying white clouds, and the broad blue lift of the
    sky,

And to halt at the chattering brook, in the tall green fern at the
    brink
  Where the harebell grows, and the gorse, and the foxgloves
    purple and white;
Where the shy-eyed delicate deer come down in a troop to drink
  When the stars are mellow and large at the coming on of the
    night.

O, to feel the beat of the rain, and the homely smell of the
    earth,
  Is a tune for the blood to jig to, a joy past power of words;
And the blessed green comely meadows are all a-ripple with
    mirth
  At the noise of the lambs at play and the dear wild cry of the
    birds.

JOHN MASEFIELD

ON INNS

There is no private house in which people can enjoy themselves so well as in a capital tavern. Let there be ever so great plenty of good things, ever so much grandeur, ever so much elegance, ever so much desire that every body should be easy; in the nature of things it cannot be; there must always be some degree of care and anxiety. The master of the house is anxious to entertain his guests; the guests are anxious to be agreeable to him: and no man, but a very impudent dog indeed, can as freely command what is in another man's house, as if it were his own. Whereas, at a tavern, there is a general freedom from anxiety. You are sure you are welcome; and the more noise you make, the more trouble you give, the more good things you call for, the welcomer you are. No servants will attend you with the alacrity which waiters do, who are excited by the prospect of an immediate reward in proportion as they please. No, Sir; there is nothing which has yet been contrived by man, by which so much happiness is produced as by a good tavern or inn.

SAMUEL JOHNSON
Quoted in *The Life of Samuel Johnson*
by James Boswell

VENICE

How light we go, how soft we skim!
And all in moonlight seem to swim.
In moonlight is it now, or shade?
In planes of sure division made,
By angles sharp of palace walls
The clear light and the shadow falls;

O sight of glory, sight of wonder!
Seen, a pictorial portent, under,

O great Rialto, the vast round
Of thy thrice-solid arch profound!—
How light we go, how softly! Ah,
Life should be as the gondola!

ARTHUR HUGH CLOUGH

A WET SHEET AND A FLOWING SEA

A wet sheet and a flowing sea,
    A wind that follows fast
And fills the white and rustling sail
    And bends the gallant mast;
And bends the gallant mast, my boys,
    While, like the eagle free,
Away the good ship flies, and leaves
    Old England on the lee.

O for a soft and gentle wind!
    I heard a fair one cry;
But give to me the snoring breeze
    And white waves heaving high;
And white waves heaving high, my boys,
    The good ship tight and free—
The world of waters is our home,
    And merry men are we.

There's tempest in yon horned moon,
    And lightning in yon cloud;
And hark the music, mariners!
    The wind is piping loud;
The wind is piping loud, my boys,
    The lightning flashes free—
While the hollow oak our palace is,
    Our heritage the sea.

ALLAN CUNNINGHAM

89

BERMUDAS

Where the remote Bermudas ride
In th' ocean's bosom unespied,
From a small boat that rowed along
The listening winds received this song:
   What should we do but sing His praise
Who led us through the watery maze,
Unto an isle so long unknown,
And yet far kinder than our own?
Where He the huge sea-monsters wracks
That lift the deep upon their backs.
He lands us on a grassy stage,
Safe from the storms and prelate's rage.
He gave us this eternal spring
Which here enamels everything;
And sends the fowls to us in care
On daily visits through the air;
He hangs in shades the orange bright,
Like golden lamps in a green night,
And does in the pomegranates close
Jewels more rich than Ormus shows.
He makes the figs our mouths to meet,
And throws the melons at our feet;
But apples plants of such a price,
No tree could ever bear them twice.
With cedars chosen by His hand
From Lebanon He stores the land;
And makes the hollow seas that roar
Proclaim the ambergris on shore.
He cast (of which we rather boast)
The Gospel's pearl upon our coast,
And in these rocks for us did frame
A temple, where to sound His name.
Oh, let our voice His praise exalt
Till it arrive at Heaven's vault,

Which then (perhaps) rebounding may
Echo beyond the Mexique bay.
   Thus sung they in the English boat
A holy and a cheerful note:
And all the way to guide their chime
With falling oars they kept the time.

ANDREW MARVELL

HOME-THOUGHTS, FROM THE SEA

Nobly, nobly Cape Saint Vincent to the North-west died away;
Sunset ran, one glorious blood-red, reeking into Cadiz Bay;
Bluish 'mid the burning water, full in face Trafalgar lay;
In the dimmest North-east distance dawn'd Gibraltar grand and
   gray;
'Here and here did England help me: how can I help England?'
   —say
Whoso turns as I, this evening, turn to God to praise and pray,
While Jove's planet rises yonder, silent over Africa.

ROBERT BROWNING

THE DOWNS

O bold majestic downs, smooth, fair and lonely;
O still solitude, only matched in the skies;
   Perilous in steep places,
   Soft in the level races,
Where sweeping in phantom silence the cloudland flies;
With lovely undulation of fall and rise;
   Entrenched with thickets thorned,
By delicate miniature dainty flowers adorned!

I climb your crown, and lo! a sight surprising
Of sea in front uprising, steep and wide:
   And scattered ships ascending
   To heaven, lost in the blending
Of distant blues, where water and sky divide,
Urging their engines against wind and tide,
   And all so small and slow
They seem to be wearily pointing the way they would go.

The accumulated murmur of soft plashing,
Of waves on rocks dashing and searching the sands,
   Takes my ear, in the veering
   Baffled wind, as rearing
Upright at the cliff, to the gullies and rifts he stands;
And his conquering surges scour out over the lands;
   While again at the foot of the downs
He masses his strength to recover the topmost crowns.

ROBERT BRIDGES

SEA FEVER

I must go down to the seas again, to the lonely sea and the sky,
And all I ask is a tall ship and a star to steer her by;
And the wheel's kick and the wind's song and the white sail's
   shaking,
And a grey mist on the sea's face, and a grey dawn breaking.

I must go down to the seas again, for the call of the running tide
Is a wild call and clear call that may not be denied;
And all I ask is a windy day with the white clouds flying,
And the flung spray and the blown spume, and the sea-gulls
   crying.

I must go down to the seas again, to the vagrant gypsy life,
To the gull's way and the whale's way where the wind's like a
    whetted knife;
And all I ask is a merry yarn from a laughing fellow-rover,
And quiet sleep and a sweet dream when the long trick's over.

JOHN MASEFIELD

GO DOWN TO KEW IN LILAC-TIME

Go down to Kew in lilac-time, in lilac-time, in lilac-time;
    Go down to Kew in lilac-time (it isn't far from London!);
And you shall wander hand in hand with love in summer's
    wonderland;
    Go down to Kew in lilac-time (it isn't far from London!).

The cherry-trees are seas of bloom and soft perfume and sweet
    perfume,
    The cherry-trees are seas of bloom (and oh, so near to
    London!);
And there they say, when dawn is high, and all the world's a
    blaze of sky,
    The cuckoo, though he's very shy, will sing a song for
    London.

The nightingale is rather rare and yet they say you'll hear him
    there
    At Kew, at Kew in lilac-time (and oh, so near to London!);
The linnet and the throstle, too, and after dark the long halloo,
    And golden-eyed tu-whit, tu-whoo of owls that ogle London.

For Noah hardly knew a bird of any kind that isn't heard
    At Kew, at Kew in lilac-time (and oh, so near to London!);
And when the rose begins to pout, and all the chestnut spires are
    out.
    You'll hear the rest without a doubt, all chorusing for
    London:—

Come down to Kew in lilac-time, in lilac-time, in lilac-time;
  Come down to Kew in lilac-time (it isn't far from London!);
And you shall wander hand in hand with love in summer's
    wonderland;
  Come down to Kew in lilac-time (it isn't far from London!).

ALFRED NOYES
From *The Barrel-Organ*

QUAYSIDE

And glad to find, on again looking at it,
It was not nearly so good as I had thought—
You know the ship is moving when you see
The boxes on the quayside sliding away
And growing smaller—and having real delight
When the port's cleared and the coast out of sight,
And ships are few, each on its proper course,
With no occasion for approach or discourse.

ROBERT GRAVES

ON CLUBS

Man is said to be a Sociable Animal, and, as an Instance of it, we may observe, that we take all Occasions and Pretences of forming ourselves into those little Nocturnal Assemblies which are commonly known by the name of Clubs. When a Sett of Men find themselves agree in any Particular, tho' never so trivial, they establish themselves into a kind of Fraternity, and meet once or twice a Week, upon the Account of such a Fantastick Resemblance. I know a considerable Market-town in which there was a Club of Fat-Men that did not come together (as you may well suppose) to entertain one another with Sprightliness and Wit, but to keep one another in Countenance: The Room, where the Club met, was something of the largest, and had two Entrances, the one by a Door of a moderate Size, and the other by a Pair of Folding-Doors. If a Candidate for this Corpulent Club could make his Entrance through the first he was looked upon as unqualified; but if he stuck in the Passage, and could not force his Way through it, the Folding-Doors were immediately thrown open for his Reception, and he was saluted as a Brother. I have heard that this Club, though it consisted but of fifteen Persons, weighed above three Tun.

In Opposition to this Society there sprung up another, composed of Scare-Crows and Skeletons, who being very meagre and envious, did all they could to thwart the Designs of their Bulky Brethren, whom they represented as Men of Dangerous Principles; till at length they worked them out of the Favour of the People, and consequently out of the Magistracy. These Factions tore the Corporation in Pieces for several Years, till at length they came to this Accommodation: that the two Bailiffs of the Town should be annually chosen out of the two Clubs; by which Means the principal Magistrates are at this Day coupled like Rabbets, one fat and one lean.

Every one has heard of the Club, or rather the Confederacy, of the Kings. This grand Alliance was formed a little after the Return of King Charles the Second, and admitted into it Men of all Qualities and Professions, provided they agreed in this Sir-name of King, which, as they imagined, sufficiently declared the Owners of it to be altogether untainted with Republican and Anti-Monarchical Principles.

A Christian Name has likewise been often used as a Badge of Distinction, and made the Occasion of a Club. That of the Georges, which used to meet at the Sign of the George, on St. George's day, and swear Before George, is still fresh in every one's Memory.

There are at present in several Parts of this City what they call Street-Clubs, in which the chief Inhabitants of the Street converse together every Night. I remember, upon my enquiring after Lodgings in Ormond-Street, the Landlord, to recommend that Quarter of the Town, told me there was at that time a very good

Club in it; he also told me, upon further Discourse with him, that two or three noisy Country Squires, who were settled there the Year before, had considerably sunk the Price of House-Rent; and that the Club (to Prevent the like Inconveniencies for the future) had thoughts of taking every House that became vacant into their own Hands, till they had found a Tenant for it of a Sociable Nature and good Conversation.

The Hum-Drum Club, of which I was formerly an unworthy Member, was made up of very honest Gentlemen, of peaceable Dispositions, that used to sit together, smoak their Pipes, and say nothing 'till Mid-night. The Mum Club (as I am informed) is an Institution of the same Nature, and as great an Enemy to Noise.

After these two innocent Societies, I cannot forbear mentioning a very mischievous one that was erected in the Reign of King Charles the Second: I mean the Club of Duellists, in which none was to be admitted that had not fought his Man. The President of it was said to have killed half a dozen in single Combat; and as for the other Members, they took their Seats according to the number of their Slain. There was likewise a Side-Table for such as had only drawn Blood, and shown a laudable Ambition of taking the first Opportunity to qualify themselves for the first Table. This Club, consisting only of Men of Honour, did not continue long, most of the Members of it being put to the Sword, or hanged, a little after its Institution.

Our Modern celebrated Clubs are founded upon Eating and Drinking, which are Points wherein most Men agree, and in which the Learned and Illiterate, the Dull and the Airy, the Philosopher and the Buffoon, can all of them bear a Part. The Kit-Cat it self is said to have taken its Original from a Mutton-Pye. The Beef-Steak and October Clubs are neither of them averse to Eating and Drinking, if we may form a Judgment of them from their respective Titles.

When Men are thus knit together, by Love of Society, not a Spirit of Faction, and do not meet to censure or annoy those that are absent, but to enjoy one another: When they are thus combined for their own Improvement, or for the Good of others, or at least to relax themselves from the Business of the Day, by an innocent and chearful Conversation, there may be something very useful in these little Institutions and Establishments.

I cannot forbear concluding this Paper with a Scheme of Laws that I met with upon a Wall in a little Ale-house: How I came thither I may inform my Reader at a more convenient time. These Laws were enacted by a Knot of Artizans and Mechanicks, who used to meet every Night; and as there is something in them which gives us a pretty Picture of low Life, I shall transcribe them Word for Word.

RULES to be observed in the Two-penny Club, erected in this Place, for the Preservation of Friendship and good Neighbourhood.

I. Every Member at his first coming in shall lay down his Two Pence.

II. Every Member shall fill his Pipe out of his own Box.

III. If any Member absents himself he shall forfeit a Penny for the Use of the Club, unless in case of Sickness or Imprisonment.

IV. If any Member swears or curses, his Neighbour may give him a Kick upon the Shins.

V. If any Member tells Stories in the Club that are not true, he shall forfeit for every third Lie an Half-Penny.

VI. If any Member strikes another wrongfully, he shall pay his Club for him.

VII. If any Member brings his Wife into the Club, he shall pay for whatever she drinks or smoaks.

VIII. If any Member's Wife comes to fetch him Home from the Club, she shall speak to him without the Door.

IX. If any Member calls another Cuckold, he shall be turned out of the Club.

X. None shall be admitted into the Club that is of the same Trade with any Member of it.

XI. None of the Club shall have his Cloaths or Shoes made or mended, but by a Brother Member.

XII. No Non-juror shall be capable of being a Member.

The Morality of this little Club is guarded by such wholesome Laws and Penalties, that I question not but my Reader will be as well pleased with them as he would have been with the Leges Convivales of Ben. Jonson, the Regulations of an old Roman Club cited by Lipsius, or the rules of a Symposium in an ancient Greek author.

JOSEPH ADDISON
From *The Spectator*

PRELUDE

Still south I went and west and south again,
Through Wicklow from the morning till the night,
And far from cities and the sights of men,
Lived with the sunshine and the moon's delight.

I knew the stars, the flowers, and the birds,
The grey and wintry sides of many glens,
And did but half remember human words,
In converse with the mountains, moors and fens.

J. M. SYNGE

FRANCE

To kinder skies, where gentler manners reign,
I turn; and France displays her bright domain.
Gay sprightly land of mirth and social ease,
Pleas'd with thyself, whom all the world can please,
How often have I led thy sportive choir,
With tuneless pipe, beside the murmuring Loire?

Where shading elms along the margin grew,
And freshen'd from the wave the Zephyr flew;
And haply, though my harsh touch faltering still,
But mock'd all tune, and marr'd the dancer's skill;
Yet would the village praise my wonderous pow'r,
And dance, forgetful of the noon-tide hour.
Alike all ages. Dames of ancient days
Have led their children through the mirthful maze,
And the gay grandsire, skill'd in gestic lore,
Has frisk'd beneath the burthen of threescore.
  So blest a life these thoughtless realms display,
Thus idly busy rolls their world away:
Theirs are those arts that mind to mind endear,
For honour forms the social temper here.
Honour, that praise which real merit gains,
Or even imaginary worth obtains,
Here passes current; paid from hand to hand,
It shifts in splendid traffic round the land:
From courts to camps, to cottages it strays,
And all are taught an avarice of praise;
They please, are pleas'd, they give to get esteem,
'Till, seeming blest, they grow to what they seem.

OLIVER GOLDSMITH
From *The Traveller*

TO THE VIRGINIAN VOYAGE

You brave heroic minds
  Worthy your country's name,
    That honour still pursue;
    Go and subdue!
Whilst loitering hinds
  Lurk here at home with shame.

Britons, you stay too long:
　　Quickly aboard bestow you,
　　　And with a merry gale
　　　Swell your stretch'd sail
With vows as strong
　　As the winds that blow you.

Your course securely steer,
　　West and by south forth keep!
　　　Rocks, lee-shores, nor shoals
　　　When Eolus scowls
You need not fear;
　　So absolute the deep.

And cheerfully at sea
　　Success you still entice
　　　To get the pearl and gold,
　　　And ours to hold
Virginia,
　　Earth's only paradise.

Where nature hath in store
　　Fowl, venison, and fish,
　　　And the fruitfull'st soil
　　　Without your toil
Three harvests more,
　　All greater than your wish.

And the ambitious vine
　　Crowns with his purple mass
　　　The cedar reaching high
　　　To kiss the sky,
The cypress, pine,
　　And useful sassafras.

To whom the Golden Age
　　Still nature's laws doth give,
　　　No other cares attend,
　　　But them to defend
From winter's rage,
　　That long there doth not live.

When as the luscious smell
　　Of that delicious land
　　　Above the seas that flows
　　　The clear wind throws,
Your hearts to swell
　　Approaching the dear strand;

In kenning of the shore
　　(Thanks to God first given)
　　　O you the happiest men,
　　　Be frolic then!
Let cannons roar,
　　Frighting the wide heaven.

And in regions far,
　　Such heroes bring ye forth
　　　As those from whom we came;
　　　And plant our name
Under that star
　　Not known unto our North.

And as there plenty grows
　　Of laurel everywhere—
　　　Apollo's sacred tree—
　　　You it may see
A poet's brows
　　To crown, that may sing there.

Thy *Voyages* attend,
 Industrious Hakluyt,
  Whose reading shall inflame
  Men to seek fame,
 And much commend
  To after times thy wit.

MICHAEL DRAYTON

THE JUMBLIES

I

They went to sea in a Sieve, they did,
 In a Sieve they went to sea:
In spite of all their friends could say,
On a winter's morn, on a stormy day,
 In a Sieve they went to sea!
And when the Sieve turned round and round,
And every one cried, 'You'll all be drowned!'
They called aloud, 'Our Sieve ain't big,
But we don't care a button, we don't care a fig!
 In a Sieve we'll go to sea!'
  Far and few, far and few,
   Are the lands where the Jumblies live;
   Their heads are green, and their hands are blue,
   And they went to sea in a Sieve.

2

They sailed away in a Sieve, they did,
 In a Sieve they sailed so fast,
With only a beautiful pea-green veil
Tied with a riband by way of a sail,
 To a small tobacco-pipe mast;
And every one said, who saw them go,
'O won't they be soon upset, you know!

For the sky is dark, and the voyage is long,
And happen what may, it's extremely wrong
  In a Sieve to sail so fast!'
    Far and few, far and few,
      Are the lands where the Jumblies live;
    Their heads are green, and their hands are blue,
      And they went to sea in a Sieve.

3

The water it soon came in, it did,
  The water it soon came in;
So to keep them dry, they wrapped their feet
In a pinky paper all folded neat.
  And they fastened it down with a pin.
And they passed the night in a crockery-jar,
And each of them said, 'How wise we are!
Though the sky be dark, and the voyage be long,
Yet we never can think we were rash or wrong,
  While round in our Sieve we spin!'
    Far and few, far and few,
      Are the lands where the Jumblies live;
    Their heads are green, and their hands are blue,
      And they went to sea in a Sieve.

4

And all night long they sailed away;
  And when the sun went down,
They whistled and warbled a moony song
To the echoing sound of a coppery gong,
  In the shade of the mountains brown.
'O Timballo! How happy we are,
When we live in a sieve and a crockery-jar,
And all night long in the moonlight pale,
We sail away with a pea-green sail,
  In the shade of the mountains brown!'

Far and few, far and few,
  Are the lands where the Jumblies live;
Their heads are green, and their hands are blue,
  And they went to sea in a Sieve.

5

They sailed to the Western Sea, they did,
  To a land all covered with trees,
And they bought an Owl, and a useful Cart,
And a pound of Rice, and a Cranberry Tart,
  And a hive of silvery Bees.
And they bought a Pig, and some green Jack-daws,
And a lovely Monkey with lollipop paws,
And forty bottles of Ring-Bo-Ree,
  And no end of Stilton Cheese.
    Far and few, far and few,
      Are the lands where the Jumblies live;
    Their heads are green, and their hands are blue,
      And they went to sea in a Sieve.

6

And in twenty years they all came back,
  In twenty years or more,
And every one said, 'How tall they've grown!
For they've been to the Lakes, and the Terrible Zone,
  And the hills of the Chankly Bore';
And they drank their health, and gave them a feast
Of dumplings made of beautiful yeast;
And every one said, 'If we only live,
We too will go to sea in a Sieve,—
  To the hills of the Chankly Bore!'
    Far and few, far and few,
      Are the lands where the Jumblies live;
    Their heads are green, and their hands are blue,
      And they went to sea in a Sieve.

EDWARD LEAR

SCOTCH RHAPSODY

'Do not take a bath in Jordan,
                    Gordon,
On the holy Sabbath, on the peaceful day!'
Said the huntsman, playing on his old bagpipe,
Boring to death the pheasant and the snipe—
Boring the ptarmigan and grouse for fun—
Boring them worse than a nine-bore gun.
Till the flaxen leaves where the prunes are ripe
Heard the tartan wind a-droning in the pipe,
And they heard MacPherson say:
'Where do the waves go? What hotels
Hide their bustles and their gay ombrelles!
And would there be room?—Would there be *room*?
  Would there be room for me?'
There is a hotel at Ostend
Cold as the wind, without an end,
Haunted by ghostly poor relations
Of Bostonian conversations
(Bagpipes rotting through the walls).
And there the pearl-ropes fall like shawls
With a noise like marine waterfalls.
And 'Another little drink wouldn't do us any harm'
Pierces through the Sabbatical calm.
And that is the place for me!
So do not take a bath in Jordan,
                    Gordon,
On the holy Sabbath, on the peaceful day—
Or you'll never go to heaven, Gordon MacPherson,
And speaking purely as a private person
That is the place—*that* is the place—that is the *place*
  for me!

EDITH SITWELL

Staying at Home

A SONG OF ENGLAND

There is a song of England that none shall ever sing;
    So sweet it is and fleet it is
That none whose words are not as fleet as birds upon the wing,
    And regal as her mountains,
    And radiant as the fountains
Of rainbow-coloured sea-spray that every wave can fling
Against the cliffs of England, the sturdy cliffs of England,
    Could more than seem to dream of it,
    Or catch one flying gleam of it,
Above the seas of England that never cease to sing.

There is a song of England that only lovers know;
    So rare it is and fair it is,
Oh, like a fairy rose it is upon a drift of snow,
    So cold and sweet and sunny,
    So full of hidden honey,
So like a flight of butterflies where rose and lily blow
Along the lanes of England, the leafy lanes of England;
    When flowers are at their vespers
    And full of little whispers,
The boys and girls of England shall sing it as they go.

There is a song of England that only love may sing,
    So sure it is and pure it is;
And seaward with the seamew it spreads a whiter wing,
    And with the skylark hovers
    Above the tryst of lovers,

Above the kiss and whisper that led the lovely Spring
Through all the glades of England, the ferny glades of England,
  Until the way enwound her
  With sprays of May, and crowned her
With stars of frosty blossom in a merry morris-ring.

There is a song of England that haunts her hours of rest;
  The calm of it and balm of it
Are breathed from every hedgerow that blushes to the West:
  From cottage doors that nightly
  Cast their welcome out so brightly
On the lanes where laughing children are lifted and caressed
By the tenderest hands in England, hard and blistered hands of
      England;
  And from the restful sighing
  Of the sleepers that are lying
With the arms of God around them on the night's contented
      breast.

There is a song of England that wanders in the wind;
  So sad it is and glad it is
That men who hear it madden and their eyes are wet and blind,
  For the lowlands and the highlands
  Of the unforgotten islands,
For the Islands of the Blessed, and the rest they cannot find
As they grope in dreams to England and the love they left in
      England;
  Little feet that danced to meet them,
  And the lips that used to greet them,
And the watcher at the window in the home they left behind.

There is a song of England that thrills the beating blood
  With burning cries and yearning
Tides of hidden aspiration hardly known or understood;
  Aspirations of the creature
  Tow'rds the unity of Nature;

Sudden chivalries revealing whence the longing is renewed
In the men that live for England, live and love and die for
    England:
  By the light of their desire
  They shall blindly blunder higher
To a wider, grander Kingdom and a deeper, nobler Good.

There is a song of England that only God can hear;
  So gloriously victorious,
It soars above the choral stars that sing the Golden Year;
  Till even the cloudy shadows
  That wander o'er her meadows
In silent purple harmonies declare His glory there,
Along the hills of England, the billowy hills of England,
  While heaven rolls and ranges
  Through all the myriad changes
That mirror God in music to the mortal eye and ear.

There is a song of England that none shall ever sing:
  So sweet it is and fleet it is
That none whose words are not as fleet as birds upon the wing,
  And regal as her mountains,
  And radiant as the fountains
Of rainbow-coloured sea-spray that every wave can fling
Against the cliffs of England, the sturdy cliffs of England,
  Could more than seem to dream of it,
  Or catch one flying gleam of it,
Above the seas of England that never cease to sing.

ALFRED NOYES

AN ITALIAN SONG

Dear is my little native vale,
The ring-dove builds and murmurs there;
Close by my cot she tells her tale
To every passing villager:
The squirrel leaps from tree to tree,
And shells his nuts at liberty.

In orange groves and myrtle bowers,
That breathe a gale of fragrance round,
I charm the fairy-footed hours
With my loved lute's romantic sound;
Or crowns of living laurel weave,
For those that win the race at eve.

The shepherd's horn at break of day,
The ballet danced in twilight glade,
The canzonet and roundelay
Sung in the silent greenwood shade;
These simple joys, that never fail,
Shall bind me to my native vale.

SAMUEL ROGERS

HOME-THOUGHTS, FROM ABROAD

O to be in England
Now that April's there,
And whoever wakes in England
Sees, some morning, unaware,
That the lowest boughs and the brushwood sheaf
Round the elm-tree bole are in tiny leaf,
While the chaffinch sings on the orchard bough
In England—now!

And after April, when May follows,
And the whitethroat builds, and all the swallows!
Hark, where my blossom'd pear-tree in the hedge
Leans to the field and scatters on the clover
Blossoms and dewdrops—at the bent spray's edge—
That's the wise thrush; he sings each song twice over,
Lest you should think he never could recapture
The first fine careless rapture!
And though the fields look rough with hoary dew,
All will be gay when noontide wakes anew
The buttercups, the little children's dower
—Far brighter than this gaudy melon-flower!

ROBERT BROWNING

HAME, HAME, HAME

Hame, hame, hame, O hame fain wad I be—
O hame, hame, hame, to my ain countree!

When the flower is i' the bud and the leaf is on the tree,
The larks shall sing me hame in my ain countree;
Hame, hame, hame, O hame fain wad I be—
O hame, hame, hame, to my ain countree!

The green leaf o' loyaltie's beginning for to fa',
The bonnie White Rose it is withering an' a';
But I'll water 't wi' the blude of usurping tyrannie,
An' green it will graw in my ain countree.

O, there's nocht now frae ruin my country can save,
But the keys o' kind heaven, to open the grave;
That a' the noble martyrs wha died for loyaltie
May rise again an' fight for their ain countree.

The great now are gane, a' wha ventured to save,
The new grass is springing on the tap o' their grave;
But the sun through the mirk blinks blythe in my e'e,
'I'll shine on ye yet in your ain countree.'

Hame, hame, hame, O hame fain wad I be—
O hame, hame, hame, to my ain countree!

ALLAN CUNNINGHAM

BLEST WINTER NIGHTS

Thrice happy days! in rural business past.
Blest winter nights! when, as the genial fire
Chears the wide hall, his cordial family
With soft domestic arts the hours beguile,
And pleasing talk that starts no timerous fame,
With witless wantoness to hunt it down:
Or thro' the fairy-land of tale or song
Delighted wander, in fictitious fates
Engag'd, and all that strikes humanity;
Till lost in fable, they the stealing hour
Of timely rest forget. Sometimes, at eve,
His neighbours lift the latch, and bless unbid
His festal roof; while, o'er the light repast,
And sprightly cups, they mix in social joy;
And, thro' the maze of conversation, trace
Whate'er amuses or improves the mind.
Sometimes at eve (for I delight to taste
The native zest and flavour of the fruit,
Where sense grows wild, and takes of no manure)
The decent, honest, chearful husbandman
Should drown his labours in my friendly bowl;
And at my table find himself at home!

JOHN ARMSTRONG
From The Art of Preserving Health

ENGLAND, MY ENGLAND

What have I done for you,
   England, my England?
What is there I would not do,
   England, my own?
With your glorious eyes austere,
As the Lord were walking near,
Whispering terrible things and dear
   As the Song on your bugles blown,
      England—
   Round the world on your bugles blown!

Where shall the watchful sun,
   England, my England,
Match the master-work you've done,
   England, my own?
When shall he rejoice agen
Such a breed of mighty men
As come forward, one to ten,
   To the Song on your bugles blown,
      England—
   Down the years on your bugles blown?

Ever the faith endures,
   England, my England:—
'Take and break us: we are yours,
   England, my own!
Life is good, and joy runs high
Between English earth and sky:
Death is death; but we shall die
   To the Song on your bugles blown,
      England—
   To the stars on your bugles blown!'

They call you proud and hard,
  England, my England:
You with worlds to watch and ward,
  England, my own!
You whose mail'd hand keeps the keys
Of such teeming destinies,
You could know nor dread nor ease
  Were the Song on your bugles blown,
    England,
  Round the Pit on your bugles blown!

Mother of Ships whose might,
  England, my England,
Is the fierce old Sea's delight,
  England, my own,
Chosen daughter of the Lord,
Spouse-in-Chief of the ancient Sword,
There's the menace of the Word
  In the Song on your bugles blown,
    England—
  Out of heaven on your bugles blown!

WILLIAM ERNEST HENLEY

HAPPY BRITANNIA

Heavens! what a goodly Prospect spreads around,
Of Hills, and Dales, and Woods, and Lawns, and Spires,
And glittering Towns, and gilded Streams, till all
The stretching Landskip into Smoke decays!
Happy Britannia! where the Queen of Arts,
Inspiring Vigor, Liberty abroad
Walks, unconfin'd, even to thy farthest Cotts,
And scatters Plenty with unsparing Hand.
  Rich is thy Soil, and merciful thy Clime;

Thy Streams unfailing in the Summer's Drought;
Unmatch'd thy Guardian-Oaks; thy Valleys float
With golden Waves; and on thy Mountains Flocks
Bleat numberless; while, roving round their Sides,
Bellow the blackening Herds in lusty Droves.
Beneath, thy Meadows glow, and rise unquell'd
Against the Mower's Scythe. On every hand,
Thy Villas shine. Thy Country teems with Wealth;
And Property assures it to the Swain,
Pleas'd, and unweary'd, in his guarded Toil.
  Full are thy Cities with the Sons of Art;
And Trade and Joy, in every busy Street,
Mingling are heard: even Drudgery himself,
As at the Car he sweats, or dusty hews
The Palace-Stone, looks gay. Thy crouded Ports,
Where rising Masts an endless Prospect yield,
With Labour burn, and echo to the Shouts
Of hurry'd Sailor, as he hearty waves
His last Adieu, and loosening every Sheet,
Resigns the spreading Vessel to the Wind.
Bold, firm, and graceful, are thy generous Youth,
By Hardship sinew'd, and by Danger fir'd,
Scattering the Nations where they go; and first
Or in the listed Plain, or wintry Seas.
Mild are thy Glories too, as o'er the Plans
Of thriving Peace thy thoughtful Sires preside;
In Genius, and substantial Learning, high;
For every Virtue, every Worth, renown'd;
Sincere, plain-hearted, hospitable, kind;
Yet like the mustering Thunder when provok'd,
The Dread of Tyrants, and the sole Resource
Of those that under grim Oppression groan.

JAMES THOMSON (the elder)
From *Summer*

O ENGLAND, COUNTRY OF MY
HEART'S DESIRE

O England, country of my heart's desire,
Land of the hedgerow and the village spire,
Land of thatched cottages and murmuring bees,
And wayside inns where one may take one's ease.
Of village green where cricket may be played,
And fat old spaniels sleeping in the shade—
O homeland, far away across the main,
How would I love to see your face again!—
Your daisied meadows and your grassy hills,
Your primrose banks, your parks, your tinkling rills,
Your copses where the purple bluebells grow,
Your quiet lanes where lovers loiter so,
Your cottage-gardens with their wallflower's scent,
Your swallows 'neath the eaves, your sweet content!
And 'mid the fleecy clouds that o'er you spread,
Listen, the skylark singing overhead—
    That's the old country, that's the old home!
    You never forget it wherever you roam.

E. V. LUCAS

THIS ENGLAND

This royal throne of kings, this sceptred isle,
This earth of majesty, this seat of Mars,
This other Eden, demi-paradise,
This fortress built by Nature for herself
Against infection and the hand of war,
This happy breed of men, this little world,
This precious stone set in the silver sea,
Which serves it in the office of a wall,
Or as a moat defensive to a house,

Against the envy of less happier lands,
This blessed plot, this earth, this realm, this England,
This nurse, this teeming womb of royal kings,
Fear'd by their breed and famous by their birth,
Renowned for their deeds as far from home,
For Christian service and true chivalry,
As is the sepulchre in stubborn Jewry
Of the world's ransom, blessed Mary's son:
This land of such dear souls, this dear, dear land . . .

WILLIAM SHAKESPEARE
From *The Tragedy of King Richard the Second*

REAL HAPPINESS

As some lone miser visiting his store,
Bends at his treasure, counts, recounts it o'er;
Hoards after hoards his rising raptures fill,
Yet still he sighs, for hoards are wanting still:
Thus to my breast alternate passions rise,
Pleas'd with each good that heaven to man supplies:
Yet oft a sigh prevails, and sorrows fall,
To see the sum of human bliss so small;
And oft I wish, amidst the scene, to find
Some spot to real happiness consign'd,
Where my worn soul, each wand'ring hope at rest,
May gather bliss to see my fellows blest.
But where to find that happiest spot below,
Who can direct, when all pretend to know?
The shudd'ring tenant of the frigid zone
Boldly proclaims that happiest spot his own,
Extols the treasures of his stormy seas,
And his long nights of revelry and ease;
The naked negroe, panting at the line,
Boasts of his golden sands and palmy wine,

Basks in the glare, or stems the tepid wave,
And thanks his Gods for all the good they gave.
Such is the patriot's boast, where'er we roam,
His first, best country ever is, at home.

And yet, perhaps, if countries we compare,
And estimate the blessings which they share,
Tho' patriots flatter, still shall wisdom find
An equal portion dealt to all mankind,
As different good, by Art or Nature given,
To different nations makes their blessings even.

OLIVER GOLDSMITH
From *The Traveller*

ENGLAND, WITH ALL THY FAULTS

England, with all thy faults, I love thee still--
My country! and, while yet a nook is left,
Where English minds and manners may be found,
Shall be constrain'd to love thee. Though thy clime
Be fickle, and thy year most part deform'd
With dripping rains, or wither'd by a frost—
I would not yet exchange thy sullen skies,
And fields without a flower, for warmer France
With all her vines; nor for Ausonia's groves
Of golden fruitage, and her myrtle bowers.
To shake thy senate, and from heights sublime
Of patriot eloquence to flash down fire
Upon thy foes, was never meant my task:
But I can feel thy fortunes, and partake
Thy joys and sorrows, with as true a heart
As any thunderer there. And I can feel
Thy follies too; and with a just disdain
Frown at effeminates, whose very looks
Reflect dishonour on the land I love.
How, in the name of soldiership and sense,

Should England prosper, when such things, as smooth
And tender as a girl, all essenced o'er
With odours, and as profligate as sweet—
Who sell their laurel for a myrtle wreath,
And love when they should fight; when such as these
Presume to lay their hand upon the ark
Of her magnificent and awful cause?
Time was when it was praise and boast enough
In every clime, and travel where we might,
That we were born her children. Praise enough
To fill th' ambition of a private man,
That Chatham's language was his mother tongue
And Wolfe's great name compatriot with his own.
Farewell those honours, and farewell with them
The hope of such hereafter! They have fall'n
Each in his field of glory; one in arms,
And one in council—Wolfe upon the lap
Of smiling Victory that moment won,
And Chatham, heart-sick of his country's shame!
They made us many soldiers. Chatham still
Consulting England's happiness at home,
Secured it by an unforgiving frown,
If any wrong'd her. Wolfe, where'er he fought,
Put so much of his heart into his act
That his example had a magnet's force,
And all were swift to follow whom all loved.
Those suns are set. Oh, rise some other such!
Or all that we have left is empty talk
Of old achievements, and despair of new.

WILLIAM COWPER

From *The Task* (Book 2: 'The Time-piece')

'Nature I Loved...'

INVOCATION

Rarely, rarely, comest thou,
　　Spirit of Delight!
Wherefore hast thou left me now
　　Many a day and night?
Many a weary night and day
'Tis since thou art fled away.

How shall ever one like me
　　Win thee back again?
With the joyous and the free
　　Thou wilt scoff at pain.
Spirit false! thou hast forgot
All but those who need thee not.

As a lizard with the shade
　　Of a trembling leaf,
Thou with sorrow art dismay'd;
　　Even the sighs of grief
Reproach thee, that thou art not near,
And reproach thou wilt not hear.

Let me set my mournful ditty
　　To a merry measure;
Thou wilt never come for pity,
　　Thou wilt come for pleasure:
Pity then will cut away
Those cruel wings, and thou wilt stay.

I love all that thou lovest,
   Spirit of Delight!
The fresh earth in new leaves drest
   And the starry night;
Autumn evening, and the morn
When the golden mists are born.

I love snow, and all the forms
   Of the radiant frost;
I love waves, and winds, and storms,
   Everything almost
Which is Nature's, and may be
Untainted by man's misery.

I love tranquil solitude,
   And such society
As is quiet, wise, and good;
   Between thee and me
What diff'rence? but thou dost possess
The things I seek, not love them less.

I love Love—though he has wings,
   And like light can flee,
But above all other things,
   Spirit, I love thee—
Thou art love and life! O come!
Make once more my heart thy home!

               PERCY BYSSHE SHELLEY

SPRING

Spring, the sweet spring, is the year's pleasant king;
Then blooms each thing, then maids dance in a ring,
Cold doth not sting, the pretty birds do sing:
   Cuckoo, jug-jug, pu-we, to-witta-woo!

The palm and may make country houses gay,
Lambs frisk and play, the shepherds pipe all day,
And we hear aye birds tune this merry lay:
   Cuckoo, jug-jug, pu-we, to-witta-woo!

The fields breathe sweet, the daisies kiss our feet,
Young lovers meet, old wives a-sunning sit;
In every street these tunes our ears do greet:
   Cuckoo, jug-jug, pu-we, to-witta-woo!
     Spring, the sweet spring!

THOMAS NASHE

PIPPA'S SONG

The year's at the spring,
And day's at the morn;
Morning's at seven;
The hill-side's dew-pearl'd;
The lark's on the wing;
The snail's on the thorn;
God's in His heaven—
All's right with the world!

ROBERT BROWNING
From Pippa Passes

A BOY'S SONG

Where the pools are bright and deep,
Where the grey trout lies asleep,
Up the river and over the lea,
That's the way for Billy and me.

Where the blackbird sings the latest,
Where the hawthorn blooms the sweetest,

Where the nestlings chirp and flee,
That's the way for Billy and me.

Where the mowers mow the cleanest,
Where the hay lies thick and greenest,
There to track the homeward bee,
That's the way for Billy and me.

Where the hazel bank is steepest,
Where the shadow falls the deepest,
Where the clustering nuts fall free,
That's the way for Billy and me.

Why the boys should drive away
Little sweet maidens from the play,
Or love to banter and fight so well,
That's the thing I never could tell.

But this I know, I love to play
Through the meadow, among the hay;
Up the water and over the lea,
That's the way for Billy and me.

JAMES HOGG

THANATOPSIS

To him who in the love of Nature holds
Communion with her visible forms, she speaks
A various language; for his gayer hours
She has a voice of gladness, and a smile
And eloquence of beauty, and she glides
Into his darker musings, with a mild
And healing sympathy, that steals away
Their sharpness, ere he is aware. When thoughts

Of the last bitter hour come like a blight
Over thy spirit, and sad images
Of the stern agony, and shroud, and pall,
And breathless darkness, and the narrow house,
Make thee to shudder, and grow sick at heart;—
Go forth, under the open sky, and list
To Nature's teachings, while from all around—
Earth and her waters, and the depths of air—
Comes a still voice—Yet a few days, and thee
The all-beholding sun shall see no more
In all his course; nor yet in the cold ground,
Where thy pale form was laid, with many tears,
Nor in the embrace of ocean, shall exist
Thy image. Earth, that nourished thee, shall claim
Thy growth, to be resolved to earth again,
And, lost each human trace, surrendering up
Thine individual being, shalt thou go
To mix for ever with the elements,
To be a brother to the insensible rock
And to the sluggish clod, which the rude swain
Turns with his share, and treads upon. The oak
Shall send his roots abroad, and pierce thy mould,
Yet not to thine eternal resting-place
Shalt thou retire alone, nor couldst thou wish
Couch more magnificent. Thou shalt lie down
With patriarchs of the infant world—with kings,
The powerful of the earth—the wise, the good,
Fair forms, and hoary seers of ages past,
All in one mighty sepulchre. The hills
Rock-ribbed and ancient as the sun,—the vales
Stretching in pensive quietness between;
The venerable woods—rivers that move
In majesty, and the complaining brooks
That make the meadows green; and, poured round all,
Old Ocean's gray and melancholy waste,—
Are but the solemn decorations all

Of the great tomb of man. The golden sun,
The planets, all the infinite host of heaven,
Are shining on the sad abodes of death,
Through the still lapse of ages. All that tread
The globe are but a handful to the tribes
That slumber in its bosom.—Take the wings
Of morning, pierce the Barcan wilderness,
Or lose thyself in the contiguous woods
Where rolls the Oregon, and hears no sound,
Save his own dashings—yet the dead are there:
And millions in those solitudes, since first
The flight of years began, have laid them down
In their last sleep—the dead reign there alone.
So shalt thou rest, and what if thou withdraw
In silence from the living, and no friend
Take note of thy departure? All that breathe
Will share thy destiny. The gay will laugh
When thou art gone, the solemn brood of care
Plod on, and each one as before will chase
His favorite phantom; yet, all these shall leave
Their mirth and their employments, and shall come
And make their bed with thee. As the long train
Of ages glide away, the sons of men,
The youth in life's green spring, and he who goes
In the full strength of years, matron and maid,
The speechless babe, and the gray-headed man—
Shall one by one be gathered to thy side,
By those, who in their turn shall follow them.

So live, that when thy summons comes to join
The innumerable caravan, which moves
To that mysterious realm, where each shall take
His chamber in the silent halls of death,
Thou go not, like the quarry-slave at night,
Scourged to his dungeon, but, sustained and soothed,
By an unfaltering trust, approach thy grave,

Like one who wraps the drapery of his couch
About him, and lies down to pleasant dreams.

WILLIAM CULLEN BRYANT

OVER HILL, OVER DALE

Over hill, over dale,
   Thorough bush, thorough briar,
Over park, over pale,
   Thorough flood, thorough fire,
I do wander everywhere,
Swifter than the moone's sphere;
And I serve the fairy queen,
To dew her orbs upon the green.
The cowslips tall her pensioners be:
In their gold coats spots you see;
Those be rubies, fairy favours,
In those freckles live their savours:
I must go seek some dewdrops here,
And hang a pearl in every cowslip's ear.
Farewell, thou lob of spirits; I'll be gone:
Our queen and all her elves come here anon.

WILLIAM SHAKESPEARE
From A Midsummer-Night's Dream

LOVELIEST OF TREES

Loveliest of trees, the cherry now
Is hung with bloom along the bough
And stands about the woodland ride
Wearing white for Eastertide.

Now, of my threescore years and ten,
Twenty will not come again,
And take from seventy springs a score,
It only leaves me fifty more.

And since to look at things in bloom
Fifty springs are little room,
About the woodlands I will go
To see the cherry hung with snow.

A. E. HOUSMAN

From *A Shropshire Lad*

SPRING FLOWERS

Along the blushing Borders, bright with Dew,
And in yon mingled Wilderness of Flowers,
Fair-handed Spring unbosoms every Grace:
Throws out the Snow-drop, and the Crocus first;
The Daisy, Primrose, Violet darkly blue,
And Polyanthus of unnumber'd Dyes;
The yellow Wall-Flower, stain'd with iron Brown;
And lavish Stock that scents the Garden round:
From the soft Wing of vernal Breezes shed,
Anemonies; Auriculas, enrich'd
With shining Meal o'er all their velvet Leaves;
And full Ranunculas, of glowing Red.
Then comes the Tulip-Race, where Beauty plays
Her idle Freaks: from Family diffus'd
To Family, as flies the Father-Dust,
The varied Colours run; and while they break
On the charm'd Eye, th' exulting Florist marks,
With secret Pride, the Wonders of his Hand,
No gradual Bloom is wanting; from the Bud,
First-born of Spring, to Summer's musky Tribes:
Nor Hyacinths, deep-purpled; nor Jonquils,

Of potent Fragrance; nor Narcissus fair,
As o'er the fabled Fountain hanging still;
Nor broad Carnations; nor gay-spotted Pinks;
Nor, shower'd from every Bush, the Damask-rose:
Infinite Numbers, Delicacies, Smells,
With Hues on Hues Expression cannot paint,
The Breath of Nature, and her endless Bloom.

JAMES THOMSON (the elder)
From *Spring*

HYMN TO THE SPIRIT OF NATURE

Life of Life! thy lips enkindle
   With their love the breath between them;
And thy smiles before they dwindle
   Make the cold air fire: then screen them
In those locks, where whoso gazes
Faints, entangled in their mazes.

Child of Light! thy limbs are burning
   Through the veil which seems to hide them,
As the radiant lines of morning
   Through thin clouds, ere they divide them;
And this atmosphere divinest
Shrouds thee wheresoe'er thou shinest.

Fair are others: none beholds thee;
   But thy voice sounds low and tender
Like the fairest, for it folds thee
   From the sight, that liquid splendour;
And all feel, yet see thee never,
As I feel now, lost for ever!

Lamp of Earth! where'er thou movest
  Its dim shapes are clad with brightness,
And the souls of whom thou lovest
  Walk upon the winds with lightness
Till they fail, as I am failing,
Dizzy, lost, yet unbewailing!

PERCY BYSSHE SHELLEY

TO THE DAISY

With little here to do or see
Of things that in the great world be,
Sweet Daisy! oft I talk to thee,
  For thou art worthy,
Thou unassuming commonplace
Of Nature, with that homely face,
And yet with something of a grace
  Which Love makes for thee!

Oft on the dappled turf at ease
I sit and play with similes,
Loose types of things through all degrees,
  Thoughts of thy raising;
And many a fond and idle name
I give to thee, for praise or blame,
As is the humour of the game,
  While I am gazing.

A nun demure, of lowly port;
Or sprightly maiden, of Love's court,
In thy simplicity the sport
  Of all temptations;
A queen in crown of rubies drest;
A starveling in a scanty vest;
Are all, as seems to suit thee best,
  Thy appellations.

A little Cyclops, with one eye
Staring to threaten and defy,
That thought comes next—and instantly
    The freak is over,
The shape will vanish, and behold!
A silver shield with boss of gold
That spreads itself, some fairy bold
    In fight to cover.

I see thee glittering from afar—
And then thou art a pretty star,
Not quite so fair as many are
    In heaven above thee!
Yet like a star, with glittering crest
Self-poised in air thou seem'st to rest;—
May peace come never to his nest
    Who shall reprove thee!

Sweet Flower! for by that name at last
When all my reveries are past
I call thee, and to that cleave fast,
    Sweet silent creature!
That breath'st with me in sun and air,
Do thou, as thou art wont, repair
My heart with gladness, and a share
    Of thy meek nature!

WILLIAM WORDSWORTH

THE DAFFODILS

I wander'd lonely as a cloud
    That floats on high o'er vales and hills,
When all at once I saw a crowd,
    A host of golden daffodils,
Beside the lake, beneath the trees,
Fluttering and dancing in the breeze.

Continuous as the stars that shine
   And twinkle on the Milky Way,
They stretch'd in never-ending line
   Along the margin of a bay:
Ten thousand saw I at a glance,
Tossing their heads in sprightly dance.

The waves beside them danced, but they
   Outdid the sparkling waves in glee:—
A poet could not but be gay
   In such a jocund company!
I gazed, and gazed, but little thought
What wealth the show to me had brought:

For oft, when on my couch I lie
   In vacant or in pensive mood,
They flash upon that inward eye
   Which is the bliss of solitude;
And then my heart with pleasure fills,
And dances with the daffodils.

                WILLIAM WORDSWORTH

PACK, CLOUDS, AWAY

Pack, clouds, away, and welcome day,
   With night we banish sorrow;
Sweet air blow soft, mount larks aloft
   To give my Love good-morrow!
Wings from the wind to please her mind
   Notes from the lark I'll borrow;
Bird, prune thy wing, nightingale sing,
   To give my Love good-morrow;
     To give my Love good-morrow
     Notes from them both I'll borrow.

Wake from thy nest, robin-redbreast,
   Sing, birds, in every furrow;
And from each hill, let music shrill
   Give my fair Love good-morrow!
Blackbird and thrush in every bush,
   Stare, linnet, and cock-sparrow!
You pretty elves, amongst yourselves
   Sing my fair Love good-morrow;
     To give my Love good-morrow
     Sing, birds, in every furrow!

THOMAS HEYWOOD

A THING OF BEAUTY

A thing of beauty is a joy for ever:
Its loveliness increases; it will never
Pass into nothingness; but still will keep
A bower quiet for us, and a sleep
Full of sweet dreams, and health, and quiet breathing.
Therefore, on every morrow, are we wreathing
A flowery band to bind us to the earth,
Spite of despondence, of the inhuman dearth
Of noble natures, of the gloomy days,
Of all the unhealthy and o'er-darkened ways
Made for our searching: yes, in spite of all,
Some shape of beauty moves away the pall
From our dark spirits. Such the sun, the moon,
Trees old and young, sprouting a shady boon
For simple sheep; and such are daffodils
With the green world they live in; and clear rills
That for themselves a cooling covert make
'Gainst the hot season; the mid-forest brake,
Rich with a sprinkling of fair musk-rose blooms:
And such too is the grandeur of the dooms
We have imagined for the mighty dead;
All lovely tales that we have heard or read:

An endless fountain of immortal drink,
Pouring unto us from the heaven's brink.

JOHN KEATS
From *Endymion*

NOTHING IS SO BEAUTIFUL
AS SPRING

Nothing is so beautiful as spring—
   When weeds, in wheels, shoot long and lovely and lush;
  Thrush's eggs look little low heavens, and thrush
Through the echoing timber does so rinse and wring
The ear, it strikes like lightnings to hear him sing;
   The glassy pear tree leaves and blooms, they brush
   The descending blue; that blue is all in a rush
With richness; the racing lambs too have fair their fling.

What is all this juice and all this joy?
   A strain of the earth's sweet being in the beginning
In Eden garden.—Have, get, before it cloy,
   Before it cloud, Christ, lord, and sour with sinning,
Innocent mind and Mayday in girl and boy,
   Most, O maid's child, thy choice and worthy the winning.

GERARD MANLEY HOPKINS

THE PASSIONATE SHEPHERD
TO HIS LOVE

Come live with me, and be my love,
And we will all the pleasures prove
That hills and valleys, dales and fields,
And all the craggy mountains yields.

And we will sit upon the rocks,
Seeing the shepherds feed their flocks

By shallow rivers, to whose falls
Melodious birds sing madrigals.

And I will make thee beds of roses,
And a thousand fragrant posies,
A cap of flowers and a kirtle
Embroider'd all with leaves of myrtle.

A gown made of the finest wool
Which from our pretty lambs we pull,
Fair lined slippers for the cold,
With buckles of the purest gold;

A belt of straw and ivy-buds,
With coral clasps and amber studs,
And if these pleasures may thee move,
Come live with me, and be my love.

Thy silver dishes for thy meat,
As precious as the gods do eat,
Shall on an ivory table be
Prepar'd each day for thee and me.

The shepherd swains shall dance and sing
For thy delight each May-morning;
If these delights thy mind may move,
Then live with me, and be my love.

CHRISTOPHER MARLOWE

WHERE THE BEE SUCKS

Where the bee sucks, there suck I:
In a cowslip's bell I lie;
There I couch when owls do cry.
On the bat's back I do fly

After summer merrily.
Merrily, merrily shall I live now
Under the blossom that hangs on the bough.

WILLIAM SHAKESPEARE
From *The Tempest*

WHEN DAFFODILS BEGIN TO PEER

When daffodils begin to peer
   With heigh! the doxy over the dale,
Why, then comes in the sweet o' the year;
   For the red blood reigns in the winter's pale.

The white sheet bleaching on the hedge,
   With heigh! the sweet birds, O! how they sing,
Doth set my pugging tooth on edge;
   For a quart of ale is a dish for a king.

The lark, that tirra-lirra chants,
   With heigh! with heigh! the thrush and the jay,
Are summer songs for me and my aunts,
   While we lie tumbling in the hay.

WILLIAM SHAKESPEARE
From *The Winter's Tale*

IMMORTAL NATURE

Roll on, Ye Stars! exult in youthful prime,
Mark with bright curves the printless steps of Time;
Near and more near your beamy cars approach
And lessening orbs on lessening orbs encroach;—
Flowers of the sky! ye too to age must yield,
Frail as your silken sisters of the field!

Star after star from Heaven's high arch shall rush,
Suns sink on suns, and systems systems crush,
Headlong, extinct, to one dark centre fall,
And Death and Night and Chaos mingle all!
—Till o'er the wreck, emerging from the storm,
Immortal Nature lifts her changeful form,
Mounts from her funeral pyre on wings of flame,
And soars and shines, another and the same.

ERASMUS DARWIN
From *The Economy of Vegetation*

SONG

The primrose in the green forest,
    The violets, they be gay;
The double daisies, and the rest
    That trimly decks the way,
Doth move the spirits with brave delights,
    Who beauty's darlings be:
With hey tricksy, trim-go-tricksy,
    Under the greenwood tree.

THOMAS DELONEY

TO AUTUMN

Season of mists and mellow fruitfulness!
    Close bosom-friend of the maturing sun;
Conspiring with him how to load and bless
    With fruit the vines that round the thatch-eaves run;
To bend with apples the moss'd cottage-trees,
    And fill all fruit with ripeness to the core;
        To swell the gourd, and plump the hazel shells
With a sweet kernel; to set budding more,
    And still more, later flowers for the bees,
    Until they think warm days will never cease,
        For Summer has o'er-brimm'd their clammy cells.

Who hath not seen thee oft amid thy store?
  Sometimes whoever seeks abroad may find
Thee sitting careless on a granary floor,
  Thy hair soft-lifted by the winnowing wind,
Or on a half-reap'd furrow sound asleep,
    Drowsed with the fume of poppies, while thy hook
      Spares the next swath and all its twined flowers;
And sometimes like a gleaner thou dost keep
  Steady thy laden head across a brook;
  Or by a cider-press, with patient look,
    Thou watchest the last oozings hours by hours.

Where are the songs of Spring? Ay, where are they?
  Think not of them, thou hast thy music too,—
While barred clouds bloom the soft-dying day,
  And touch the stubble-plains with rosy hue;
Then in a wailful choir the small gnats mourn
  Among the river sallows, borne aloft
    Or sinking as the light wind lives or dies;
And full-grown lambs loud bleat from hilly bourn;
  Hedge-crickets sing; and now with treble soft
  The redbreast whistles from a garden-croft;
    And gathering swallows twitter in the skies.

JOHN KEATS

CHOOSING A MAST

This mast, new-shaved, through whom I rive the ropes,
Says she was once an oread of the slopes,
Graceful and tall upon the rocky highlands,
A slender tree, as vertical as noon,
And her low voice was lovely as the silence
Through which a fountain whistles to the moon,
Who now of the white spray must take the veil
And, for her songs, the thunder of the sail.

I chose her for her fragrance, when the spring
With sweetest resins swelled her fourteenth ring
And with live amber welded her young thews:
I chose her for the glory of the Muse,
Smoother of forms, that her hard-knotted grain,
Grazed by the chisel, shaven by the plane,
Might from the steel as cool a burnish take
As from the bladed moon a windless lake.

I chose her for her eagerness of flight
Where she stood tiptoe on the rocky height
Lifted by her own perfume to the sun,
While through her rustling plumes with eager sound
Her eagle spirit, with the gale at one,
Spreading wide pinions, would have spurned the ground
And her own sleeping shadow, had they not
With thymy fragrance charmed her to the spot.

Lover of song, I chose this mountain pine
Not only for the straightness of her spine
But for her songs: for there she loved to sing
Through a long noon's repose of wave and wing—
The fluvial swirling of her scented hair
Sole rill of song in all that windless air
And her slim form the naiad of the stream
Afloat upon the languor of its theme;

And for the soldier's fare on which she fed—
Her wine the azure, and the snow her bread;
And for her stormy watches on the height—
For only out of solitude or strife
Are born the sons of valour and delight;
And lastly for her rich exulting life
That with the wind stopped not its singing breath
But carolled on, the louder for its death.

Under a pine, when summer days were deep,
We loved the most to lie in love or sleep;
And when in long hexameters the west
Rolled his grey surge, the forest for his lyre,
It was the pines that sang us to our rest
Loud in the wind and fragrant in the fire,
With legioned voices swelling all night long,
From Pelion to Provence, their storm of song.

It was the pines that fanned us in the heat,
The pines, that cheered us in the time of sleet,
For which sweet gifts I set one dryad free—
No longer to the wind a rooted foe,
This nymph shall wander where she longs to be
And with the blue north wind arise and go,
A silver huntress with the moon to run
And fly through rainbows with the rising sun;

And when to pasture in the glittering shoals
The guardian mistral drives his thundering foals,
And when like Tartar horsemen racing free
We ride the snorting fillies of the sea,
My pine shall be the archer of the gale
While on the bending willow curves the sail
From whose great bow the long keel shooting home
Shall fly, the feathered arrow of the foam.

ROY CAMPBELL

'... and, next to Nature, Art'

ON FIRST LOOKING INTO
CHAPMAN'S HOMER

Much have I travell'd in the realms of gold,
  And many goodly states and kingdoms seen;
  Round many western islands have I been
Which bards in fealty to Apollo hold.
Oft of one wide expanse had I been told
  That deep-brow'd Homer ruled as his demesne:
  Yet did I never breathe its pure serene
Till I heard Chapman speak out loud and bold:
Then felt I like some watcher of the skies
  When a new planet swims into his ken;
Or like stout Cortez, when with eagle eyes
  He stared at the Pacific—and all his men
Look'd at each other with a wild surmise—
  Silent, upon a peak in Darien.

JOHN KEATS

ODE ON A GRECIAN URN

Thou still unravish'd bride of quietness,
  Thou foster-child of Silence and slow Time,
Sylvan historian, who canst thus express
  A flowery tale more sweetly than our rhyme:
What leaf-fringed legend haunts about thy shape

Of deities or mortals, or of both.
In Tempé or the dales of Arcady?
What men or gods are these? What maidens loth?
What mad pursuit? What struggle to escape?
What pipes and timbrels? What wild ecstasy?

Heard melodies are sweet, but those unheard
Are sweeter, therefore, ye soft pipes, play on;
Not to the sensual ear, but, more endear'd,
Pipe to the spirit ditties of no tone:
Fair youth, beneath the trees, thou canst not leave
Thy song, nor ever can those trees be bare;
Bold Lover, never, never canst thou kiss,
Though winning near the goal—yet, do not grieve;
She cannot fade, though thou hast not thy bliss,
For ever wilt thou love, and she be fair!

Ah, happy, happy boughs! that cannot shed
Your leaves, nor ever bid the Spring adieu;
And, happy melodist, unwearied,
For ever piping songs for ever new;
More happy love! more happy, happy love!
For ever warm and still to be enjoy'd,
For ever panting and for ever young;
All breathing human passion far above,
That leaves a heart high-sorrowful and cloy'd,
A burning forehead, and a parching tongue.

Who are these coming to the sacrifice?
To what green altar, O mysterious priest,
Lead'st thou that heifer lowing at the skies,
And all her silken flanks with garlands drest?
What little town by river or sea-shore,
Or mountain-built with peaceful citadel,
Is emptied of its folk, this pious morn?
And, little town, thy streets for evermore

Will silent be; and not a soul, to tell
   Why thou art desolate, can e'er return.

O Attic shape! fair attitude? with brede
   Of marble men and maidens overwrought,
With forest branches and the trodden weed;
   Thou, silent form! dost tease us out of thought
As doth eternity. Cold Pastoral!
   When old age shall this generation waste,
   Thou shalt remain, in midst of other woe
Than ours, a friend to man, to whom thou say'st,
   'Beauty is truth, truth beauty,—that is all
   Ye know on earth, and all ye need to know.'

JOHN KEATS

THE AIMS OF ART

Upon the whole it seems to me, that the object and intention of all the Arts is to supply the natural imperfection of things, and often to gratify the mind by realising and embodying what never existed but in the imagination.

It is allowed on all hands, that facts, and events, however they may bind the historian, have no dominion over the poet or the painter. With us, history is made to bend and conform to this great idea of art. And why? Because these arts, in their highest province, are not addressed to the gross senses; but to the desires of the mind, to that spark of divinity which we have within, impatient of being circumscribed and pent up by the world which is about us. Just so much as our art has of this, just so much of dignity, I had almost said of divinity, it exhibits; and those of our artists who possessed this mark of distinction in the highest degree, acquired from thence the glorious appelation, of Divine.

SIR JOSHUA REYNOLDS
From *Discourses*

WILLIAM SHAKESPEARE

Not, if men's tongues and angels' all in one
   Spake, might the world be said that might speak Thee.
   Streams, winds, woods, flowers, fields, mountains, yea, the sea,
What power is in them all to praise the sun?
His praise is this,—he can be praised of none.
   Man, woman, child, praise God for him; but he
   Exults not to be worshipped, but to be.
He is; and, being, beholds his work well done.
All joy, all glory, all sorrow, all strength, all mirth,
Are his: without him, day were night on earth.
   Time knows not his from time's own period.
All lutes, all harps, all viols, all flutes, all lyres,
Fall dumb before him ere one string suspires.
   All stars are angels; but the sun is God.

ALGERNON CHARLES SWINBURNE

DICKENS IN CAMP

Above the pines the moon was slowly drifting,
   The river sang below;
The dim Sierras, far beyond, uplifting
   Their minarets of snow.

The roaring camp-fire, with rude humor, painted
   The ruddy tints of health
On haggard face and form that dropped and fainted
   In the fierce race for wealth.

Till one arose, and from his pack's scant treasure
   A hoarded volume drew,
And cards were dropped from hands of listless leisure
   To hear the tale anew.

And then, while round them shadows gathered faster,
   And as the firelight fell,
He read aloud the book wherein the Master
   Had writ of 'Little Nell.'

Perhaps 'twas boyish fancy—for the reader
   Was youngest of them all—
But, as he read, from clustering pine and cedar
   A silence seemed to fall;

The fir-trees, gathering closer in the shadows,
   Listened in every spray,
While the whole camp with 'Nell' on English meadows
   Wandered, and lost their way.

And so in mountain solitudes—o'ertaken
   As by some spell divine—
Their cares drop from them like the needles shaken
   From out the gusty pine.

Lost is that camp, and wasted all its fire;
   And he who wrought that spell?—
Ah, towering pine and stately Kentish spire,
   Ye have one tale to tell!

Lost is that camp! but let its fragrant story
   Blend with the breath that thrills
With hop-vines' incense all the pensive glory
   That fills the Kentish hills.

And on that grave where English oak and holly
   And laurel wreaths entwine,
Deem it not all a too presumptuous folly—
   This spray of Western pine!

FRANCIS BRET HARTE

ON GUSTO

Gusto in art is power or passion defining any object.—It is not so difficult to explain this term in what relates to expression (of which it may be said to be the highest degree) as in what relates to things without expression, to the natural appearances of objects, as mere colour or form. In one sense, however, there is hardly any object entirely devoid of expression, without some character of power belonging to it, some precise association with pleasure or pain: and it is in giving this truth of character from the truth of feeling, whether in the highest or the lowest degree, but always in the highest degree of which the subject is capable, that gusto consists.

There is a gusto in the colouring of Titian. Not only do his heads seem to think—his bodies seem to feel. This is what the Italians mean by the *morbidezza* of his flesh-colour. It seems sensitive and alive all over; not merely to have the look and texture of flesh, but the feeling in itself. For example, the limbs of his female figures have a luxurious softness and delicacy, which appears conscious of the pleasure of the beholder. As the objects themselves in nature would produce an impression on the sense, distinct from every other object, and having something divine in it, which the heart owns and the imagination consecrates, the objects in the picture preserve the same impression, absolute, unimpaired, stamped with all the truth of passion, the pride of the eye, and the charm of beauty. Rubens makes his flesh-colour like flowers; Albano's is like ivory; Titian's is like flesh, and like nothing else. It is as different from that of other painters as the skin is from a piece of white or red drapery thrown over it. The blood circulates here and there, the blue veins just appear, the rest is distinguished throughout only by that sort of tingling sensation to the eye, which the body feels within itself. This is gusto,—Vandyke's flesh-colour, though it has great truth and purity, wants gusto. It has not the internal character, the living principle in it. It is a smooth surface, not a warm, moving

146

mass. It is painted without passion, with indifference. The hand only has been concerned. The impression slides off from the eye, and does not, like the tones of Titian's pencil, leave a sting behind it in the mind of the spectator. The eye does not acquire a taste of appetite for what it sees. In a word, gusto in painting is where the impression made on one sense excites by affinity those of another.

Michael Angelo's forms are full of gusto. They everywhere obtrude the sense of power upon the eye. His limbs convey an idea of muscular strength, of moral grandeur, and even of intellectual dignity; they are firm, commanding, broad, and massy, capable of executing with ease the determined purposes of the will. His faces have no other expression than his figures, conscious power and capacity. They appear only to think what they shall do, and to know that they can do it. This is what is meant by saying that his style is hard and masculine. It is the reverse of Correggio's, which is effeminate. That is, the gusto of Michael Angelo consists in expressing energy of will without proportionate sensibility, Correggio's in expressing exquisite sensibility without energy of will. In Correggio's faces as well as figures we see neither bones nor muscles, but then what a soul is there, full of sweetness and of grace—pure, playful, soft, angelical! There is sentiment enough in a hand painted by Correggio to set up a school of history painters. Whenever we look at the hands of Correggio's women or of Raphael's, we always wish to touch them.

Again, Titian's landscapes have a prodigious gusto, both in the colouring and forms. We shall never forget one that we saw many years ago in the Orleans Gallery of Acteon hunting. It had a brown, mellow autumnal look. The sky was of the colour of stone. The winds seemed to sing through the rustling branches of the trees, and already you might hear the twanging of bows resound through the tangled mazes of the wood. Mr. West, we understand, has this landscape. He will know if this description of it is just. The landscape background of the St. Peter Martyr is another well-known instance of the power of this great painter to give a romantic interest and an appropriate character to the objects of his pencil, where every circumstance adds to the effect of the scene—the bold trunks of the tall forest trees, the trailing ground plants, with that cold convent spire rising in the distance, amidst the blue sapphire mountains and the golden sky.

Rubens has a great deal of gusto in his Fauns and Satyrs, and in all that expresses motion, but in nothing else. Rembrandt has it in everything; everything in his pictures has a tangible character. If he puts a diamond in the ear of a Burgomaster's wife, it is of the first water; and his furs and stuffs are proof against a Russian winter. Raphael's gusto was only in expression; he had no idea of the character of anything but the human form. The dryness and poverty of his style in other respects is a phenomenon in the art. His trees are like sprigs of grass stuck in a book of botanical specimens. Was it that Raphael never had time to go beyond the walls of Rome? That he was always in the streets, at church, or in the bath? He was not one of the society of Arcadians. . . .

WILLIAM HAZLITT

MONA LISA

She is older than the rocks among which she sits;
Like the Vampire,
She has been dead many times,
And learned the secrets of the grave;
And has been a diver in deep seas,
And keeps their fallen day about her;
And trafficked for strange webs with Eastern merchants;
And, as Leda,
Was the mother of Helen of Troy,
And, as St. Anne,
Was the mother of Mary;
And all this has been to her but as the sound of lyres and flutes,
And lives
Only in the delicacy
With which it has moulded the changing lineaments,
And tinged the eyelids and the hands.

WALTER PATER

A LITTLE LEARNING

A little learning is a dangerous thing;
Drink deep, or taste not the Pierian spring:
There shallow draughts intoxicate the brain,
And drinking largely sobers us again.
Fired at first sight with what the Muse imparts,
In fearless youth we tempt the heights of arts,
While from the bounded level of our mind,
Short views we take, nor see the lengths behind;
But more advanced, behold with strange surprise
New distant scenes of endless science rise!
So pleased at first the towering Alps we try,
Mount o'er the vales and seem to tread the sky,
The eternal snows appear already pass'd,
And the first clouds and mountains seem the last:
But, those attain'd, we tremble to survey
The growing labours of the lengthen'd way,
The increasing prospect tires our wandering eyes,
Hills peep o'er hills, and Alps on Alps arise!

ALEXANDER POPE
From *Essay on Criticism*

VERSES ON THE PROSPECT OF PLANTING ARTS AND LEARNING IN AMERICA

The Muse, disgusted at an age and clime
    Barren of every glorious theme,
In distant lands now waits a better time,
    Producing subjects worthy fame:

In happy climes, where from the genial sun
    And virgin earth such scenes ensue,
The force of art by nature seems outdone,
    And fancied beauties by the true:

149

In happy climes the seat of innocence,
  Where nature guides and virtue rules,
Where men shall not impose for truth and sense,
  The pedantry of courts and schools:

There shall be sung another golden age,
  The rise of empire and of arts,
The good and great inspiring epic rage,
  The wisest heads and noblest hearts.

Not such as Europe breeds in her decay;
  Such as she bred when fresh and young,
When heav'nly flame did animate her clay,
  By future poets shall be sung.

Westward the course of empire takes its way;
  The four first acts already past,
A fifth shall close the drama with the day;
  Time's noblest offspring is the last.

GEORGE BERKELEY, BISHOP OF CLOYNE

UPON WESTMINSTER BRIDGE

Earth has not anything to show more fair:
  Dull would he be of soul who could pass by
  A sight so touching in its majesty:
This City now doth like a garment wear
The beauty of the morning; silent, bare,
  Ships, towers, domes, theatres, and temples lie
  Open unto the fields, and to the sky;
All bright and glittering in the smokeless air.

Never did sun more beautifully steep
  In his first splendour valley, rock, or hill;
Ne'er saw I, never felt, a calm so deep!
  The river glideth at his own sweet will:
  Dear God! the very houses seem asleep;
  And all that mighty heart is lying still!

WILLIAM WORDSWORTH

Freedom

CHARACTER OF A HAPPY LIFE

How happy is he born and taught
That serveth not another's will;
Whose armour is his honest thought,
And simple truth his utmost skill!

Whose passions not his masters are;
Whose soul is still prepared for death,
Not tied unto the world with care
Of public fame, or private breath;

Who envies none that chance doth raise,
Or vice; who never understood
How deepest wounds are given by praise,
Nor rules of state, but rules of good;

Who hath his life from rumours freed,
Whose conscience is his strong retreat;
Whose state can neither flatterers feed,
Nor ruin make accusers great;

Who God doth late and early pray
More of His grace than gifts to lend;
And entertains the harmless day
With a well-chosen book or friend;

—This man is freed from servile bands
Of hope to rise, or fear to fall;
Lord of himself, though not of lands;
And having nothing, yet hath all.

SIR HENRY WOTTON

WHAT ART THOU, FREEDOM?

What art thou, Freedom? O! could slaves
Answer from their living graves
This demand—tyrants would flee
Like a dream's dim imagery:

Thou art not, as impostors say,
A shadow soon to pass away,
A superstition, and a name
Echoing from the cave of Fame.

For the labourer thou art bread,
And a comely table spread
From his daily labour come
In a neat and happy home.

Thou art clothes, and fire, and food
For the trampled multitude—
No—in countries that are free
Such starvation cannot be
As in England now we see.

To the rich thou art a check,
When his foot is on the neck
Of his victim, thou dost make
That he treads upon a snake.

Thou art Justice—ne'er for gold
May thy righteous laws be sold
As laws are in England—thou
Shield'st alike the high and low.

Thou art Wisdom—Freemen never
Dream that God will damn for ever
All who think those things untrue
Of which Priests make such ado.

Thou art Peace—never by thee
Would blood and treasure wasted be
As tyrants wasted them, when all
Leagued to quench thy flame in Gaul.

What if English toil and blood
Was poured forth, even as a flood?
It availed, oh, Liberty,
To dim, but not extinguish thee.

Thou art Love—the rich have kissed
Thy feet, and like him following Christ,
Give their substance to the free
And through the rough world follow thee,

Or turn their wealth to arms, and make
War for thy beloved sake
On wealth, and war, and fraud—whence they
Drew the power which is their prey.

Science, Poetry and Thought
Are thy lamps; they make the lot
Of the dwellers in a cot
So serene, they curse it not.

Spirit, Patience, Gentleness,
All that can adorn and bless
Art thou—let deeds, not words, express
  Thine exceeding loveliness.

PERCY BYSSHE SHELLEY
From *The Mask of Anarchy*

TO ALTHEA FROM PRISON

When Love with unconfined wings
   Hovers within my gates;
And my divine Althea brings
   To whisper at the grates;
When I lie tangled in her hair
   And fettered to her eye;
The birds that wanton in the air
   Know no such liberty.

When flowing cups run swiftly round
   With no allaying Thames,
Our careless heads with roses bound,
   Our hearts with loyal flames;
When thirsty grief in wine we steep,
   When healths and draughts go free,
Fishes that tipple in the deep
   Know no such liberty.

When, like committed linnets, I
   With shriller voice shall sing
The sweetness, mercy, majesty
   And glories of my King;
When I shall voice aloud, how good
   He is, how great should be;
Enlarged winds that curl the flood
   Know no such liberty.

Stone walls do not a prison make,
   Nor iron bars a cage;
Minds innocent and quiet take
   That for an hermitage;
If I have freedom in my love,
   And in my soul am free;
Angels alone, that soar above
   Enjoy such liberty.   RICHARD LOVELACE

A SHEPHERD'S BLISS

But ah! let me under some Kentish hill
Near rolling Medway 'mong my shepherd peers,
With fearless merry-make and piping still,
Securely pass my few and slow-paced years:
    While yet the great Augustus of our nation
    Shuts up old Janus in the long cessation,
Strengthening our pleasing ease, and gives us sure vacation.

There may I, master of a little flock,
Feed my poor lambs, and often change their fare:
My lovely mate shall tend my sparing stock,
And nurse my little ones with pleasing care;
    Whose love and look shall speak their father plain.
    Health be my feast, Heaven hope, content my gain:
So in my little house my lesser heart shall reign.

The beech shall yield a cool safe canopy,
While down I sit, and chant to th' echoing wood:
Ah, singing might I live and singing die!
So by fair Thames or silver Medway's flood,
    The dying swan, when years her temples pierce,
    In music-strains breathes out her life and verse;
And chanting her own dirge rides on her wat'ry hearse.

What shall I then need seek a patron out,
Or beg a favour from a mistress' eyes,
To fence my song against the vulgar rout,
Or shine upon me with her Geminis?
    What care I, if they praise my slender song?
    Or reck I, if they do me right or wrong?
A shepherd's bliss nor stands nor falls to ev'ry tongue.

PHINEAS FLETCHER
From *The Purple Land*

STANZAS ON FREEDOM

Men! whose boast it is that ye
Come of fathers brave and free,
If there breathe on earth a slave,
Are ye truly free and brave?
If ye do not feel the chain
When it works a brother's pain,
Are ye not base slaves indeed,
Slaves unworthy to be freed?

Women! who shall one day bear
Sons to breathe New England air,
If ye hear, without a blush,
Deeds to make the roused blood rush
Like red lava through your veins,
For your sisters now in chains,—
Answer! are ye fit to be
Mothers of the brave and free?

Is true Freedom but to break
Fetters for our own dear sake,
And, with leathern hearts, forget
That we owe mankind a debt?
No! true Freedom is to share
All the chains our brothers wear,
And, with heart and hand, to be
Earnest to make others free!

They are slaves who fear to speak
For the fallen and the weak;
They are slaves who will not choose
Hatred, scoffing, and abuse,

Rather than in silence shrink
From the truth they needs must think;
They are slaves who dare not be
In the right with two or three.

JAMES RUSSELL LOWELL

OF OLD SAT FREEDOM ON
THE HEIGHTS

Of old sat Freedom on the heights,
  The thunders breaking at her feet:
Above her shook the starry lights:
  She heard the torrents meet.

There in her place she did rejoice,
  Self-gather'd in her prophet-mind,
But fragments of her mighty voice
  Came rolling on the wind.

Then stept she down thro' town and field
  To mingle with the human race,
And part by part to men reveal'd
  The fullness of her face—

Grave mother of majestic works,
  From her isle-altar gazing down,
Who, God-like, grasps the triple forks,
  And King-like, wears the crown:

Her open eyes desire the truth.
  The wisdom of a thousand years
Is in them. May perpetual youth
  Keep dry their light from tears;

That her fair form may stand and shine,
   Make bright our days and lights our dreams,
Turning to scorn with lips divine
   The falsehood of extremes!

LORD TENNYSON

WHY I AM A LIBERAL

'Why?' Because all I haply can and do,
   All that I am now, all I hope to be,—
   Whence comes it save from fortune setting free
Body and soul the purpose to pursue,
God traced, for both? If fetters, not a few,
   Of prejudice, convention, fall from me,
   These shall I bid men—each in his degree
Also God-guided—bear, and gayly, too?

But little do or can the best of us:
   That little is achieved through Liberty.
Who, then, dares hold, emancipated thus,
   His fellow shall continue bound? Not I,
Who live, love, labour freely, nor discuss
   A brother's right to freedom. That is 'Why.'

ROBERT BROWNING

ONE MAN'S OPINION

If all mankind minus one were of one opinion, and only one person
were of the contrary opinion, mankind would be no more justified
in silencing that one person than he, if he had the power, would
be justified in silencing mankind. Were an opinion a personal
possession of no value except to the owner; if to be obstructed
in the enjoyment of it were simply a private injury, it would make
some difference whether the injury was inflicted only on a few

persons or on many. But the peculiar evil of silencing the expression of an opinion is that it is robbing the human race; posterity as well as the existing generation; those who dissent from the opinion, still more than those who hold it. If the opinion is right, they are deprived of the opportunity of exchanging error for truth; if wrong, they lose, what is almost as great a benefit, the clearer perception and livelier impression of truth, produced by its collision with error.

It is necessary to consider separately these two hypotheses, each of which has a distinct branch of the argument corresponding to it. We can never be sure that the opinion we are endeavouring to stifle is a false opinion; and if we were sure, stifling it would be an evil still.   JOHN STUART MILL
From *On Liberty*

LET'S STOP SOMEBODY FROM
DOING SOMETHING!

Councillor Busy and Mr. Nose, the Member for
    Misery Wood,
And the Secretaree for the Societee for Making the
    Public Good,
Were walking up and down the town with a frown,
    for everywhere they saw
The bold, bad Britisher doing things which weren't
    against the law;
    And 'This won't do!' said Councillor Busy;
    'This won't do!' said the Honourable Nose;
    'It certainly won't!' said the Secretaree of the S.M.B.P.G.

'Let's stop somebody from doing something!
    Everybody does too much.
People seem to think they've a right to eat and drink,
Talk and walk and respirate and rink,
    Bicycle and bathe and such.

So let's have lots of little regulations,
Let's make laws and jobs for our relations,
There's too much kissing at the railway stations,
Let's find out what everyone is doing,
  And then stop everyone from doing it.'

Councillor Busy and Mr. Nose walked on through
  the summer night,
And a young man looked at his lady friend and
  suddenly smiled outright;
And he hadn't applied for a licence, or been to the
  County Hall,
Or made a report at the magistrate's court, or filled
  up a form at all;
  And 'Did you see that?' said Councillor Busy;
  'Did you see *that*?' said the Honourable Nose;
  'I did see that,' said the Secretaree of the S.M.B.P.G.

'Let's stop somebody from doing something!
  There's too much smiling in the city.
You don't see me in conversation with a she;
We don't osculate, and why should he?
    Send for the Watch Committee!
  Let's make the girls wear high-necked blouses,
  Let's put microphones in people's houses,
  Let's imprison gentlemen who hug their spouses;
Let's find out what everyone is doing,
  And then stop everyone from doing it.'

Councillor Busy went up to Heaven (from eating too
  much fruit),
And the Secretaree took an overdose of tea, and
  Nose soon followed suit;
But they didn't much like the tone of Heaven, for
  the tone was far too gay.
The angels seemed to enjoy themselves, and the
  young folk laughed all day.

And 'This won't do,' said Councillor Busy;
'Did you see *that*?' said the Honourable Nose;
'No self-control!' said the Secretaree of the S.M.B.P.G.

'Let's stop somebody from doing something!
    There's too much liberty here,
Constant song is obviously wrong,
Let's get a plainclothes constable along—
    Somebody should interfere.
Let's stop love and lollipops and smoking,
Let's stamp out unregulated joking,
We've got noses and they're made for poking,
Let's find out what everyone is doing,
    And then stop everyone from doing it.'

A. P. HERBERT

JOAN'S SPEECH TO THE INQUISITOR

It is not the bread and water I fear: I can live on bread: when
have I asked for more? It is no hardship to drink water if the
water be clean. Bread has no sorrow for me, and water no afflic-
tion. But to shut me from the light of the sky and the sight of the
fields and flowers; to chain my feet so that I can never again ride
with the soldiers nor climb the hills; to make me breathe foul
damp darkness, and keep from me everything that brings me
back to the love of God when your wickedness and foolishness
tempt me to hate Him: all this is worse than the furnace in the
Bible that was heated seven times. I could do without my war-
horse; I could drag about in a skirt; I could let the banners and
the trumpets and the knights and soldiers pass me and leave me
behind as they leave the other women, if only I could still hear
the wind in the trees, the larks in the sunshine, the young lambs
crying through the healthy frost, and the blessed blessed church
bells that send my angel voices floating to me on the wind. But

without these things I cannot live; and by your wanting to take them away from me, or from any human creature, I know that your counsel is of the devil, and that mine is of God.

GEORGE BERNARD SHAW

From *Saint Joan*

INDEPENDENCE

Thy spirit, Independence, let me share!
Lord of the lion-heart and eagle-eye,
Thy steps I follow with my bosom bare,
Nor heed the storm that howls along the sky.
Deep in the frozen regions of the north,
A goddess violated brought thee forth,
Immortal Liberty, whose look sublime
Hath bleached the tyrant's cheek in every varying clime.

TOBIAS GEORGE SMOLLETT

SLAVES CANNOT BREATHE IN ENGLAND

Slaves cannot breathe in England; if their lungs
Receive our air, that moment they are free;
They touch our country, and their shackles fall;
That's noble, and bespeaks a nation proud
And jealous of the blessing. Spread it then,
And let it circulate through ev'ry vein
Of all your empire; that where Britain's pow'r
Is felt, mankind may feel her mercy too.

WILLIAM COWPER

From *The Task*

THE SWISS PEASANT

Once Man entirely free, alone and wild,
Was bless'd as free—for he was Nature's child
He, all superior but his God disdain'd,
Walk'd none restraining, and by none restrain'd,
Confess'd no law but what his reason taught,
Did all he wish'd, and wish'd but what he ought.
As Man in his primaeval dower array'd
The image of his glorious sire display'd,
Ev'n so, by vestal Nature guarded, here
The traces of primaeval Man appear.
The native dignity no forms debase,
The eye sublime, and surly lion-grace.
The slave of none, of beasts alone the lord,
He marches with his flute, his book, and sword,
Well taught by that to feel his rights, prepar'd
With this 'the blessings he enjoys to guard.'

WILLIAM WORDSWORTH
From *Descriptive Sketches*

THE ISLES OF GREECE

The isles of Greece, the isles of Greece!
    Where burning Sappho loved and sung,
Where grew the arts of war and peace,
    Where Delos rose, and Phoebus sprung!
Eternal summer gilds them yet,
But all, except their sun, is set.

The Scian and the Teian muse,
    The hero's harp, the lover's lute,
Have found the fame your shores refuse:
    Their place of birth alone is mute
To sounds which echo further west
Than your sires' 'Islands of the Blest.'

The mountains look on Marathon—
  And Marathon looks on the sea;
And musing there an hour alone,
  I dream'd that Greece might still be free;
For standing on the Persians' grave,
I could not deem myself a slave.

A king sate on the rocky brow
  Which looks o'er sea-born Salamis;
And ships, by thousands, lay below,
  And men in nations—all were his!
He counted them at break of day—
And when the sun set where were they?

And where are they? and where art thou,
  My country? On thy voiceless shore
The heroic lay is tuneless now—
  The heroic bosom beats no more!
And must thy lyre, so long divine,
Degenerate into hands like mine?

'Tis something in the dearth of fame,
  Though link'd among a fetter'd race,
To feel at least a patriot's shame,
  Even as I sing, suffuse my face;
For what is left the poet here?
For Greeks a blush—for Greece a tear.

Must we but weep o'er days more blest?
  Must we but blush?—Our fathers bled.
Earth! render back from out thy breast
  A remnant of our Spartan dead!
Of the three hundred grant but three,
To make a new Thermopylae!

What, silent still? and silent all?
    Ah! no;—the voices of the dead
Sound like a distant torrent's fall,
    And answer, 'Let one living head,
But one arise,—we come, we come!'
    'Tis but the living who are dumb.

In vain—in vain: strike other chords;
    Fill high the cup with Samian wine!
Leave battles to the Turkish hordes,
    And shed the blood of Scio's vine!
Hark! rising to the ignoble call—
How answers each bold Bacchanal!

You have the Pyrrhic dance as yet;
    Where is the Phyrrhic phalanx gone?
Of two such lessons, why forget
    The nobler and the manlier one?
You have the letters Cadmus gave—
Think ye he meant them for a slave?

Fill high the bowl with Samian wine!
    We will not think of themes like these!
It made Anacreon's song divine:
    He served—but served Polycrates—
A tyrant; but our masters then
Were still, at least, our countrymen.

The tyrant of the Chersonese
    Was freedom's best and bravest friend;
That tyrant was Miltiades!
    Oh! that the present hour would lend
Another despot of the kind!
Such chains as his were sure to bind.

Fill high the bowl with Samian wine!
　On Suli's rock, and Parga's shore,
Exists the remnant of a line
　Such as the Doric mothers bore;
And there, perhaps, some seed is sown,
The Heracleidan blood might own.

Trust not for freedom to the Franks—
　They have a king who buys and sells;
In native swords, and native ranks,
　The only hope of courage dwells:
But Turkish force, and Latin fraud,
Would break your shield, however broad.

Fill high the bowl with Samian wine!
　Our virgins dance beneath the shade,—
I see their glorious black eyes shine;
　But gazing on each glowing maid,
My own the burning tear-drop laves,
To think such breasts must suckle slaves.

Place me on Sunium's marbled steep,
　Where nothing, save the waves and I,
May hear our mutual murmurs sweep;
　There, swan-like, let me sing and die:
A land of slaves shall ne'er be mine—
Dash down you cup of Samian wine!

LORD BYRON
From *Don Juan*

ITALY AND BRITAIN

How has kind Heav'n adorn'd the happy Land,
And scatter'd Blessings with a wastful Hand!
But what avail her unexhausted Stores,
Her blooming Mountains and her sunny Shores,

With all the Gifts that Heav'n and Earth impart,
The Smiles of Nature, and the Charms of Art,
While proud Oppression in her Vallies reigns,
And Tyranny usurps her happy Plains?
The poor Inhabitant beholds in vain
The red'ning Orange and the swelling Grain:
Joyless he sees the growing Oils and Wines,
And in the Myrtle's fragrant Shade repines:
Starves in the midst of Nature's Bounty curst,
And in the loaden Vine-yard dies for Thirst,
　　Oh Liberty, thou Goddess Heav'nly bright,
Profuse of Bliss, and pregnant with Delight,
Eternal Pleasures in thy Presence reign,
And smiling Plenty leads thy wanton Train!
Eas'd of her load Subjection grows more light,
And Poverty looks cheerful in thy sight;
Thou mak'st the gloomy Face of Nature gay,
Giv'st Beauty to the Sun, and Pleasure to the Day.
　　Thee, Goddess, Thee, Britannia's Isle adores;
How has she oft exhausted all her Stores,
How oft in Fields of Death thy Presence sought?
Nor thinks the mighty Prize too dearly bought:
On Foreign Mountains may the Sun refine
The Grape's soft Juice, and mellow it to Wine,
With Citron Groves adorn a distant Soil,
And the fat Olive swell with floods of Oil:
We envy not the warmer Clime that lies
In ten Degrees of more indulgent Skies,
Nor at the Courseness of our Heav'n repine,
Tho' o're our Heads the frozen Pleiads shine:
'Tis Liberty that Crowns Britannia's Isle,
And makes her barren Rocks and her bleak
　　Mountains smile.

JOSEPH ADDISON
From *A Letter from Italy*

SONNET ON CHILLON

Eternal Spirit of the chainless Mind!
  Brightest in dungeons, Liberty! thou art,
  For there thy habitation is the heart—
The heart which love of Thee alone can bind,
And when thy sons to fetters are consign'd,
  To fetters, and the damp vault's dayless gloom,
  Their country conquers with their martyrdom,
And Freedom's fame finds wings on every wind.
Chillon! thy prison is a holy place
  And thy sad floor an altar, for 'twas trod,
Until his very steps have left a trace
  Worn as if thy cold pavement were a sod,
By Bonnivard! May none those marks efface!
  For they appeal from tyranny to God.

LORD BYRON

WRITTEN AT AN INN AT HENLEY

To thee, fair freedom, I retire
  From flattery, cards, and dice, and din;
Nor art thou found in mansions higher
  Than the low cot, or humble inn.

'Tis here with boundless power I reign;
  And every health which I begin,
Converts dull port to bright champagne;
  Such freedom crowns it at an inn.

I fly from pomp, I fly from plate,
  I fly from falsehood's specious grin!
Freedom I love, and form I hate,
  And choose my lodgings at an inn.

Here, waiter, take my sordid ore,
   Which lackeys else might hope to win;
It buys, what courts have not in store;
   It buys me freedom at an inn.

Whoe'er has travelled life's dull round,
   Where'er his stages may have been,
May sigh to think he still has found
   The warmest welcome at an inn.

WILLIAM SHENSTONE

LIFE, LIBERTY, AND THE PURSUIT OF HAPPINESS

We hold these truths to be sacred and undeniable; that all men are created equal and independent, that from that equal creation they derive rights inherent and inalienable, among which are the preservation of life, and liberty, and the pursuit of happiness.

THOMAS JEFFERSON
From the original draft for the American
Declaration of Independence

ADDRESS AT GETTYSBURG

Fourscore and seven years ago our fathers brought forth upon this continent a new nation, conceived in liberty, and dedicated to the proposition that all men are created equal. Now we are engaged in a great civil war, testing whether that nation, or any nation so conceived and so dedicated, can long endure. We are met on a great battle-field of that war. We have come to dedicate a portion of that field as a final resting-place of those who here gave their lives that that nation might live. It is altogether fitting and proper that we should do this. But in a larger sense we cannot dedicate, we cannot consecrate, we cannot hallow this ground. The brave men, living and dead, who struggled here, have consecrated it far above our power to add or detract. The world will little note, nor long remember, what we say here, but it can never forget what they did here. It is for us, the living, rather to be dedicated here to the unfinished work they have thus far so nobly advanced. It is rather for us to be here dedicated to the great task remaining before us, that from these honored dead we take increased devotion to that cause for which they here gave the last full measure of devotion; that we here highly resolve that the dead shall not have died in vain, that the nation shall, under God, have a new birth of freedom, and that the government of the people, by the people, and for the people, shall not perish from the earth.

ABRAHAM LINCOLN

Service

HOW ARE THY SERVANTS BLEST, O LORD!

How are thy Servants blest, O Lord!
  How sure is their Defence!
Eternal Wisdom is their Guide,
  Their Help Omnipotence.

In foreign Realms, and Lands remote,
  Supported by Thy Care,
Through burning Climes I pass'd unhurt,
  And breath'd in tainted Air.

Thy Mercy sweetned ev'ry Soil,
  Made ev'ry Region please;
The hoary Alpine Hills it warm'd,
  And smoak'd the Tyrrhene Seas:

Think, O my Soul, devoutly think,
  How with affrighted Eyes
Thou saw'st the wide extended Deep
  In all its Horrors rise!

Confusion dwelt in ev'ry Face,
  And Fear in ev'ry Heart;
When Waves on Waves, and Gulphs in Gulphs,
  O'ercame the Pilot's Art.

Yet then from all my Griefs, O Lord,
  Thy Mercy set me free,
Whilst in the Confidence of Pray'r
  My Soul took Hold on Thee;

For tho' in dreadful Whirles we hung
   High on the broken Wave,
I knew Thou wert not slow to hear,
   Nor Impotent to save.

The Storm was laid, the Winds retir'd,
   Obedient to Thy Will;
The Sea, that roar'd at Thy Command,
   At Thy Command was still.

In Midst of Dangers, Fears and Death,
   Thy Goodness I'll adore,
And praise Thee for Thy Mercies past;
   And humbly hope for more.

My Life, if Thou preserv'st my Life,
   Thy Sacrifice shall be;
And Death, if Death must be my Doom,
   Shall join my Soul to Thee!

JOSEPH ADDISON

I VOW TO THEE, MY COUNTRY

I vow to thee, my country—all earthly things above—
Entire and whole and perfect, the service of my love,
The love that asks no questions: the love that stands the test,
That lays upon the altar the dearest and the best:
The love that never falters, the love that pays the price,
The love that makes undaunted the final sacrifice.
And there's another country, I've heard of long ago—
Most dear to them that love her, most great to them that know—
We may not count her armies: we may not see her King—
Her fortress is a faithful heart, her pride is suffering—
And soul by soul and silently her shining bounds increase,
And her ways are ways of gentleness and all her paths are peace.

CECIL SPRING-RICE

IN HOSPITAL

STAFF-NURSE: OLD STYLE

The great masters of the commonplace,
Rembrandt and good Sir Walter—only these
Could paint her all to you: experienced ease
And antique liveliness and ponderous grace;
The sweet old roses of her sunken face;
The depth and malice of her sly, grey eyes;
The broad Scots tongue that flatters, scolds, defies;
The thick Scots wit that fells you like a mace,
These thirty years has she been nursing here,
Some of them under Syme, her hero still.
Much is she worth, and even more is made of her.
Patients and students hold her very dear.
The doctors love her, tease her, use her skill.
They say 'The Chief' himself is half-afraid of her.

LADY-PROBATIONER

Some three, or five, or seven, and thirty years;
A Roman nose; a dimpling double-chin;
Dark eyes and shy that, ignorant of sin,
Are yet acquainted, it would seem, with tears;
A comely shape; a slim, high-coloured hand,
Graced, rather oddly, with a signet ring;
A bashful air, becoming everything;
A well-bred silence always at command.
Her plain print gown, prim cap, and bright steel chain
Look out of place on her, and I remain
Absorbed in her, as in a pleasant mystery.
Quick, skilful, quiet, soft in speech and touch . . .
'Do you like nursing?' 'Yes, Sir, very much.'
Somehow I rather think she has a history.

'THE CHIEF'

His brow spreads large and placid, and his eye
Is deep and bright, with steady looks that still.
Soft lines of tranquil thought his face fulfil—
His face at once benign and proud and shy.
If envy scout, if ignorance deny,
His faultless patience, his unyielding will,
Beautiful gentleness and splendid skill,
Innumerable gratitudes reply.
His wise, rare smile is sweet with certainties,
And seems in all his patients to compel
Such love and faith as failure cannot quell;
We hold him for another Herakles,
Battling with custom, prejudice, disease,
As once the son of Zeus with Death and Hell.

SCRUBBER

She's tall and gaunt, and in her hard, sad face
With flashes of the old fun's animation
There lowers the fixed and peevish resignation
Bred of a past where troubles came apace.
She tells me that her husband, ere he died,
Saw seven of their children pass away,
And never knew the little lass at play
Out on the green, in whom he's deified.
Her kin dispersed, her friends forgot and gone,
All simple faith her honest Irish mind,
Scolding her spoiled young saint, she labours on:
Telling her dreams, taking her patients' part,
Trailing her coat sometimes: and you shall find
No rougher, quainter speech, nor kinder heart.

WILLIAM ERNEST HENLEY

TO LUCASTA, GOING TO THE WARS

Tell me not, Sweet, I am unkind,
    That from the nunnery
Of thy chaste breast and quiet mind
    To war and arms I fly.

True, a new mistress now I chase,
    The first foe in the field;
And with a stronger faith embrace
    A sword, a horse, a shield.

Yet this inconstancy is such
    As thou too shalt adore;
I could not love thee, Dear, so much,
    Loved I not Honour more.

RICHARD LOVELACE

SOCIAL UNEQUALS

My Lady, I am the son of a butler and a lady's-maid—perhaps
the happiest of all combinations; and to me the most beautiful
thing in the world is a haughty, aristocratic English house, with
every one kept in his place. Though I were equal to your ladyship,
where would the pleasure be to me? It would be counterbalanced
by the pain of feeling that Thomas and John were equal to me.

J. M. BARRIE
From The Admirable Crichton

THE DIVINE OFFICE OF THE KITCHEN

Lord of the pots and pipkins, since I have no time to be
A saint by doing lovely things and Vigilling with Thee,
By watching in the twilight dawn, and storming Heaven's gates,
Make me a saint by getting meals and washing up the plates.

CECILY R. HALLACK

FREELY WE SERVE

Son of heav'n and earth,
Attend: that thou art happy, owe to God;
That thou continu'st such, owe to thyself,
That is, to thy obedience; therein stand.
This was that caution given thee; be advised.
God made thee perfect, not immutable;
And good He made thee, but to persevere
He left it in thy power; ordain'd thy will
By nature free, not over-ruled by fate
Inextricable, or strict necessity:
Our voluntary service he requires,
Not our necessitated, such with him
Finds no acceptance, nor can find; for how
Can hearts, not free, be tried whether they serve
Willing or no, who will but what they must
By destiny, and can no other choose?
Myself and all th' angelic host, that stand
In sight of God enthroned, our happy state
Hold, as you yours, while our obedience holds,
On other surety none; freely we serve,
Because we freely love, as in our will
To love or not; in this we stand or fall.

JOHN MILTON
From Paradise Lost

PRAYER FOR PEACE

O God, which art the author of peace, and lover of concord,
in knowledge of whom standeth our eternal life, whose service
is perfect freedom: Defend us thy humble servants in all assaults
of our enemies; that we, surely trusting in thy defence, may not
fear the power of any adversaries, through the might of Jesus
Christ our Lord. *Amen.*

The Book of Common Prayer

Ecstasy

THE KISS

O, that joy so soon should waste!
  Or so sweet a bliss
    As a kiss
Might not for ever last!
So sugared, so melting, so soft, so delicious,
  The dew that lies on roses,
  When the morn herself discloses,
    Is not so precious.
O, rather than I would it smother,
Were I to taste such another,
  It should be my wishing
  That I might die kissing.

BEN JONSON
From *Cynthia's Revels*

THE WILLING MISTRESS

Amyntas led me to a grove
  Where all the trees did shade us;
The sun itself though it had strove
  It could not have betrayed us.
The place secured from human eyes
  No other fear allows,
But when the winds that gently rise
  Do kiss the yielding boughs.

Down there we sat upon the moss,
  And did begin to play
A thousand amorous tricks, to pass
  The heat of all the day.
A many kisses he did give,
  And I returned the same,
Which made me willing to receive
  That which I dare not name.

His charming eyes no aid required
  To tell their softening tale;
On her that was already fired
  'Twas easy to prevail.
He did but kiss and clasp me round,
  Whilst those his thoughts exprest;
And laid me gently on the ground:
  Ah, who can guess the rest?

APHRA   BEHN

IMAGINATION

Were it not for imagination, Sir, a man would be as happy in
the arms of a chambermaid as of a Duchess.

SAMUEL JOHNSON
Quoted in The Life of Samuel Johnson
by James Boswell

LET'S SPORT A WHILE

Being set, let's sport a while, my fair;
I will tie love-knots in thy hair.
See, Zephyr through the leaves doth stray
And has free liberty to play,
And braids thy locks; and shall I find
Less favour than a saucy wind?
Now let me sit and fix my eyes
On thee that art my paradise.

Thou art my all. The Spring remains
In the fair violets of thy veins;
And that it is a Summer's day,
Ripe cherries in thy lips display;
And when for Autumn I would seek,
'Tis in the apples of thy cheek;
But that which only moves my smart,
Is to see Winter in thy heart.
Strange, when at once in one appear
All the four seasons of the year!
I'll clasp that neck, where should be set,
A rich and orient carcanet;
But swains are poor; admit of, then,
More natural chains, the arms of men.
Come, let me touch those breasts that swell
Like two fair mountains, and may well
Be styled the Alps, but that I fear
The snow has less of whitness there.
But stay, my love; a fault I spy.
Why are these two fair mountains dry?
Which, if they run, no Muse would please
To taste of any spring but these.
And Ganymede employed should be
To fetch his Jove nectar from thee.
Thou shalt be nurse, fair Venus swears,
To the next Cupid that she bears.
Were it not then discreetly done
To ope one spring to let two run?
Fie, fie, this belly, beauty's mint,
Blushes to see no coin stamped in't.
Employ it then, for though it be
Our wealth, it is your royalty;
And beauty will have current grace
That bears the image of your face.
How to the touch the ivory thighs
Vail gently, and again to rise,

As pliable to impression
As virgin wax or Parian stone
Dissolved to softness, plump and full,
More white and soft than Cotswold wool,
Or cotton from the Indian tree,
Or pretty silkworm's housewifery,
These on two marble pillars raised,
Make me in doubt which should be praised,
They or their columns, most; but when
I view those feet which I have seen
So nimbly trip it o'er the lawns
That all the satyrs and the fawns
Have stood amazed when they would pass
Over the leas, and not a grass
Would feel the weight, nor rush nor bent,
Dropping betray which way you went;
Oh then I felt my hot desires
Burn more and flame with double fires.

Now let us kiss. Would you be gone?
Manners at least allows me one.
Blush you at this, pretty one? Stay,
And I will take that kiss away
Thus, with a second, and that too
A third wipes off; so will we go
To numbers that the stars outrun
And all the atoms in the sun.
For though we kiss till Phoebus' ray
Sink in the seas, and kissing stay
Till his bright beams return again,
There can of all but one remain;
And if for one good manners call,
In one good manners grant me all.

THOMAS RANDOLPH
From *A Pastoral Courtship*

KISSING

Come hither Womankind and all their worth,
Give me thy kisses as I call them forth.
Give me the billing-kiss, that of the dove,
    A kiss of love;
The melting-kiss, a kiss that doth consume
    To a perfume;
The extract-kiss, of every sweet a part,
    A kiss of art;
The kiss which ever stirs some new delight,
    A kiss of might;
The twaching smacking kiss, and when you cease
    A kiss of peace;
The music-kiss, crotchet and quaver time,
    The kiss of rhyme;
The kiss of eloquence, which doth belong
    Unto the tongue;
The kiss of all the sciences in one,
    The Kiss alone.
So 'tis enough.

LORD HERBERT

From VENUS AND ADONIS

Sometimes she shakes her head, and then his hand;
Now gazeth she on him, now on the ground;
Sometimes her arms infold him like a band:
She would, he will not in her arms be bound;
  And when from thence he struggles to be gone,
  She locks her lily fingers one in one.

'Fondling,' she saith, 'since I have hemm'd thee here
Within the circuit of this ivory pale,
I'll be a park, and thou shalt be my deer;
Feed where thou wilt, on mountain or in dale:

185

Graze on my lips, and if those hills be dry,
  Stray lower, where the pleasant fountains lie.

'Within this limit is relief enough,
Sweet bottom-grass and high delightful plain,
Round rising hillocks, brakes obscure and rough,
To shelter thee from tempest and from rain:
    Then be my deer, since I am such a park;
    No dog shall rouse thee, though a thousand bark.'

  . . . . . .

'Fair Queen,' quoth he, 'if any love you owe me,
Measure my strangeness with my unripe years:
Before I know myself, seek not to know me;
No fisher but the ungrown fry forbears:
    The mellow plum doth fall, the green sticks fast,
    Or being early pluck'd is sour to taste.

'Look! the world's comforter, with weary gait,
His day's hot task hath ended in the west;
The owl, night's herald, shrieks, 'tis very late;
The sheep are gone to fold, birds to their nest,
    And coal-black clouds that shadow heaven's light
    Do summon us to part and bid good night.

'Now let me say good night, and so say you;
If you will say so, you shall have a kiss.'
'Good night,' quoth she; and ere he says adieu,
The honey fee of parting tender'd is:
    Her arms do lend his neck a sweet embrace;
    Incorporate then they seem, face grows to face.

Till, breathless, he disjoin'd and backward drew
The heavenly moisture, that sweet coral mouth,
Whose precious taste her thirsty lips well knew,
Whereon they surfeit, yet complain on drouth:

He with her plenty press'd, she faint with dearth,
Their lips together glued, fall to the earth.

Now quick desire hath caught the yielding prey,
And glutton-like she feeds, yet never filleth;
Her lips are conquerors, his lips obey,
Paying what ransom the insulter willeth;
  Whose vulture thought doth pitch the price so high,
  That she will draw his lips' rich treasure dry.

And having felt the sweetness of the spoil,
With blindfold fury she begins to forage;
Her face doth reek and smoke, her blood doth boil,
And careless lust stirs up a desperate courage;
  Planting oblivion, beating reason back,
  Forgetting shame's pure blush and honour's wrack.

Hot, faint, and weary, with her hard embracing,
Like a wild bird being tam'd with too much handling,
Or as the fleet-foot roe that's tir'd with chasing,
Or like the froward infant still'd with dandling,
  He now obeys, and now no more resisteth,
  While she takes all she can, not all she listeth.

WILLIAM SHAKESPEARE

THE DESPERATE LOVER

After the pangs of a desperate lover,
  When day and night I have sighed all in vain;
Ah, what a pleasure it is to discover
  In her eyes pity, who causes my pain!

When with unkindness our love at a stand is,
  And both have punished ourselves with the pain,
Ah, what a pleasure the touch of her hand is,
  Ah, what a pleasure to press it again!

When the denial comes fainter and fainter,
   And her eyes give what her tongue does deny,
Ah, what a trembling I feel when I venture,
   Ah, what a trembling does usher my joy!

When with a sigh she accords me the blessing,
   And her eyes twinkle 'twixt pleasure and pain,
Ah, what a joy 'tis beyond all expressing,
   Ah, what a joy to hear: Shall we again?

JOHN DRYDEN
From *An Evening's Love*

SONG OF SONGS

Behold, thou art fair, my love; behold, thou art fair; thou hast doves' eyes within thy locks: thy hair is as a flock of goats that appear from mount Gilead.

Thy teeth are like a flock of sheep that are even shorn, which came up from the washing; whereof every one bear twins, and none is barren among them.

Thy lips are like a thread of scarlet, and thy speech is comely: thy temples are like a piece of a pomegranate within thy locks.

Thy neck is like the tower of David, builded for an armoury whereon there hang a thousand bucklers, all shields of mighty men.

Thy two breasts are like two young roes that are twins, which feed among the lilies.

Until the day break, and the shadows flee away, I will get me to the mountain of myrrh, and to the hill of frankincense.

Thou art all fair, my love; there is no spot in thee.

Come with me from Lebanon, my spouse, with me from Lebanon: look from the top of Amana, from the top of Shenir and Hermon, from the lions' dens, from the mountains of the leopards.

Thou hast ravished my heart, my sister, my spouse; thou hast ravished my heart with one of thine eyes, with one chain of thy neck.

How fair is thy love, my sister, my spouse! how much better is thy love than wine! and the smell of thine ointments than all spices!

Thy lips, O my spouse, drop as the honeycomb; honey and milk are under thy tongue; and the smell of thy garments is like the smell of Lebanon.

A garden inclosed is my sister, my spouse; a spring shut up, a fountain sealed.

Thy plants are an orchard of pomegranates with pleasant fruits; camphire, with spikenard.

Spikenard and saffron; calamus and cinnamon, with all trees of frankincense; myrrh and aloes, with all the chief spices;

A fountain of gardens, a well of living waters, and streams from Lebanon.

Awake, O north wind; and come, thou south; blow upon my garden, that the spices thereof may flow out. Let my beloved come into his garden, and eat his pleasant fruits.

.   .   .   .   .   .

How beautiful are thy feet with shoes, O prince's daughter! the joints of thy thighs are like jewels, the work of the hands of a cunning workman.

Thy navel is like a round goblet, which wanteth not liquor; thy belly is like an heap of wheat set about with lilies:

Thy two breasts are like two young roes that are twins.

Thy neck is as a tower of ivory; thine eyes like the fishpools in Heshbon, by the gate of Bathrabbim; thy nose is as the tower of Lebanon, which looketh toward Damascus:

Thine head upon thee is like Carmel, and the hair of thine head like purple: the king is held in the galleries.

How fair and how pleasant art thou, O love, for delights!

This thy stature is like to a palm tree, and thy breasts to clusters of grapes.

I said, I will go up to the palm tree, I will take hold of the boughs thereof; now also thy breasts shall be as clusters of the vine, and the smell of thy nose like apples;

And the roof of thy mouth like the best wine for my beloved, that goeth down sweetly, causing the lips of those that are asleep to speak.

I am my beloved's, and his desire is toward me.

Come, my beloved, let us go forth into the field; let us lodge in the villages.

Let us get up early to the vineyards: let us see if the vine flourish, whether the tender grape appear and the pomegranates bud forth: there will I give thee my loves.

The mandrakes give a smell, and at our gates are all manner of pleasant fruits, new and old, which I have laid up for thee, O my beloved.

The Song of Solomon

SYLVIA THE FAIR

Sylvia the fair, in the bloom of fifteen,
Felt an innocent warmth as she lay on the green;
She had heard of a pleasure, and something she guessed
By the towsing and tumbling and touching her breast;
She saw the men eager, but was at a loss
What they meant by their sighing and kissing so close;
   By their praying and whining,
   And clasping and twining,
   And panting and wishing,
   And sighing and kissing,
   And sighing and kissing so close.

Ah, she cried, ah, for a languishing maid
In a country of Christians to die without aid!
Not a Whig or a Tory or Trimmer at least,
Or a Protestant parson or Catholic priest,
To instruct a young virgin that is at a loss
What they meant by their sighing and kissing so close;
    By their praying and whining,
    And clasping and twining,
    And panting and wishing,
    And sighing and kissing,
    And sighing and kissing so close.

Cupid in shape of a swain did appear;
He saw the sad wound, and in pity drew near,
Then showed her his arrow and bid her not fear,
For the pain was no more than a maiden may bear;
When the balm was infused, she was not at a loss
What they meant by their sighing and kissing so close;
    By their praying and whining,
    And clasping and twining,
    And panting and wishing,
    And sighing and kissing,
    And sighing and kissing so close.

JOHN DRYDEN

LOVE

    All thoughts, all passions, all delights,
    Whatever stirs this mortal frame,
    All are but ministers of Love,
        And feed his sacred flame.

    Oft in my waking dreams do I
    Live o'er again that happy hour,
    When midway on the mount I lay,
        Beside the ruin'd tower.

The moonshine, stealing o'er the scene,
Had blended with the lights of eve;
And she was there, my hope, my joy,
My own dear Genevieve!

She lean'd against the armed man,
The statute of the armed Knight;
She stood and listen'd to my lay,
Amid the lingering light.

Few sorrows hath she of her own,
My hope! my joy! my Genevieve!
She loves me best whene'er I sing
The songs that make her grieve.

I play'd a soft and doleful air;
I sang an old and moving story—
An old rude song, that suited well
That ruin wild and hoary.

She listen'd with a flitting blush,
With downcast eyes and modest grace;
For well she knew I could not choose
But gaze upon her face.

I told her of the Knight that wore
Upon his shield a burning brand;
And that for ten long years he woo'd
The Lady of the Land.

I told her how he pined: and ah!
The deep, the low, the pleading tone
With which I sang another's love,
Interpreted my own.

She listen'd with a flitting blush,
With downcast eyes, and modest grace;
And she forgave me, that I gazed
    Too fondly on her face!

But when I told the cruel scorn
That crazed that bold and lovely Knight,
And that he cross'd the mountain-woods,
    Nor rested day nor night;

That sometimes from the savage den,
And sometimes from the darksome shade,
And sometimes starting up at once
    In green and sunny glade—

There came and look'd him in the face
An angel beautiful and bright;
And that he knew it was a Fiend,
    This miserable Knight!

And that, unknowing what he did,
He leap'd amid a murderous band,
And saved from outrage worse than death
    The Lady of the Land;—

And how she wept and clasp'd his knees;
And how she tended him in vain—
And ever strove to expiate
    The scorn that crazed his brain;—

And that she nursed him in a cave;
And how his madness went away,
When on the yellow forest leaves
    A dying man he lay;—

His dying words—but when I reach'd
That tenderest strain of all the ditty,
My faltering voice and pausing harp
 Disturb'd her soul with pity!

All impulses of soul and sense
Had thrill'd my guileless Genevieve;
The music and the doleful tale,
 The rich and balmy eve;

And hopes, and fears that kindle hope,
An undistinguishable throng,
And gentle wishes long subdued,
 Subdued and cherish'd long!

She wept with pity and delight,
She blush'd with love and virgin shame;
And like the murmur of a dream,
 I heard her breathe my name.

Her bosom heaved—she stepp'd aside,
As conscious of my look she stept—
Then suddenly, with timorous eye
 She fled to me and wept.

She half enclosed me with her arms,
She press'd me with a meek embrace;
And bending back her head, look'd up,
 And gazed upon my face.

'Twas partly love, and partly fear,
And partly 'twas a bashful art,
That I might rather feel, than see.
 The swelling of her heart.

I calm'd her fears, and she was calm,
And told her love with virgin pride;
And so I won my Genevieve,
    My bright and beauteous Bride.

SAMUEL TAYLOR COLERIDGE

I WILL ENJOY THEE NOW

I will enjoy thee now, my Celia, come,
And fly with me to Love's Elysium.
The giant, Honour, that keeps cowards out
Is but a masquer, and the servile rout
Of baser subjects only bend in vain
To the vast idol; whilst the nobler train
Of valiant lovers daily sail between
The huge Colossus' legs, and pass unseen
Unto the blissful shore. Be bold and wise,
And we shall enter; the grim Swiss denies
Only to tame fools a passage, that not know
He is but form and only frights in show
The duller eyes that look from far; draw near
And thou shalt scorn what we were wont to fear.
We shall see how the stalking pageant goes
With borrow'd legs, a heavy load to those
That made and bear him; not, as we once thought,
The seed of gods, but a weak model wrought
By greedy men, that seek to enclose the common,
And within private arms empale free woman.

Come, then, and mounted on the wings of Love
We'll cut the flitting air and soar above
The monster's head, and in the noblest seats
Of those blest shades quench and renew our heats.
There shall the queens of love and innocence,
Beauty and Nature, banish all offence

From our close ivy-twines; there I'll behold
Thy bared snow and thy unbraided gold;
There my enfranchised hand on every side
Shall o'er thy naked polish'd ivory slide.
No curtain there, though of transparent lawn,
Shall be before thy virgin-treasure drawn;
But the rich mine, to the enquiring eye
Exposed, shall ready still for mintage lie,
And we will coin young Cupids. There a bed
Of roses and fresh myrtles shall be spread,
Under the cooler shades of cypress groves;
Our pillows of the down of Venus' doves,
Whereon our panting limbs we'll gently lay,
In the faint respites of our active play;
That so our slumbers may in dreams have leisure
To tell the nimble fancy our past pleasure,
And so our souls, that cannot be embraced,
Shall the embraces of our bodies taste.
Meanwhile the bubbling stream shall court the shore,
Th' enamour'd chirping wood-choir shall adore
In varied tunes the deity of love;
The gentle blasts of western winds shall move
The trembling leaves, and through their close
   boughs breathe
Still music, whilst we rest ourselves beneath
Their dancing shade; till a soft murmur, sent
From souls entranced in amorous languishment,
Rouse us, and shoot into our veins fresh fire,
Till we in their sweet ecstasy expire.

Then, as the empty bee that lately bore
Into the common treasure all her store,
Flies 'bout the painted field with nimble wing,
Deflow'ring the fresh virgins of the spring,
So will I rifle all the sweets that dwell
In my delicious paradise, and swell

My bag with honey, drawn forth by the power
Of fervent kisses from each spicy flower.
I'll seize the rose-buds in their perfumed bed,
The violet knots, like curious mazes spread
O'er all the garden, taste the ripen'd cherry,
The warm firm apple, tipp'd with coral berry;
Then will I visit with a wand'ring kiss
The vales of lilies and the bower of bliss;
And where the beauteous region doth divide
Into two milky ways, my lips shall slide
Down those smooth alleys, wearing as they go
A track for lovers on the printed snow;
Thence climbing o'er the swelling Apennine,
Retire into thy grove of eglantine,
Where I will all those ravish'd sweets distill
Through Love's alembic, and with chemic skill
From the mix'd mass one sovereign balm derive,
Then bring that great elixir to thy hive.

THOMAS CAREW
From *A Rapture*

COME, CHLOE, AND GIVE ME
SWEET KISSES

Come, Chloe, and give me sweet kisses,
    For sweeter sure never girl gave:
But why in the midst of my blisses
    Do you ask me how many I'd have?
I'm not to be stinted in pleasure,
    Then pr'ythee my charmer be kind,
For whilst I love thee above measure,
    To numbers I'll ne'er be confin'd.

Count the bees that on Hybla are playing,
　　Count the flow'rs that enamel its fields,
Count the flocks that on Tempe are straying,
　　Or the grain that rich Sicily yields;
Go number the stars in the heaven,
　　Count how many sands on the shore,
When so many kisses you've given
　　I still shall be craving for more.

To a heart full of love let me hold thee,
　　To a heart which, dear Chloe, is thine
With my arms I'll for ever enfold thee,
　　And twist round thy limbs like a vine.
What joy can be greater than this is?
　　My life on thy lips shall be spent;
But the wretch that can number his kisses
　　With few will be ever content.

SIR CHARLES HANBURY WILLIAMS

THE CONSTANT LOVER

Out upon it, I have loved
　　Three whole days together!
And am like to love three more,
　　If it prove fair weather.

Time shall moult away his wings
　　Ere he shall discover
In the whole wide world again
　　Such a constant lover.

But the spite on 't is, no praise
　　Is due at all to me:
Love with me had made no stays,
　　Had it any been but she.

Had it any been but she,
　　And that very face,
There had been at least ere this
　　A dozen dozen in her place.

SIR JOHN SUCKLING

CEAN DUBH DEELISH
(DARLING BLACK HEAD)

Put your head, darling, darling, darling,
　　Your darling black head my heart above;
O mouth of honey, with thyme for fragrance,
　　Who, with heart in breast, could deny you love?

O many and many a young girl for me is pining,
　　Letting her locks of gold to the cold wind free,
For me, the foremost of our gay young fellows;
　　But I'd leave a hundred, pure love, for thee!

Then put your head, darling, darling, darling,
　　Your darling black head my heart above;
O mouth of honey, with thyme for fragrance,
　　Who, with heart in breast, could deny you love?

SIR SAMUEL FERGUSON

FREEDOM AND LOVE

How delicious is the winning
Of a kiss at Love's beginning,
When two mutual hearts are sighing
For the knot there's no untying!

Yet remember, 'midst your wooing,
Love has bliss, but Love has ruing;
Other smiles may make you fickle,
Tears for other charms may trickle.

199

Love he comes, and Love he tarries,
Just as fate or fancy carries;
Longest stays when sorest chidden,
Laughs and flies when press'd and bidden.

Bind the sea to slumber stilly,
Bind its odour to the lily,
Bind the aspen ne'er to quiver,
Then bind Love to last for ever.

Love's a fire that needs renewal
Of fresh beauty for its fuel;
Love's wing moults when caged and captured,
Only free he soars enraptured.

Can you keep the bee from ranging,
Or the ringdove's neck from changing?
No! nor fetter'd Love from dying
In the knot there's no untying.

THOMAS CAMPBELL

JUAN AND HAIDÉE

They look'd up to the sky, whose floating glow
    Spread like a rosy ocean, vast and bright;
They gazed upon the glittering sea below,
    Whence the broad moon rose circling into sight;
They heard the waves splash, and the wind so low,
    And saw each other's dark eyes darting light
Into each other—and, beholding this,
Their lips drew near, and clung into a kiss;

A long, long kiss, a kiss of youth, and love,
    And beauty, all concentrating like rays
Into one focus, kindled from above;
    Such kisses as belong to early days,

200

Where heart, and soul, and sense, in concert move,
    And the blood's lava, and the pulse a blaze,
Each kiss a heart-quake,—for a kiss's strength,
I think it must be reckon'd by its length.

By length I mean duration; theirs endured
    Heaven knows how long—no doubt they never reckon'd;
And if they had, they could not have secured
    The sum of their sensations to a second:
They had not spoken; but they felt allured,
    As if their souls and lips each other beckon'd,
Which, being join'd, like swarming bees they clung—
Their hearts the flowers from whence the honey sprung.

They were alone, but not alone as they
    Who shut in chambers think it loneliness;
The silent ocean, and the starlight bay,
    The twilight glow, which momently grew less,
The voiceless sands, and dropping caves, that lay
    Around them, made them to each other press,
As if there were no life beneath the sky
Save theirs, and that their life could never die.

They fear'd no eyes nor ears on that lone beach,
    They felt no terrors from the night; they were
All in all to each other; though their speech
    Was broken words, they thought a language there,—
And all the burning tongues the passions teach
    Found in one sigh the best interpreter
Of nature's oracle—first love,—that all
Which Eve has left her daughters since her fall.

Haidée spoke not of scruples, ask'd no vows,
    Nor offer'd any; she had never heard
Of plight and promises to be a spouse,
    Or perils by a loving maid incurr'd;

She was all which pure ignorance allows,
    And flew to her young mate like a young bird,
And never having dreamt of falsehood, she
Had not one word to say of constancy.

She loved, and was beloved—she adored,
    And she was worshipp'd; after nature's fashion,
Their intense souls, into each other pour'd,
    If souls could die, had perish'd in that passion,—
But by degrees their senses were restored,
    Again to be o'ercome again to dash on;
And, beating 'gainst his bosom, Haidée's heart
Felt as if never more to beat apart.

Alas! they were so young, so beautiful,
    So lonely, loving, helpless, and the hour
Was that in which the heart is always full,
    And, having o'er itself no further power,
Prompts deeds eternity cannot annul,
    But pays off moments in an endless shower
Of hell-fire—all prepared for people giving
Pleasure or pain to one another living.

Alas! for Juan and Haidée! they were
    So loving and so lovely—till then never,
Excepting our first parents, such a pair
    Had run the risk of being damn'd for ever;
And Haidée, being devout as well as fair,
    Had doubtless heard about the Stygian river,
And hell and purgatory—but forgot
Just in the very crisis she should not.

They look upon each other, and their eyes
    Gleam in the moonlight; and her white arm clasps
Round Juan's head, and his around her lies
    Half buried in the tresses which it grasps;

She sits upon his knee, and drinks his sighs,
   He hers, until they end in broken gasps;
And thus they form a group that's quite antique,
Half naked, loving, natural, and Greek.

And when those deep and burning moments pass'd,
   And Juan sunk to sleep within her arms,
She slept not, but all tenderly, though fast,
   Sustain'd his head upon her bosom's charms;
And now and then her eye to heaven is cast,
   And then on the pale cheek her breast now warms,
Pillow'd on her o'erflowing heart, which pants
With all it granted, and with all its grants.

An infant when it gazes on a light,
   A child the moment when it drains the breast,
A devotee when soars the Host in sight,
   An Arab with a stranger for a guest,
A sailor when the prize has struck in fight,
   A miser filling his most hoarded chest,
Feel rapture; but not such true joy are reaping
As they who watch o'er what they love while sleeping.

For there it lies so tranquil, so beloved,
   All that it hath of life with us is living;
So gentle, stirless, helpless, and unmoved,
   And all unconscious of the joy 't is giving;
All it hath felt, inflicted, pass'd, and proved,
   Hush'd into depths beyond the watcher's diving;
There lies the thing we love with all its errors
And all its charms, like death without its terrors.

The lady watch'd her lover—and that hour
   Of Love's, and Night's, and Ocean's solitude,
O'erflow'd her soul with their united power;
   Amidst the barren sand and rocks so rude

She and her wave-worn love had made their bower,
  Where nought upon their passion could intrude,
And all the stars that crowded the blue space
Saw nothing happier than her glowing face.

LORD BYRON
From Don Juan

THE LICORICE FIELDS AT PONTEFRACT

In the licorice fields at Pontefract
  My love and I did meet
And many a burdened licorice bush
  Was blooming round our feet;
Red hair she had and golden skin,
Her sulky lips were shaped for sin,
Her sturdy legs were flannel-slack'd.
The strongest legs in Pontefract.

The light and dangling licorice flowers
  Gave off the sweetest smells;
From various black Victorian towers
  The Sunday evening bells
Came pealing over dales and hills
And tanneries and silent mills
And lowly streets where country stops
And little shuttered corner shops.

She cast her blazing eyes on me
  And plucked a licorice leaf;
I was her captive slave and she
  My red-haired robber chief.

Oh love! for Love I could not speak,
It left me winded, wilting, weak
And held in brown arms strong and bare
And wound with flaming ropes of hair.

JOHN BETJEMAN

THE LAST KISS

Join once again, my Celia, join
Thy rosy lips to these of mine,
   Which, though they be not such,
Are full as sensible of bliss,
That is, as soon can taste a kiss,
   As thine of softer touch.

Each kiss of thine creates desire,
Thy odorous breath inflames Love's fire,
   And wakes the sleeping coal;
Such a kiss to be I find
The conversation of the mind,
   And whisper of the soul.

Thanks, sweetest, now thou'rt perfect grown,
For by this last kiss I'm undone;
   Thou breathest silent darts;
Henceforth each little touch will prove
A dangerous stratagem in love,
   And thou wilt blow up hearts.

CHARLES COTTON

Poignancy

WHEN WE TWO PARTED

When we two parted
  In silence and tears,
Half-broken hearted
  To sever for years,
Pale grew thy cheek and cold
  Colder thy kiss;
Truly that hour foretold
  Sorrow to this.

The dew of the morning
  Sunk chill on my brow—
It felt like the warning
  Of what I feel now.
Thy vows are all broken,
  And light is thy fame;
I hear thy name spoken,
  And share in its shame.

They name thee before me,
  A knell to mine ear;
A shudder comes o'er me—
  Why wert thou so dear?
They know not I knew thee,
  Who knew thee too well—
Long, long shall I rue thee,
  Too deeply to tell.

In secret we met—
    In silence I grieve
That thy heart could forget,
    Thy spirit deceive.
If I should meet thee
    After long years,
How should I greet thee?
    With silence and tears.

LORD BYRON

REMEMBER

Remember me when I am gone away,
Gone far away into the silent land;
When you can no more hold me by the hand,
Nor I half turn to go yet turning stay.
Remember me when no more day by day
You tell me of our future that you plann'd:
Only remember me; you understand
It will be late to counsel then or pray.
Yet if you should forget me for a while
And afterwards remember, do not grieve:
For if the darkness and corruption leave
A vestige of the thoughts that once I had,
Better by far you should forget and smile
Than that you should remember and be sad.

CHRISTINA GEORGINA ROSSETTI

SWEETEST LOVE, I DO NOT GO

Sweetest love, I do not go,
    For weariness of thee,
Nor in hope the world can show
    A fitter love for me;

But since that I
Must die at last, 'tis best
To use myself in jest
    Thus by feigned deaths to die.

Yesternight the sun went hence,
    And yet is here to-day;
He hath no desire nor sense,
    Nor half so short a way;
        Then fear not me,
But believe that I shall make
Speedier journeys, since I take
    More wings and spurs than he.

O how feeble is man's power,
    That if good fortune fall,
Cannot add another hour
    Nor a lost hour recall!
        But come bad chance,
And we join to it our strength,
And we teach it art and length,
    Itself o'er us to advance.

When thou sigh'st, thou sigh'st not wind,
    But sigh'st my soul away;
When thou weep'st, unkindly kind,
    My life's blood doth decay.
        It cannot be
That thou lov'st me, as thou say'st,
If in thine my life thou waste,
    That art the best of me.

Let not thy divining heart
    Forethink me any ill,
Destiny may take thy part,
    And may thy fears fulfil;

But think that we
Are but turned aside to sleep;
They who one another keep
Alive, ne'er parted be.

JOHN DONNE

LA BELLE DAME SANS MERCI

Ah, what can ail thee, wretched wight,
    Alone and palely loitering?
The sedge is wither'd from the lake,
    And no birds sing.

Ah, what can ail thee, wretched wight,
    So haggard and so woe-begone?
The squirrel's granary is full,
    And the harvest's done.

I see a lily on thy brow,
    With anguish moist and fever dew;
And on thy cheek a fading rose
    Fast withereth too.

I met a lady in the meads
    Full beautiful, a faery's child;
Her hair was long, her foot was light,
    And her eyes were wild.

I set her on my pacing steed,
    And nothing else saw all day long;
For sideways would she lean, and sing
    A faery's song.

I made a garland for her head,
    And bracelets too, and fragrant zone;
She look'd at me as she did love,
    And made sweet moan.

She found me roots of relish sweet,
    And honey wild, and manna dew;
And sure in language strange she said,
    I love thee true.

She took me to her elfin grot,
    And there she gaz'd and sighed deep,
And there I shut her wild sad eyes—
    So kiss'd to sleep.

And there we slumber'd on the moss,
    And there I dream'd, ah woe betide,
The latest dream I ever dream'd
    On the cold hill side.

I saw pale kings, and princes too,
    Pale warriors, death-pale were they all;
Who cry'd—'La belle Dame sans merci
    Hath thee in thrall!'

I saw their starv'd lips in the gloam
    With horrid warning gaped wide,
And I awoke, and found me here
    On the cold hill side.

And this is why I sojourn here
    Alone and palely loitering,
Though the sedge is wither'd from the lake,
    And no birds sing.

JOHN KEATS

SYMPATHY

The maid I love ne'er thought of me
Amid the scenes of gaiety;
But when her heart or mine sank low,
Ah, then it was no longer so.

From the slant palm she raised her head,
And kiss'd the cheek whence youth had fled,
Angels! some future day for this,
Give her as sweet and pure a kiss.

WALTER SAVAGE LANDOR

THE ENCHANTMENT

I did but look and love awhile,
    'Twas but for one half-hour;
Then to resist I had no will,
    And now I have no power.

To sigh and wish is all my ease;
    Sighs which do heat impart
Enough to melt the coldest ice
    Yet cannot warm your heart.

O would your pity give my heart
    One corner of your breast,
'Twould learn of yours the winning art
    And quickly steal the rest.

THOMAS OTWAY

I HAVE BEEN FAITHFUL TO THEE,
CYNARA! IN MY FASHION

Last night, ah, yesternight, betwixt her lips and mine
There fell thy shadow, Cynara! thy breath was shed
Upon my soul between the kisses and the wine;
And I was desolate and sick of an old passion,
    Yea, I was desolate and bowed my head:
I have been faithful to thee, Cynara! in my fashion.

All night upon mine heart I felt her warm heart beat,
Night-long within mine arms in love and sleep she lay;
Surely the kisses of her bought red mouth were sweet;
But I was desolate and sick of an old passion,
    When I awoke and found the dawn was grey:
I have been faithful to thee, Cynara! in my fashion.

I have forgot much, Cynara! gone with the wind,
Flung roses, roses riotously with the throng,
Dancing, to put thy pale, lost lilies out of mind;
But I was desolate and sick of an old passion,
    Yea, all the time, because the dance was long:
I have been faithful to thee, Cynara! in my fashion.

I cried for madder music and for stronger wine,
But when the feast is finished and the lamps expire,
Then falls thy shadow, Cynara! the night is thine;
And I am desolate and sick of an old passion,
    Yea, hungry for the lips of my desire:
I have been faithful to thee, Cynara! in my fashion.

ERNEST DOWSON

ANNABEL LEE

It was many and many a year ago,
　　In a kingdom by the sea,
That a maiden there lived whom you may know
　　By the name of Annabel Lee.
And this maiden she lived with no other thought
　　Than to love and be loved by me.

I was a child and she was a child
　　In this kingdom by the sea:
But we loved with a love that was more than love—
　　I and my Annabel Lee,
With a love that the winged seraphs of heaven
　　Coveted her and me.

And this was the reason that, long ago,
　　In this kingdom by the sea,
A wind blew out of a cloud, chilling
　　My beautiful Annabel Lee,
So that her high-born kinsmen came
　　And bore her away from me,
To shut her up in a sepulchre
　　In this kingdom by the sea.

The angels, not half so happy in heaven,
　　Went envying her and me—
Yes! that was the reason (as all men know,
　　In this kingdom by the sea)
That the wind came out of the cloud one night,
　　Chilling and killing my Annabel Lee.

But our love it was stronger by far than the love
　　Of those who were older than we—
　　Of many far wiser than we—
And neither the angels in heaven above,

Nor the demons down under the sea,
Can ever dissever my soul from the soul
　Of the beautiful Annabel Lee:

For the moon never beams without bringing me dreams
　Of the beautiful Annabel Lee;
And the stars never rise, but I feel the bright eyes
　Of the beautiful Annabel Lee;
And so, all the night-tide, I lie down by the side
Of my darling—my darling—my life and my bride,
　In the sepulchre there by the sea,
　In her tomb by the sounding sea.

EDGAR ALLAN POE

LOVE'S SECRET

Never seek to tell thy love,
　Love that never told can be;
For the gentle wind doth move
　Silently, invisibly.

I told my love, I told my love,
　I told her all my heart,
Trembling, cold, in ghastly fears.
　Ah! she did depart!

Soon after she was gone from me,
　A traveller came by,
Silently, invisibly:
　He took her with a sigh.

WILLIAM BLAKE

AH, HOW SWEET IT IS TO LOVE!

Ah, how sweet it is to love!
  Ah, how gay is young Desire!
And what pleasing pains we prove
  When we first approach Love's fire!
Pains of love be sweeter far
Than all other pleasures are.

Sighs which are from lovers blown
  Do but gently heave the heart:
Ev'n the tears they shed alone
  Cure, like trickling balm, their smart:
Lovers, when they lose their breath,
Bleed away in easy death.

Love and Time with reverence use,
  Treat them like a parting friend;
Nor the golden gifts refuse
  Which in youth sincere they send:
For each year their price is more,
And they less simple than before.

Love, like spring-tides full and high,
  Swells in every youthful vein;
But each tide does less supply,
  Till they quite shrink in again:
If a flow in age appear,
'Tis but rain, and runs not clear.

JOHN DRYDEN

TO MARY WOLLSTONECRAFT GODWIN

Mine eyes were dim with tears unshed;
   Yes, I was firm—thus wert not thou;—
My baffled looks did fear yet dread
   To meet thy looks—I could not know
How anxiously they sought to shine
With soothing pity upon mine.

To sit and curb the soul's mute rage
   Which preys upon itself alone;
To curse the life which is the cage
   Of fettered grief that dares not groan,
Hiding from many a careless eye
The scorned load of agony.

Whilst thou alone, then not regarded,
   The   thou alone should be,
To spend years thus, and be rewarded,
   As thou, sweet love, requited me
When none were near—Oh! I did wake
From torture for that moment's sake.

Upon my heart thy accents sweet
   Of peace and pity fell like dew
On flowers half dead;—thy lips did meet
   Mine tremblingly; thy dark eyes threw
Their soft persuasion on my brain,
Charming away its dream of pain.

We are not happy, sweet! our state
   Is strange and full of doubt and fear;
More need of words that ills abate;—
   Reserve or censure come not near
Our sacred friendship, lest there be
No solace left for thee and me.

Gentle and good and mild thou art,
Nor can I live if thou appear
Aught but thyself, or turn thine heart
Away from me, or stoop to wear
The mask of scorn, although it be
To hide the love thou feel'st for me.

PERCY BYSSHE SHELLEY

LOVE'S FAREWELL

Since there's no help, come let us kiss and part,—
Nay I have done, you get no more of me;
And I am glad, yea, glad with all my heart,
That thus so cleanly I myself can free.

Shake hands for ever, cancel all our vows;
And when we meet at any time again,
Be it not seen in either of our brows
That we one jot of former love retain.

Now at the last gasp of love's latest breath,
When his pulse failing, passion speechless lies,
When faith is kneeling by his bed of death,
And innocence is closing up his eyes,

—Now if thou wouldst, when all have given him over,
From death to life thou mightst him yet recover!

MICHAEL DRAYTON

Creatures Great
and Small

ANIMAL LIFE

I think I could turn and live with animals, they are so placid
    and self-contain'd,
I stand and look at them long and long.

They do not sweat and whine about their condition,
They do not lie awake in the dark and weep for their sins,
They do not make me sick discussing their duty to God,
Not one is dissatisfied, not one is demented with the mania of
    owning things,
Not one kneels to another, nor to his kind that lived thousands
    of years ago,
Not one is respectable or unhappy over the whole earth.

WALT WHITMAN
From *Song of Myself*

THE WINGED HORSE

It's ten years ago to-day you turned me out o' doors
To cut my feet on flinty lands and stumble down the shores,
And I thought about the all-in-all, oh more than I can tell!
But I caught a horse to ride upon and I rode him very well,
He had flame behind the eyes of him and wings upon his side.
    And I ride, and I ride!

I rode him out of Wantage and I rode him up the hill,
And there I saw the Beacon in the morning standing still,
Inkpen and Hackpen and southward and away
High through the middle airs in the strengthening of the day,
And there I saw the channel-glint and England in her pride.
        And I ride, and I ride!

And once a-top of Lambourne down toward the hill of Clere
I saw the Host of Heaven in rank and Michael with his spear,
And Turpin out of Gascony and Charlemagne the Lord,
And Roland of the marches with his hand upon his sword
For the time he should have need of it, and forty more beside.
        And I ride, and I ride!

For you that took the all-in-all the things you left were three.
A loud voice for singing and keen eyes to see,
And a spouting well of joy within that never yet was dried!
        And I ride.

HILAIRE BELLOC

HORSES ON THE CAMARGUE

In the grey wastes of dread,
The haunt of shattered gulls where nothing moves
But in a shroud of silence like the dead,
I heard a sudden harmony of hooves,
And, turning, saw afar
A hundred snowy horses unconfined,
The silver runaways of Neptune's car
Racing, spray-curled, like waves before the wind.
Sons of the Mistral, fleet
As him with whose strong gusts they love to flee,
Who shod the flying thunders on their feet
And plumed them with the snortings of the sea;

Theirs is no earthly breed
Who only haunt the verges of the earth
And only on the sea's salt herbage feed—
Surely the great white breakers gave them birth.
For when for years a slave,
A horse of the Camargue, in alien hands,
Should catch some far-off fragrance of the wave
Carried far inland from his native sands,
Many have told the tale
Of how in fury, foaming at the rein,
He hurls his rider; and with lifted tail,
With coal-red eyes and cataracting mane,
Heading his course for home,
Though sixty foreign leagues before him sweep,
Will never rest until he breathes the foam
And hears the native thunder of the deep.
But when the great gusts rise
And lash their anger on these arid coasts,
When the scared gulls career with mournful cries
And whirl across the waste like driven ghosts:
When hail and fire converge,
The only souls to which they strike no pain
Are the white-crested fillies of the surge
And the white horses of the windy plain.
Then in their strength and pride
The stallions of the wilderness rejoice;
They feel their Master's trident in their side,
And high and shrill they answer to his voice.
With white tails smoking free,
Long streaming manes, and arching necks, they show
Their kinship to their sisters of the sea—
And forward hurl their thunderbolts of snow.
Still out of hardship bred,
Spirits of power and beauty and delight
Have ever on such frugal pastures fed
And loved to course with tempests through the night.

221

ROY CAMPBELL

SOCIABLE ANIMALS

There is a wonderful spirit of sociality in the brute creation, independent of sexual attachment: the congregating of gregarious birds in the winter is a remarkable instance.

Many horses, though quiet with company, will not stay one minute in a field by themselves: the strongest fences cannot restrain them. My neighbour's horse will not only not stay by himself abroad, but he will not bear to be left alone in a strange stable without discovering the utmost impatience, and endeavouring to break the rack and manger with his fore feet. He has been known to leap out at stable-window, through which dung was thrown, after company; and yet in other respects is remarkably quiet. Oxen and cows will not fatten by themselves; but will neglect the finest pasture that is not recommended by society. It would be needless to instance in sheep, which constantly flock together.

But this propensity seems not to be confined to animals of the same species; for we know a doe, still alive, that was brought up from a little fawn with a dairy of cows; with them it goes a-field, and with them it returns to the yard. The dogs of the house take no notice of this deer, being used to her; but, if strange dogs come by, a chase ensues; while the master smiles to see his favourite securely leading her pursuers over hedge, or gate, or stile, till she returns to the cows, who, with fierce lowings and menacing horns, drive the assailants quite out of the pasture.

Even great disparity of kind and size does not always prevent social advances and mutual fellowship. For a very intelligent and observant person has assured me that, in the former part of his life, keeping but one horse, he happened also on a time to have but one solitary hen. These two incongruous animals spent much of their time together in a lonely orchard, where they saw no creature but each other. By degrees an apparent regard began to take place between these two sequestered individuals. The fowl would approach the quadruped with notes of complacency, rubbing herself gently against his legs; while the horse would look down with satisfaction, and move with the greatest caution and circumspection, lest he should trample on his diminutive companion. Thus, by mutual good offices, each seemed to console the vacant hours of the other; so that Milton, when he puts the following sentiment in the mouth of Adam, seems to be somewhat mistaken:

> Much less can *bird* with *beast*, or fish with fowl
> So well converse, nor with the ox the ape.

GILBERT WHITE
From The Natural History of Selborne

INSCRIPTION ON THE MONUMENT OF A NEWFOUNDLAND DOG

When some proud son of man returns to earth,
Unknown to glory, but upheld by birth,
The sculptor's art exhausts the pomp of woe,
And storied urns record who rest below:
When all is done, upon the tomb is seen,
Not what he was, but what he should have been;
But the poor dog, in life the firmest friend,
The first to welcome, foremost to defend,
Whose honest heart is still his master's own,
Who labours, fights, lives, breathes, for him alone,
Unhonour'd falls unnoticed all his worth,
Denied in heaven the soul he held on earth:
While man, vain insect! hopes to be forgiven,
And claims himself a sole exclusive heaven.
Oh man! thou feeble tenant of an hour,
Debased by slavery, or corrupt by power,
Who knows thee well must quit thee with disgust,
Degraded mass of animated dust!
Thy love is lust, thy friendship all a cheat,
Thy smiles hypocrisy, thy words deceit!

By nature vile, ennobled but by name,
Each kindred brute might bid thee blush for shame.
Ye! who perchance behold this simple urn,
Pass on—it honours none you wish to mourn:
To mark a friend's remains these stones arise;
I never knew but one,—and here he lies.

LORD BYRON

HODGE THE CAT

I never shall forget the indulgence with which he treated Hodge, his cat; for whom he himself used to go out and buy oysters, lest the servant having that trouble should take a dislike to the poor creature. I am, unluckily, one of those who have an antipathy to a cat, so that I am uneasy when in the room with one; and I own, I frequently suffered a good deal from the presence of the same Hodge. I recollect him one day scrambling up Dr. Johnson's breast, apparently with much satisfaction, while my friend, smiling and half-whistling, rubbed down his back, and pulled him by the tail; and when I observed he was a fine cat saying, 'Why, yes, Sir, but I have had cats whom I liked better than this'; and then, as if perceiving Hodge to be out of countenance, adding, 'but he is a very fine cat, a very fine cat indeed.'

JAMES BOSWELL
From The Life of Samuel Johnson

MILK FOR THE CAT

When the tea is brought at five o'clock,
And all the neat curtains are drawn with care,
The little black cat with bright green eyes
Is suddenly purring there.

At first she pretends, having nothing to do,
She has come in merely to blink by the grate,
But, though tea may be late or the milk may be sour,
She is never late.

And presently her agate eyes
Take a soft large milky haze,
And her independent casual glance
Becomes a stiff, hard gaze.

Then she stamps her claws or lifts her ears,
Or twists her tail and begins to stir,
Till suddenly all her lithe body becomes
One breathing, trembling purr.

The children eat and wriggle and laugh;
The two old ladies stroke their silk:
But the cat is grown small and thin with desire,
Transformed to a creeping lust for milk.

The white saucer like some full moon descends
At last from the clouds of the table above;
She sighs and dreams and thrills and glows,
Transfigured with love.

She nestles over the shining rim,
Buries her chin in the creamy sea;
Her tail hangs loose; each drowsy paw
Is doubled under each bending knee.

A long, dim ecstasy holds her life;
Her world is an infinite shapeless white,
Till her tongue has curled the last holy drop,
Then she sinks back into the night,

Draws and dips her body to heap
Her sleepy nerves in the great arm-chair,
Lies defeated and buried deep
Three or four hours unconscious there.

HAROLD MONRO

THE OWL AND THE PUSSY-CAT

The Owl and the Pussy-Cat went to sea
   In a beautiful pea-green boat.
They took some honey, and plenty of money
   Wrapped up in a five-pound note.
The Owl looked up to the stars above,
   And sang to a small guitar,
'O lovely Pussy! O Pussy, my love,
What a beautiful Pussy you are,
    You are,
    You are!
What a beautiful Pussy you are.'

Pussy said to the Owl, 'You elegant fowl!
   How charmingly sweet you sing!
O let us be married! too long we have tarried:
   But what shall we do for a ring?'
They sailed away, for a year and a day,
   To the land where the Bong-Tree grows,
And there in a wood a Piggy-wig stood,
With a ring at the end of his nose,
    His nose,
    His nose!
With a ring at the end of his nose.

'Dear Pig, are you willing to sell for one shilling
   Your ring?' Said the Piggy, 'I will.'
So they took it away, and were married next day
   By the Turkey who lives on the hill.

They dined on mince, and slices of quince,
  Which they ate with a runcible spoon;
And hand in hand, on the edge of the sand
They danced by the light of the moon,
    The moon,
    The moon,
They danced by the light of the moon.

EDWARD LEAR

TIGER, TIGER

Tiger, tiger, burning bright
In the forests of the night,
What immortal hand or eye
Could frame thy fearful symmetry?

In what distant deeps or skies
Burnt the fire of thine eyes?
On what wings dare he aspire?
What the hand dare seize the fire?

And what shoulder and what art
Could twist the sinews of thy heart?
And, when thy heart began to beat,
What dread hand form'd thy dread feet?

What the hammer? What the chain?
In what furnace was thy brain?
What the anvil? What dread grasp
Dare its deadly terrors clasp?

When the stars threw down their spears,
And water'd heaven with their tears,
Did He smile His work to see?
Did He who made the lamb make thee?

Tiger, tiger, burning bright
In the forests of the night,
What immortal hand or eye
Dare frame thy fearful symmetry?

WILLIAM BLAKE

THE SKYLARK

Bird of the wilderness,
Blithesome and cumberless,
Sweet be thy matin o'er moorland and lea!
Emblem of happiness,
Blest is thy dwelling-place—
Oh, to abide in the desert with thee!

Wild is thy lay and loud,
Far in the downy cloud;
Love gives it energy, love gave it birth.
Where, on thy dewy wing,
Where art thou journeying?
Thy lay is in heaven, thy love is on earth.

O'er fell and fountain sheen,
O'er moor and mountain green,
O'er the red streamer that heralds the day,
Over the cloudlet dim,
Over the rainbow's rim,
Musical cherub, soar, singing, away!

Then, when the gloaming comes,
Low in the heather blooms,
Sweet will thy welcome and bed of love be!
Emblem of happiness,
Blest is thy dwelling-place—
Oh, to abide in the desert with thee!

JAMES HOGG

TO THE CUCKOO

Hail, beauteous stranger of the grove!
  Thou messenger of Spring!
Now Heaven repairs thy rural seat,
  And woods thy welcome ring.

What time the daisy decks the green,
  Thy certain voice we hear:
Hast thou a star to guide thy path,
  Or mark the rolling year?

Delightful visitant! with thee
  I hail the time of flowers,
And hear the sound of music sweet
  From birds among the bowers.

The school-boy, wandering through the wood
  To pull the primrose gay,
Starts, the new voice of Spring to hear,
  And imitates thy lay.

What time the pea puts on the bloom,
  Thou fli'st thy vocal vale,
An annual guest in other lands,
  Another Spring to hail.

Sweet bird! thy bower is ever green,
  Thy sky is ever clear;
Thou hast no sorrow in thy song,
  No Winter in thy year!

O could I fly, I'd fly with thee!
  We'd make, with joyful wing,
Our annual visit o'er the globe,
  Companions of the Spring.

JOHN LOGAN

THE DARKLING THRUSH

I leant upon a coppice gate
    When Frost was spectre-gray,
And Winter's dregs made desolate
    The weakening eye of day.
The tangled bine-stems scored the sky
    Like strings from broken lyres,
And all mankind that haunted nigh
    Had sought their household fires.

The land's sharp features seemed to be
    The Century's corpse outleant,
His crypt the cloudy canopy,
    The wind his death-lament.
The ancient pulse of germ and birth
    Was shrunken hard and dry,
And every spirit upon earth
    Seemed fervourless as I.

At once a voice burst forth among
    The bleak twigs overhead
In a full-hearted evensong
    Of joy illimited;
An aged thrush, frail, gaunt, and small,
    In blast-beruffled plume,
Had chosen thus to fling his soul
    Upon the growing gloom.

So little cause for carollings
    Of such ecstatic sound
Was written on terrestrial things
    Afar or nigh around,
That I could think there trembled through
    His happy good-night air
Some blessed Hope, whereof he knew
    And I was unaware.

THOMAS HARDY

NIGHTINGALES

Beautiful must be the mountains whence ye come,
And bright in the fruitful valleys the streams wherefrom
      Ye learn your song:
Where are those starry woods? O might I wander there,
  Among the flowers, which in that heavenly air
      Bloom the year long!

Nay, barren are those mountains and spent the streams:
Our song is the voice of desire, that haunts our dreams,
      A throe of the heart,
Whose pining visions dim, forbidden hopes profound,
  No dying cadence nor long sigh can sound,
      For all our art.

Alone, aloud in the raptured ear of men
We pour our dark nocturnal secret; and then,
      As night is withdrawn
From these sweet-springing meads and bursting boughs of
      May,
  Dream, while the innumerable choir of day
      Welcome the dawn.

                    ROBERT BRIDGES

FLYING CROOKED

The butterfly, the cabbage-white,
(His honest idiocy of flight)
Will never now, it is too late,
Master the art of flying straight,
Yet has—who knows so well as I?—
A just sense of how not to fly:

231

He lurches here and here by guess
And God and hope and hopelessness.
Even the aerobatic swift
Has not his flying-crooked gift.

ROBERT GRAVES

THE GRASSHOPPER AND THE CRICKET

Green little vaulter in the sunny grass,
Catching your heart up at the feel of June,
Sole voice that's heard amidst the lazy noon,
When even the bees lag at the summoning brass;
And you, warm little housekeeper, who class
With those who think the candles come too soon,
Loving the fire, and with your tricksome tune
Nick the glad silent moments as they pass.

O sweet and tiny cousins, that belong,
One to the fields, the other to the hearth,
Both have your sunshine; both, though small, are strong
At your clear hearts; and both seem given to earth
To ring in thoughtful ears this natural song—
Indoors and out, summer and winter, Mirth.

LEIGH HUNT

THE YAK

As a friend to the children commend me the Yak.
  You will find it exactly the thing:
It will carry and fetch, you can ride on its back,
  Or lead it about with a string.

232

The Tartar who dwells on the plains of Thibet
  (A desolate region of snow)
Has for centuries made it a nursery pet,
  And surely the Tartar should know!

Then tell your papa where the Yak can be got,
  And if he is awfully rich
He will buy you the creature—or else he will not.
  (I cannot be positive which.)

HILAIRE BELLOC

THE DONKEY

When fishes flew and forests walked,
  And figs grew upon thorn,
Some moments when the moon was blood,
  Then surely I was born;

With monstrous head and sickening cry
  And ears like errant wings,
The devil's walking parody
  On all four-footed things.

The tattered outlaw of the earth,
  Of ancient crooked will;
Starve, scourge, deride me: I am dumb,
  I keep my secret still.

Fools! For I also had my hour;
  One far fierce hour and sweet:
There was a shout about my ears,
  And palms before my feet.

G. K. CHESTERTON

Victory over Adversity

ON HIS BLINDNESS

When I consider how my light is spent
  Ere half my days, in this dark world and wide,
  And that one talent which is death to hide
Lodged with me useless, though my soul more bent
To serve therewith my Maker, and present
  My true account, lest He returning chide,—
  Doth God exact day-labour, light denied?
I fondly ask—But Patience, to prevent
That murmur, soon replies: God doth not need
  Either man's work, or His own gifts; who best
Bear His mild yoke, they serve Him best. His state
Is kingly; thousands at His bidding speed
  And post o'er land and ocean without rest:—
They also serve who only stand and wait.

JOHN MILTON

THE RATIONAL DELIGHTS

For my own part, when an accident, which everyone but myself
deemed a misfortune, forced me into retirement at the age of
nineteen, the incapacity of enjoying those many exercises and
amusements, which my youth and vigour of body and mind
would have naturally led me into, presented study as the only
means of employing the activity of my spirits, and beguiling that

time which otherwise must have hung heavy on my hands: and though necessity, not choice, first put me on this pursuit of knowledge, choice very soon became the principal motive and incentive to my studies; and the rational delights of reflection, contemplation and conversation soon made me insensible of any loss I had suffered from the want of sight.

SIR JOHN FIELDING
From *The Universal Mentor*

THE GOSPEL OF ST. DUNSTAN'S

We who are blind cannot see the glory of the sunrise, the splendour of the sunlit days nor the pageant of the sunset; we cannot see the tender beauties of the moonlit night nor the brightness of the stars; the hills, the woods and the fields, the sea and the winding courses of the rivers are hidden from us; we cannot see the buildings of our cities, nor our homes, nor the movements of life, nor the faces of our dear ones. There is much that we cannot see; there is one thing we will not see, if we can help it, and that is the gloomy side of our lives. This is the gospel of St. Dunstan's.

SIR ARTHUR PEARSON
From *Victory over Blindness*

RIDING BLIND

I know of no pleasure greater than a good ride, particularly if it's in a country that I know—the feel and smell of the horse, and the leather, the fresh air, and the scents of plough and hedgerow and perhaps even of fox, the exercise and the companionship; and from time to time, a pause on the top of a hill when my companion looks at the view, and I imagine it as I used to see it years ago. 'Can you see the sea from here today?' 'Yes, there's a good deal of cloud over us here, but the sun is shining through, and you can just see the horizon with the high cliff on its left.' I remember that picture.

I thought that kind of recollection would cause me pain or regret. Perhaps it did at first, but long since I have learned to take comfort from it, and to get real pleasure out of it. Adjustment to blindness is very largely a matter of passing by the things you can no longer enjoy, and enjoying to the full the many things that are still yours.

LORD FRASER OF LONSDALE
From *Whereas I was Blind*

THE BLIND BOY

O Say! what is that thing call'd Light,
    Which I can ne'er enjoy;
What is the blessing of the sight,
    O tell your poor blind boy!

You talk of wond'rous things you see,
    You say the sun shines bright;
I feel him warm, but how can he
    Then make it day or night?

My day or night myself I make,
    Whene'er I wake or play,
And could I ever keep awake,
    It would be always day.

With heavy sighs, I often hear,
    You mourn my hopeless woe;
But sure, with patience I may bear
    A loss I ne'er can know.

Then let not what I cannot have
My Chear of Mind destroy;
Whilst thus I sing, I am a King,
Altho' a poor Blind Boy.

COLLEY CIBBER

LIFE IS SWEET

Fifteen years ago I had two hands and ten fingers. Today I have
an ugly fingerless paw for a left hand, and only a few misshapen
stumps for fingers on my right hand. Where once my face was
fresh and smooth, it is now scarred and disfigured. Compared
with my fellows I am a freak, and people sometimes stare at me
with shock, or turn away eyes brimming with pity. Yet inside I
am as normal as anyone else. I have a good job and a healthy,
happy family. Indeed, I am just as well off—if not better—than
I would have been had I been able to go on flying with the R.A.F.
Whereas then I was literally and mentally up in the clouds, today
I am down to earth with a vengeance. My life is not restricted in
any way—it is full to overflowing, free and independent. Life is
sweet—and as for my injuries, my disabilities, I don't give a
damn. . . .

We who are disabled or disfigured do not ask much of society.
Our wants are simple: a fair chance free from prejudice, and
understanding without sentimentality. Good will without understanding is not enough, or rather it can be too much; kindly
soft-hearted people show pity for us perhaps because they think
we must be sorry for ourselves. A few may be, but most of us
certainly are not. Whatever our outward appearance, we are
normal inside. We have normal hopes and fears, normal thoughts
and emotions and ambitions. We are more conscious of our
remaining abilities than of our obvious or hidden disabilities.
We do not want anyone to feel sorry for us. We just want to be

238

treated as equals, and allowed and where necessary helped to live normal lives.

To compete on equal terms with the normal and the physically sound we have to struggle hard, particularly in the first few years while the shock is still new; but the struggle can be won, as the post-war careers of the Guinea Pigs and thousands of others clearly show. We are out in the open. We have completed our journey back into life. And we find life sweet, satisfying and purposeful.

WILLIAM SIMPSON
From *I Burned My Fingers*

VICTORY FOR DAVID BELL

Men like Tommy Gaygan and John Proctor, and the young Scotsman named David Bell who was in the process of clearing an enemy minefield in Libya in 1942 when a booby trap blew up in his face, have known what it is to suffer and to conquer. When David recovered consciousness they told him he would never see or touch anything again. Yet there is no bitterness as he talks of life, as he knew it and as it is to-day. 'Life is an art,' he declares, 'there is much to be crammed into a short spell, whether it be twenty years or a hundred and I want to make the most of my time. It is no good crying over spilt milk and the ifs and might-have-beens. I have cried, but that is over, and I now realize that I am luckier than a good many people. I have my wife and children, my business'—he is a successful shopkeeper in Edin-burgh—'and my studies'—he gained his Master of Arts degree since he went blind. 'But apart from those material things, I have acquired a great gift. I can now see with my brain, right through into people. After all, the eyes are only messengers of the brain; they miss a lot and often are deceived.'

But you may ask, how could this blind and handless man, courageous though he may be, take an M.A. degree at Edinburgh

239

University when he could not even use Braille text-books for his studies? Well, his fellow students went through their notes with him and his wife read aloud from his text-books. 'When examination time came along,' he will tell you, 'my spoonfuls of breakfast were mixed with spoonfuls of Plato and Adam Smith!' Like all St. Dunstaners, this blind M.A. started with only courage and will-power; courage to face up to the cruel trick fate had played him; will-power to turn his handicap to good account.

BASIL CURTIS

LIFE WITHOUT LEGS

Apart from occasional games of tennis in the summer with my friends, my chief game now is golf, which I play to a handicap of six. Golf undoubtedly is the game that a physically handicapped person can play on equal terms with others. The great thing about golf is that you can play it anywhere. Whether you have one arm, or no legs, or whatever it is, the handicapping system is such that you can always have a good game and a lot of fun. I would say that it is probably the game that is played most by disabled people in preference to any other. I have met some splendid one-armed players, and ones with legs missing. When I first started this game I used to swing the club very fast and fell over every time, but after a bit I discovered that swinging slowly and gripping the club lightly enabled me to keep my arms clear of my body and therefore avoid upsetting my balance. I still overbalance occasionally, but so does everybody else! Only on rare occasions does one get a stance, for instance, in the left-hand corner of a bunker, which is more difficult for a disabled man than the ordinary chap, the reason being that you cannot take weight on your above-knee when it is bent.

As life goes on with the disability certain things automatically solve themselves. In the initial stages one is very sensitive to other people offering help. When you have got used to a disability, and your friends know that you have it, you not only accept help, but ask for it when needed. This is much the best way of carrying on and saves embarrassment for everybody. For instance, if I am walking up a slope on a golf course I get someone to give me a pull because it helps. If I am walking down, I hang on to someone to stop myself running away. In the early days, determined to be unnecessarily independent, I would never do this. Any heavy weight, like a suitcase, your friend will carry for you—it is easier. You are carrying yourself on your legs, so there is no point in adding weight to them and making it more difficult. For the same reason, wear the lightest shoes you can get. A lot of nonsense used to be talked years ago about an artificial leg needing to weigh a certain amount, so as not to get blown about in the wind. This is not true. An artificial leg ideally should weigh nothing, because everything artificial is dead weight.

The most tiring thing you can do with artificial legs is to stand. Sit whenever you can. You can do this unobtrusively by sitting on the edge of a chair arm or a table, thereby taking the weight off your feet, or, if you are with friends, simply sitting down.

The little things are the awkward ones like getting out of a chair in a confined space. I once had a letter from a man asking me how to get out of a chair without arms on the sides. This had never been one of my problems. Automatically you raise yourself from an armchair by placing your hands on the arms and pushing. Likewise, if there are no arms to the chair, you merely push from the seat. The principle is the same—that you have got to get your weight moving forwards before you can stand up. Where you tend to be clumsy is in moving around a confined space, like a drawing-room.

The goal of a disabled person surely is to get back to normal as far as is reasonably possible. Clearly some things which you formerly did are physically impossible to do minus your leg. Therefore you don't try to do them. On the other hand, there are plenty of other things you can continue to do. If you are athletically inclined, you cannot play football, but you can play golf. If you never played games, there is no reason to suggest that you should start playing them merely because someone else with the same disability does so. People's ideas of a normal life vary, and what you wish to achieve is your idea of a normal life. Whatever it is, one thing above all is essential, and that is to decide not to be a burden on your friends and relations. Remember that they know of your disability, and will help you physically whenever you may want such help. To my way of thinking, a disabled man who has achieved independence is no longer disabled.

DOUGLAS BADER

LIVING WITH POLIO

Infantile paralysis in middle life left me with two paralysed legs and a very weak back. This might have been the end of me, but it wasn't. I was blessed with a good wife, a woman of great character, and together we fought through. Poverty, frustration, discouragement—we managed to overcome them; I could not let her down. A sense of humour, too, helped quite a lot. To-day, though well past the prime of life, I put in a working week averaging eighty hours; I drive my car all over the country, visiting our seventy-odd branches and groups and covering over 12,000 miles a year in fine weather and in foul, and I find life interesting and worth while, although I cannot walk.

I consider I have made a success of things since polio struck me, because I manage to be a useful human being, leading a very full and busy life, proud of the fact that, up and down the country, there are many disabled men and women who think well of me and who look to me for guidance and help. And when I say all this I am not being boastful; in the still watches of the night, in my moments of self-appraisement, I have no illusion as to my shortcomings, yet I feel it would be foolish not to take pride in achievement and to simulate an entirely dishonest humility.

A disability is not necessarily a passport to heaven; physical handicaps do not make people more virtuous. They can—in many cases they do—make the afflicted difficult to live with, bringing out all the weak points of their characters, and in extreme cases such people may become as twisted in their minds as they are in their bodies. All the suspiciousness born of frustration, all the irritation, all the hurts, real and imaginary, engendered by hypersensitiveness, turned to spite by too much leisure to brood, all these factors frequently combine to produce most unpleasant results.

This is the debit side. And, of course—and this is important to understand—a physical handicap may have, and often, indeed, has, the very opposite effect. So much depends upon the original make up of the afflicted. If nature has been kind and sent him into the world with a good sense of humour there is every possibility of his bearing his burden with dignity and some measure of happiness.

FREDERICK MORENA

OF ADVERSITY

It was a high speech of Seneca (after the manner of the Stoics), that the good things which belong to prosperity are to be wished; but the good things that belong to adversity are to be admired. . . . The virtue of Prosperity is temperance, the virtue of Adversity is fortitude; which in morals is the more heroical virtue. Prosperity is the blessing of the Old Testament; Adversity is the blessing of the New; which carrieth the greater benediction, and the clearer revelation of God's favour. Yet even in the Old Testament, if you listen to David's harp, you shall hear as many hearse-like airs as carols; and the pencil of the Holy Ghost hath laboured more in describing the afflictions of Job than the felicities of Salomon. Prosperity is not without many fears and distastes; and Adversity is not without comforts and hopes. We see in needleworks and embroideries, it is more pleasing to have a lively work upon a sad and solemn ground, than to have a dark and melancholy work upon a lightsome ground: judge therefore of the pleasure of the heart by the pleasure of the eye. Certainly virtue is like precious odours, most fragrant when they are incensed or crushed: for Prosperity doth best discover vice, but Adversity doth best discover virtue.

FRANCIS BACON, BARON VERULAM

LIFE WITH THREE SENSES

Necessity gives to the eye a precious power of seeing, and in the same way it gives a precious power of feeling to the whole body. Sometimes it seems as if the very substance of my flesh were so many eyes looking out at will upon a world new created every day. The silence and darkness which are said to shut me in, open my door most hospitably to countless sensations that distract, inform, admonish, and amuse. With my three trusty guides, touch, smell, and taste, I make many excursions into the borderland of experience which is in sight of the city of Light. Nature accommodates itself to every man's necessity. If the eye is maimed, so that it does not see the beauteous face of day, the touch becomes more poignant and discriminating. Nature proceeds through practice to strengthen and augment the remaining senses. For this reason the blind often hear with greater ease and distinctness than other people. The sense of smell becomes almost a new faculty to penetrate the tangle and vagueness of things. Thus, according to an immutable law, the senses assist and reinforce one another.

HELEN KELLER
From *The World I live in*

INVICTUS

Out of the night that covers me,
  Black as the pit from pole to pole,
I thank whatever gods may be
  For my unconquerable soul.

In the fell clutch of circumstance
  I have not winced nor cried aloud.
Under the bludgeonings of chance
  My head is bloody, but unbowed.

Beyond this place of wrath and tears
  Looms but the Horror of the shade,
And yet the menace of the years
  Finds, and shall find, me unafraid.

It matters not how strait the gate,
  How charged with punishments the scroll,
I am the master of my fate:
  I am the captain of my soul.

WILLIAM ERNEST HENLEY

Compassion

THE QUALITY OF MERCY

The quality of mercy is not strain'd,
It droppeth as the gentle rain from heaven
Upon the place beneath: it is twice bless'd;
It blesseth him that gives and him that takes:
'Tis mightiest in the mightiest; it becomes
The throned monarch better than his crown;
His sceptre shows the force of temporal power,
The attribute to awe and majesty,
Wherein doth sit the dread and fear of kings;
But mercy is above this sceptred sway,
It is enthroned in the hearts of kings,
It is an attribute to God himself,
And earthly power doth then show likest God's
When mercy seasons justice.

WILLIAM SHAKESPEARE
From *The Merchant of Venice*

FORGIVENESS

And one of the Pharisees desired that he would eat with him.
And he went into the Pharisee's house, and sat down to meat.

And, behold, a woman in the city, which was a sinner, when
she knew that Jesus sat at meat in the Pharisee's house, brought
an alabaster box of ointment, and stood at his feet behind him
weeping, and began to wash his feet with tears, and did wipe
them with the hairs of her head, and kissed his feet, and anointed
them with the ointment.

Now when the Pharisee which had bidden him saw it, he spake within himself, saying, This man, if he were a prophet, would have known who and what manner of woman this is that toucheth him; for she is a sinner.

And Jesus, answering, said unto him, Simon, I have somewhat to say unto thee. And he saith, Master, say on.

There was a certain creditor which had two debtors: the one owed five hundred pence, and the other fifty: and when they had nothing to pay, he frankly forgave them both. Tell me, therefore, which of them will love him most?

Simon answered and said, I suppose that he, to whom he forgave most. And he said unto him, Thou has rightly judged.

And he turned to the woman, and said unto Simon, Seest thou this woman? I entered into thine house, thou gavest me no water for my feet; but she hath washed my feet with tears, and wiped them with the hairs of her head. Thou gavest me no kiss: but this woman, since the time I came in, hath not ceased to kiss my feet. My head with oil thou didst not anoint: but this woman hath anointed my feet with ointment. Wherefore I say unto thee, Her sins, which are many, are forgiven; for she loved much: but to whom little is forgiven, the same loveth little.

And he said unto her, Thy sins are forgiven.

And they that sat at meat with him began to say within themselves, Who is this that forgiveth sins also?

And he said to the woman, Thy faith hath saved thee: go in peace.

The Gospel according to St. Luke

HE PRAYETH WELL

He prayeth well, who loveth well
Both man and bird and beast,
He prayeth best, who loveth best
All things both great and small;
For the dear God who loveth us,
He made and loveth all.

SAMUEL TAYLOR COLERIDGE
From *The Rime of the Ancient Mariner*

HE THAT IS WITHOUT SIN . . .

Jesus went unto the mount of Olives. And early in the morning he came again to the temple, and all the people came unto him; and he sat down, and taught them. And the scribes and Pharisees brought unto him a woman taken in adultery: and when they had set her in the midst, They say unto him, Master, this woman was taken in adultery, in the very act. Now Moses in the law commanded us that such should be stoned; but what sayest thou?

This they said, tempting him, that they might have to accuse him. But Jesus stooped down, and with his finger wrote on the ground, as though he heard them not. So when they continued asking him, he lifted up himself, and said unto them, He that is without sin among you, let him first cast a stone at her. And again he stooped down, and wrote on the ground.

And they, which heard it, being convicted by their own conscience, went out one by one, beginning at the eldest even unto the last: and Jesus was left alone, and the woman standing in the midst.

When Jesus had lifted up himself, and saw none but the woman, he said unto her, Woman, where are those thine accusers? hath no man condemned thee?

She said, No man, Lord. And Jesus said unto her, Neither do I condemn thee: go, and sin no more.

The Gospel according to St. John

THE WOUND-DRESSER

An old man bending I come among new faces,
Years looking backward resuming in answer to children,
Come tell us old man, as from young men and maidens that
    love me,
(Arous'd and angry, I'd thought to beat the alarum, and urge
    relentless war,
But soon my fingers fail'd me, my face droop'd and I resign'd
    myself
To sit by the wounded and soothe them, or silently watch the
    dead;)
Years hence of these scenes, of these furious passions, these
    chances,
Of unsurpass'd heroes (was one side so brave? the other was
    equally brave;)
Now be witness again, paint the mightiest armies of earth,
Of those armies so rapid so wondrous what saw you to tell us?

What stays with you latest and deepest? of curious panics,
Of hard-fought engagements or sieges tremendous what deepest
    remains?

O maidens and young men I love and that love me,
What you ask of my days those the strangest and sudden your
    talking recalls,
Soldier alert I arrive after a long march cover'd with sweat and
    dust,
In the nick of time I come, lunge in the fight, loudly shout in
    the rush of successful charge,
Enter the captur'd works—yet lo, like a swift-running river they
    fade,
Pass and are gone, they fade—I dwell not on soldiers' perils or
    soldiers' joys,
(Both I remember well—many the hardships, few the joys, yet I
    was content.)

But in silence, in dreams' projections,
While the world of gain and appearance and mirth goes on,
So soon what is over forgotten, and waves wash the imprints off
   the sand,
With hinged knees returning I enter the doors (while for you up
   there,
Whoever you are, follow without noise and be of strong heart.)
Bearing the bandages, water and sponge,
Straight and swift to my wounded I go,
Where they lie on the ground after the battle brought in,
Where their priceless blood reddens the grass, the ground,
Or to the rows of the hospital tent, or under the roof'd
   hospital,
To the long row of cots up and down each side I return,
To each and all one after another I draw near, not one do I
   miss,
An attendant follows holding a tray, he carries a refuse pail,
Soon to be filled with clotted rags and blood, emptied, and fill'd
   again.

I onward go, I stop,
With hinged knees and steady hand to dress wounds,
I am firm with each, the pangs are sharp but unavoidable,
One turns to me his appealing eyes—poor boy! I never knew
   you,
Yet I think I could not refuse this moment to die for you, if
   that would save you.

On, on I go (open doors of time! open hospital doors!)
The crush'd head I dress (poor crazed hand tear not the
   bandage away)
The neck of the cavalry-man with the bullet through and
   through I examine,
Hard the breathing rattles, quite glazed already the eye, yet
   life struggles hard,

(Come sweet death! be persuaded O beautiful death! in mercy
    come quickly.)
From the stump of the arm, the amputated hand,
I undo the clotted lint, remove the slough, wash off the matter
    and blood,
Back on the pillow the soldier bends with curv'd neck and side-
    falling head,
His eyes are closed, his face is pale, he dares not look on the
    bloody stump,
And has not yet look'd on it.

I dress a wound in the side, deep, deep,
But a day or two more, for see the frame all wasted and sinking,
And the yellow-blue countenance see.

I dress the perforated shoulder, the foot with the bullet-wound,
Cleanse the one with a gnawing and putrid gangrene, so
    sickening, so offensive,
While the attendant stands behind aside me holding the tray
    and pail.
I am faithful, I do not give out,
The fractur'd thigh, the knee, the wound in the abdomen,
These and more I dress with impassive hand (yet deep in my
    breast a fire, a burning flame).

Thus in silence in dreams' projections,
Returning, resuming, I thread my way through the hospitals,
The hurt and wounded I pacify with soothing hand,
I sit by the restless all the dark night, some are so young,
Some suffer so much, I recall the experience sweet and sad,
(Many a soldier's loving arms about this neck have cross'd
    and rested,
Many a soldier's kiss dwells on these bearded lips.)

WALT WHITMAN

ALL THY MERCIES

When all thy Mercies, O my God,
  My rising Soul surveys;
Transported with the View, I'm lost
  In Wonder, Love, and Praise.

O how shall Words with equal Warmth
  The Gratitude declare
That glows within my Ravish'd Heart!
  But thou canst read it there.

Thy Providence my Life sustain'd
  And all my Wants redrest,
When in the silent Womb I lay,
  And hung upon the Breast.

To all my weak Complaints and Cries
  Thy Mercy lent an Ear,
Ere yet my feeble Thoughts had learnt
  To form themselves in Pray'r.

Unnumber'd Comforts to my Soul
  Thy tender Care bestow'd,
Before my Infant Heart conceiv'd
  From whom those Comforts flow'd.

When in the slipp'ry Paths of Youth
  With heedless Steps I ran,
Thine Arm unseen convey'd me safe
  And led me up to Man;

Through hidden Dangers, Toils, and Deaths,
  It gently clear'd my Way,
And through the pleasing Snares of Vice,
  More to be fear'd than they.

When worn with Sickness, oft hast thou
    With Health renew'd my Face,
And when in Sins and Sorrows sunk,
    Revived my Soul with Grace.

Thy bounteous Hand with worldly Bliss
    Has made my Cup run o'er,
And in a kind and faithful Friend
    Has doubled all my Store.

Ten thousand thousand precious Gifts
    My Daily Thanks employ,
Nor is the least a cheerful Heart,
    That tastes those Gifts with Joy.

Through ev'ry Period of my Life
    Thy Goodness I'll pursue,
And after Death in distant Worlds
    The glorious Theme renew.

When Nature fails, and Day and Night
    Divide thy Works no more,
My Ever-grateful Heart, O Lord,
    Thy Mercy shall adore.

Through all Eternity to Thee
    A joyful Song I'll raise,
For oh! Eternity's too short
    To utter all thy Praise.

JOSEPH ADDISON

THE DIVINE IMAGE

To Mercy, Pity, Peace, and Love
All pray in their distress;
And to these virtues of delight
Return their thankfulness.

For Mercy, Pity, Peace, and Love
Is God, our father dear,
And Mercy, Pity, Peace, and Love
Is Man, his child and care.

For Mercy has a human heart,
Pity a human face,
And Love, the human form divine,
And Peace, the human dress.

Then every man, of every clime,
That prays in his distress,
Prays to the human form divine,
Love, Mercy, Pity, Peace.

And all must love the human form,
In heathen, turk, or jew;
Where Mercy, Love, and Pity dwell
There God is dwelling too.

WILLIAM BLAKE

LOVE DIVINE, ALL LOVES EXCELLING

Love divine, all loves excelling,
   Joy of heaven, to earth come down;
Fix in us Thy humble dwelling,
   All Thy faithful mercies crown.

Jesus, Thou art all compassion,
  Pure unbounded love Thou art;
Visit us with Thy salvation,
  Enter every trembling heart.

Come, almighty to deliver,
  Let us all Thy grace receive;
Suddenly return, and never,
  Never more Thy temples leave.
Thee we would be always blessing,
  Serve Thee as Thy hosts above,
Pray, and praise Thee, without ceasing
  Glory in Thy perfect love.

Finish then Thy new creation,
  Pure and spotless let us be;
Let us see Thy great salvation,
  Perfectly restored in Thee;
Changed from glory into glory,
  Till in heaven we take our place,
Till we cast our crowns before Thee,
  Lost in wonder, love, and praise.

CHARLES WESLEY

Friendship

A FAITHFUL FRIEND

A faithful friend is a strong defence:
And he that hath found such an one hath found a treasure.
Nothing doth countervail a faithful friend,
And his excellency is invaluable.
A faithful friend is the medicine of life;
And they that fear the Lord shall find him.
Whoso feareth the Lord shall direct his friendship aright:
For as he is, so shall his neighbour be also.

Ecclesiasticus

OF FRIENDSHIP

It had been hard for him that spake it to have put more truth and untruth together in a few words, than in that speech, Whosoever is delighted in solitude is either a wild beast or a god. For it is most true that a natural and secret hatred and aversation towards society in any man, hath somewhat of the savage beast; but it is most untrue that it should have any character at all of the divine nature except it proceed, not out of a pleasure in solitude, but out of a love and desire to sequester a man's self for a higher conversation. . . . But little do men perceive what solitude is, and how far it extendeth. For a crowd is not company; and faces are but a gallery of pictures; and talk but a tinkling cymbal, where there is no love. . . .

A principal fruit of friendship is the ease and discharge of the fulness and swellings of the heart, which passions of all kinds do cause and induce. We know diseases of stoppings and suffocations are the most dangerous in the body; and it is not much otherwise in the mind; you may take sarza to open the liver, steel to open the spleen, flower of sulphur for the lungs, castoreum for the brain; but no receipt openeth the heart, but a true friend; to whom you may impart griefs, joys, fears, hopes, suspicions, counsels, and whatsoever lieth upon the heart to oppress it, in a kind of civil shrift or confession. . . .

FRANCIS BACON, BARON VERULAM

MY FRIEND AND I

Oh! when my Friend and I
In some thick Wood have wander'd heedless on,
Hid from the vulgar Eye; and sat us down
Upon the sloping Cowslip-cover'd Bank,
Where the pure limpid Stream has slid along
In grateful Errors thro' the Under-wood
Sweet-murmuring: Methought! the shrill-tongued
 Thrush
Mended his Song of Love; the sooty Black-bird
Mellow'd his Pipe, and soften'd ev'ry Note:
The Eglantine smell'd sweeter, and the Rose
Assum'd a Dye more deep; whilst ev'ry Flower
Vy'd with its Fellow-Plant in Luxury
Of Dress. Oh! then the longest Summer's Day
Seem'd too, too much in Haste: Still the full Heart
Had not imparted half: 'Twas Happiness
Too exquisite to last. Of Joys departed
Not to return, how painful the Remembrance!

ROBERT BLAIR
From *The Grave*

TRUE AFFECTION

That a man should lay down his life for his Friend, seems strange to vulgar affections, and such as confine themselves within that Worldly principle, *Charity begins at home*. For mine own part I could never remember the relations that I held unto my self, nor the respect that I owe unto my own nature, in the cause of God, my Country, and my Friends. Next to these three, I do embrace my self.

I confess I do not observe that order that the Schools ordain our affections, to love our Parents, Wives, Children and then our Friends; for, excepting the injunctions of Religion, I do not find in my self such a necessary and indissoluble Sympathy to all those of my blood. I hope I do not break the fifth Commandment, if I conceive I may love my friend before the nearest of my blood, even those to whom I owe the principles of life. I never yet cast a true affection on a woman; but I have loved my friend as I do virtue, my soul, my God. From hence me thinks I do conceive how God loves man, what happiness there is in the love of God.

Omitting all other, there are three most mystical unions: 1. two natures in one person; 2. three persons in one nature; 3. one soul in two bodies; for though indeed they be really divided, yet are they so united, as they seem but one, and make rather a duality than two distinct souls.

There are wonders in true affection: it is a body of *Enigma's*, mysteries, and riddles; wherein two so become one, as they both become two. I love my friend before my self, and yet me-thinks I do not love him enough: some few months hence my multiplied affection will make me believe I have not loved him at all. When I am from him, I am dead till I be with him; when I am with him, I am not satisfied, but would still be nearer him. United souls are not satisfied with imbraces, but desire to be truly each other; which being impossible, their desires are infinite, and must proceed without a possibility of satisfaction.

Another misery there is in affection, that whom we truly love like our own selves, we forget their looks, nor can our memory retain the Idea of their faces; and it is no wonder, for they are our selves, and our affection makes their looks our own. This noble affection falls not on vulgar and common constitutions, but on such as are mark'd for virtue: he that can love his friend with this noble ardour will in a competent degree affect all.

Now, if we can bring our affections to look beyond the body, and cast an eye upon the soul, we have found out the true object, not only of friendship, but Charity; and the greatest happiness that we can bequeath the soul, is that wherein we all do place our last felicity, Salvation; which though it be not in our power to bestow, it is in our charity and pious invocations to desire, if not procure and further. I cannot contentedly frame a prayer for my self in particular, without a catalogue for my friends; nor request a happiness, wherein my sociable disposition doth not desire the fellowship of my neighbour.

SIR THOMAS BROWNE
From *Religio Medici*

SONNET ON FRIENDSHIP

When we were idlers with the loitering rills,
    The need of human love we little noted:
Our love was nature; and the peace that floated
On the white mist, and dwelt upon the hills,
To sweet accord subdued our wayward wills:
    One soul was ours, one mind, one heart devoted,
    That, wisely doting, ask'd not why it doted,
And ours the unknown joy, which knowing kills.
But now I find how dear thou wert to me;
    That man is more than half of nature's treasure,
Of that fair beauty which no eye can see,
    Of that sweet music which no ear can measure;
    And now the streams may sing for others' pleasure,
The hills sleep on in their eternity.

HARTLEY COLERIDGE

A FRIEND

All that he came to give,
He gave and went again:
I have seen one man live,
I have seen one man reign,
With all the graces in his train.

As one of us, he wrought
Things of the common hour:
Whence was the charmed soul brought
That gave each act such power;
The natural beauty of a flower?

Magnificence and grace,
Excellent courtesy:
A brightness on the face,
Airs of high memory:
Whence came all these, to such as he?

Like young Shakespearean kings,
He won the adoring throng:
And as Apollo sings,
He triumphed with a song:
Triumphed, and sang, and passed along.

With a light word, he took
The hearts of men in thrall:
And, with a golden look,
Welcomed them, at his call
Giving their love, their strength, their all.

No man less proud than he,
Nor cared for homage less:
Only, he could not be
Far off from happiness:
Nature was bound to his success.

Weary, the cares, the jars,
The lets, of every day:
But the heavens filled with stars,
Chanced he upon the way:
And where he stayed, all joy would stay.

Now when the night draws down,
When the austere stars burn;
Roaming the vast live town,
My thoughts and memories yearn
Toward him, who never will return.

Yet have I seen him live,
And owned my friend, a king:
All that he came to give,
He gave and I, who sing
His praise, bring all I have to bring.

LIONEL JOHNSON

A RUDDY DROP OF MANLY BLOOD

A ruddy drop of manly blood
The surging sea outweighs,
The world uncertain comes and goes;
The lover rooted stays.
I fancied he was fled,—
And, after many a year,
Glowed unexhausted kindliness,
Like daily sunrise there.
My careful heart was free again,
O friend, my bosom said,
Through thee alone the sky is arched,
Through thee the rose is red;

All things through thee take nobler form,
And look beyond the earth,
The mill-round of our fate appears
A sun-path in thy worth.
Me too thy nobleness has taught
To master my despair;
The fountains of my hidden life
Are through thy friendship fair.

RALPH WALDO EMERSON

THE MEADOWS IN SPRING

'Tis a dull sight
  To see the year dying,
When winter winds
  Set the yellow wood sighing:
    Sighing, oh! sighing.

When such a time cometh,
  I do retire
Into an old room
  Beside a bright fire:
    Oh, pile a bright fire!

And there I sit
  Reading old things,
Of knights and lorn damsels,
  While the wind sings—
    Oh, drearily sings!

I never look out
  Nor attend to the blast;
For all to be seen
  Is the leaves falling fast:
    Falling, falling!

But close at the hearth,
　　Like a cricket, sit I,
Reading of summer
　　And chivalry—
　　　　Gallant chivalry!

Then with an old friend
　　I talk of our youth!
How 'twas gladsome, but often
　　Foolish, forsooth:
　　　　But gladsome, gladsome!

Or to get merry
　　We sing some old rhyme,
That made the wood ring again
　　In summer time—
　　　　Sweet summer time!

Then go we to smoking,
　　Silent and snug:
Naught passes between us,
　　Save a brown jug—
　　　　Sometimes!

And sometimes a tear
　　Will rise in each eye,
Seeing the two old friends
　　So merrily—
　　　　So merrily!

And ere to bed
　　Go we, go we,
Down on the ashes
　　We kneel on the knee,
　　　　Praying together!

264

Thus, then, live I,
  Till, 'mid all the gloom
By heaven! the bold sun
  Is with me in the room
    Shining, shining!

Then the clouds part,
  Swallows soaring between;
The spring is alive,
  And the meadows are green!

I jump up, like mad,
  Break the old pipe in twain,
And away to the meadows,
  The meadows again.

EDWARD FITZGERALD

JOHN ANDERSON, MY JO

John Anderson, my jo, John,
  When we were first acquent,
Your locks were like the raven,
  Your bonie brow was brent;
But now your brow is beld, John,
  Your locks are like the snow;
But blessings on your frosty pow,
  John Anderson, my jo.

John Anderson, my jo, John,
  We clamb the hill thegither;
And mony a cantie day, John,
  We've had wi' ane anither:
Now we maun totter down, John,
  And hand in hand we'll go,
And sleep thegither at the foot,
  John Anderson, my jo.   ROBERT BURNS

FRIENDSHIP AND FREEDOM

There can be no friendship where there is no freedom. Friendship loves a free air, and will not be penned up in straight and narrow enclosures. It will speak freely, and act so too; and take nothing ill where no ill is meant; nay, where it is, 'twill easily forgive, and forget too, upon small acknowledgments.

A true friend unbosoms freely, advises justly, assists readily, adventures boldly, takes all patiently, defends courageously, and continues a friend unchangeably.

They have a right to censure, that have a heart to help: the rest is cruelty, not justice.

WILLIAM PENN

From *Some Fruits of Solitude*

FAME IS A FOOD THAT DEAD MEN EAT

Fame is a food that dead men eat,—
I have no stomach for such meat.
In little light and narrow room,
They eat it in the silent tomb,
With no kind voice of comrade near
To bid the feaster be of cheer.

But Friendship is a nobler thing,—
Of Friendship it is good to sing.
For truly, when a man shall end,
He lives in memory of his friend,
Who doth his better part recall
And of his fault make funeral.

AUSTIN DOBSON

Love

FOR LOVE'S SAKE ONLY

If thou must love me, let it be for nought
Except for love's sake only. Do not say
'I love her for her smile—her look—her way
Of speaking gently,—for a trick of thought
That falls in well with mine, and certes brought
A sense of pleasant ease on such a day'—
For these things in themselves, beloved, may
Be changed, or change for thee,—and love, so wrought,
May be unwrought so. Neither love me for
Thine own dear pity's wiping my cheeks dry,—
A creature might forget to weep, who bore
Thy comfort long, and lose thy love thereby!
But love me for love's sake, that evermore
Thou mayst love on, through love's eternity.

ELIZABETH BARRETT BROWNING

GIVE ALL TO LOVE

Give all to love;
Obey thy heart;
Friends, kindred, days,
Estate, good-fame,
Plans, credit and the Muse,—
Nothing refuse.

'Tis a brave master;
Let it have scope;
Follow it utterly,
Hope beyond hope:

High and more high
It dives into noon,
With wing unspent,
Untold intent;
But it is a god,
Knows its own path
And the outlets of the sky.

It was never for the mean;
It requireth courage stout.
Souls above doubt,
Valor unbending,
It will reward,—
They shall return
More than they were,
And ever ascending.

Leave all for love;
Yet, hear me, yet,
One word more thy heart behoved,
One pulse more of firm endeavor,—
Keep thee to-day,
To-morrow, forever,
Free as an Arab
Of thy beloved.

Cling with life to the maid;
But when the surprise,
First vague shadow of surmise,
Flits across her bosom young,
Of a joy apart from thee,
Free be she, fancy-free;
Nor thou detain her vesture's hem,
Nor the palest rose she flung
From her summer diadem.

Though thou loved her as thyself,
As a self of purer clay,
Though her parting dims the day,
Stealing grace from all alive;
Heartily know,
When half-gods go,
The gods arrive.

RALPH WALDO EMERSON

THE CANONIZATION

For God's sake hold your tongue, and let me love;
  Or chide my palsy, or my gout,
My five grey hairs, or ruined fortune flout;
    With wealth your state, your mind with arts improve,
      Take you a course, get you a place,
      Observe his Honour, or his Grace,
Or the King's real, or his stamped face
  Contemplate; what you will, approve,
  So you will let me love.

Alas, alas, who's injured by my love?
  What merchant's ships have my sighs drowned?
Who says my tears have overflowed his ground?
  When did my colds a forward spring remove?
    When did the heats which my veins fill
    Add one more to the plaguy bill?
Soldiers find wars, and lawyers find out still
  Litigious men, which quarrels move,
  Though she and I do love.

Call us what you will, we are made such by love;
  Call her one, me another fly,
We're tapers too, and at our own cost die,
  And we in us find the Eagle and the Dove.

The Phoenix riddle hath more wit
By us; we two being one, are it.
So to one neutral thing both sexes fit,
  We die and rise the same, and prove
  Mysterious by this love.

We can die by it, if not live by love,
  And if unfit for tombs and hearse
Our legend be, it will be fit for verse;
  And if no piece of Chronicle we prove,
    We'll build in sonnets pretty rooms;
    As well a well-wrought urn becomes
The greatest ashes, as half-acre tombs,
  And by these hymns all shall approve
  Us canonized for Love:

And thus invoke us: You whom reverend love
  Made one another's hermitage;
You, to whom love was peace, that now is rage;
  Who did the whole world's soul contract, and drove
    Into the glasses of your eyes
    (So made such mirrors, and such spies,
That they did all to you epitomise),
  Countries, Towns, Courts: beg from above
  A pattern of your love!

                                        JOHN DONNE

WHAT IS LOVE?

Tell me, dearest, what is love?
'Tis a lightning from above;
  'Tis an arrow, 'tis a fire,
  'Tis a boy they call Desire.
    'Tis a grave
    Gapes to have
Those poor fools that long to prove.

Tell me more, are women true?
Yes, some are, and some as you.
   Some are willing, some are strange,
   Since you men first taught to change.
    And till troth
    Be in both,
All shall love, to love anew.

Tell me more, yet, can they grieve?
Yes, and sicken sore, but live:
   And be wise, and delay,
   When you men are as wise as they.
    Then I see,
    Faith will be,
Never till they both believe.

JOHN FLETCHER
From *The Captain*

LET ME NOT TO THE MARRIAGE
OF TRUE MINDS

Let me not to the marriage of true minds
  Admit impediments. Love is not love
Which alters when it alteration finds,
  Or bends with the remover to remove.
O, no! it is an ever-fixed mark,
  That looks on tempests and is never shaken;
It is the star to every wandering bark,
  Whose worth's unknown, although his height be taken.
Love's not Time's fool, though rosy lips and cheeks
  Within his bending sickle's compass come;
Love alters not with his brief hours and weeks,
  But bears it out even to the edge of doom.
    If this be error, and upon me proved,
    I never writ, nor no man ever loved.

WILLIAM SHAKESPEARE

SHALL I COMPARE THEE TO A
SUMMER'S DAY?

Shall I compare thee to a summer's day?
   Thou art more lovely and more temperate:
Rough winds do shake the darling buds of May,
   And summer's lease hath all too short a date:
Sometimes too hot the eye of heaven shines,
   And often is his gold complexion dimmed;
And every fair from fair sometime declines,
   By chance, or nature's changing course untrimmed;
But thy eternal summer shall not fade,
   Nor lose possession of that fair thou owest,
Nor shall death brag thou wander'st in his shade,
   When in eternal lines to time thou growest;
      So long as men can breathe, or eyes can see,
      So long lives this, and this gives life to thee.

                    WILLIAM SHAKESPEARE

LET ME COUNT THE WAYS

How do I love thee? Let me count the ways.
I love thee to the depth and breadth and height
My soul can reach, when feeling out of sight
For the ends of Being and ideal Grace,
I love thee to the level of every day's
Most quiet need, by sun and candle-light.
I love thee freely, as men strive for Right;
I love thee purely, as they turn from Praise.
I love thee with the passion put to use
In my old griefs, and with my childhood's faith.
I love thee with a love I seemed to lose
With my lost saints,—I love thee with the breath,
Smiles, tears, of all my life!—and, if God choose,
I shall but love thee better after death.

              ELIZABETH BARRETT BROWNING

HOW MANY TIMES DO I LOVE
THEE, DEAR?

How many times do I love thee, dear?
　Tell me how many thoughts there be
　　In the atmosphere
　　Of a new-fall'n year,
Whose white and sable hours appear
　The latest flake of Eternity:—
So many times do I love thee, dear.

How many times do I love again?
　Tell me how many beads there are
　　In a silver chain
　　Of evening rain,
Unravelled from the tumbling main,
　And threading the eye of a yellow star:—
So many times do I love again.

THOMAS LOVELL BEDDOES

MADRIGAL

　How should I love my best?
What though my love unto that height be grown
　That taking joy in you alone
　　I utterly this world detest;
Should I not love it as the only place
　Where beauty hath his perfect grace
　　And is possest?

　But I beauties despise;
You universal beauty seem to me,
　Giving and showing form and degree
　　To all the rest in your fair eyes;
Yet should I not love them as parts whereon
　Your beauty, their perfection
　　And top, doth rise?

But even myself I hate;
So far my love is from the least delight
  That at my very self I spite,
    Senseless of any happy state;
Yet may I not with justest reason fear
  How hating her I truly her
    Can celebrate?

    Thus unresolved still,
Although world, life, nay what is fair beside
  I cannot for your sake abide,
    Methinks I love not to my fill;
Yet if a greater love you can devise
  To love you some other wise,
    Believe't, I will.

LORD HERBERT

NEVER LOVE UNLESS . . .

Never love unless you can
Bear with all the faults of man:
Men sometimes will jealous be
Though but little cause they see;
And hang the head as discontent,
And speak what straight they will repent.

Men that but one saint adore
Make a show of love to more;
Beauty must be scorned in none,
Though but truly served in one:
For what is courtship but disguise?
True hearts may have dissembling eyes.

274

Men, when their affairs require,
Must awhile themselves retire;
Sometimes hunt, and sometimes hawk,
And not ever sit and talk.
If these and such-like you can bear,
Then like, and love, and never fear!

THOMAS CAMPION

TO CYNTHIA
(On concealment of her beauty)

Do not conceal thy radiant eyes,
The star-light of serenest skies,
Lest wanting of their heavenly light,
They turn to Chaos' endless night.

Do not conceal those tresses fair,
The silken snares of thy curled hair,
Lest finding neither gold nor ore
The curious silkworm work no more.

Do not conceal those breasts of thine,
More snow-white than the Apennine,
Lest if there be like cold or frost
The lily be for ever lost.

Do not conceal that fragrant scent,
Thy breath, which to all flowers hath lent
Perfumes, lest it being supprest
No spices grow in all the East.

Do not conceal thy heavenly voice,
Which makes the hearts of gods rejoice,
Lest Music hearing no such thing
The Nightingale forget to sing.

Do not conceal nor yet eclipse
Thy pearly teeth with coral lips,
Lest that the seas cease to bring forth
Gems which from thee have all their worth.

Do not conceal no beauty-grace,
That's either in thy mind or face,
Lest virtue overcome by vice
Make men believe no Paradise.

SIR FRANCIS KYNASTON

WOOING SONG

Love is the blossom where there blows
Every thing that lives or grows:
Love doth make the Heav'ns to move,
And the Sun doth burn in love:
Love the strong and weak doth yoke,
And makes the ivy climb the oak,
Under whose shadows lions wild,
Soften'd by love, grow tame and mild:
Love no med'cine can appease,
He burns the fishes in the seas:
Not all the skill his wounds can stench,
Not all the sea his fire can quench.
Love did make the bloody spear
Once a leavy coat to wear,
While in his leaves there shrouded lay
Sweet birds, for love that sing and play
And of all love's joyful flame
I the bud and blossom am.
> Only bend thy knee to me,
> Thy wooing shall thy winning be!

See, see the flowers that below
Now as fresh as morning blow;

And of all the virgin rose
That as bright Aurora shows;
How they all unleaved die,
Losing their virginity!
Like unto a summer shade,
But now born, and now they fade.
Everything doth pass away;
There is danger in delay:
Come, come, gather then the rose,
Gather it, or it you lose!
All the sand of Tagus' shore
Into my bosom casts his ore:
All the valleys' swimming corn
To my house is yearly borne:
Every grape of every vine
Is gladly bruised to make me wine:
While ten thousand kings, as proud,
To carry up my train have bow'd,
And a world of ladies send me
In my chambers to attend me:
All the stars in Heav'n that shine,
And ten thousand more, are mine:
    Only bend thy knee to me,
    Thy wooing shall thy winning be!

GILES FLETCHER

TO CHLOE
Who for his sake wished herself younger

There are two births; the one when light
   First strikes the new awaken'd sense;
The other when two souls unite,
   And we must count our life from thence:
When you loved me and I loved you
Then both of us were born anew.

Love then to us new souls did give
  And in those souls did plant new powers;
Since when another life we live,
  The breath we breathe is his, not ours:
Love makes those young whom age doth chill,
And whom he finds young keeps young still.

WILLIAM CARTWRIGHT

NOW SLEEPS THE CRIMSON PETAL

Now sleeps the crimson petal, now the white;
Nor waves the cypress in the palace walk;
Nor winks the gold fin in the porphyry font:
The firefly wakens: waken thou with me.

Now droops the milk-white peacock like a ghost,
And like a ghost she glimmers on to me.

Now lies the Earth all Danaë to the stars,
And all thy heart lies open unto me.

Now slides the silent meteor on, and leaves
A shining furrow, as thy thoughts in me.

Now folds the lily all her sweetness up,
And slips into the bosom of the lake:
So fold thyself, my dearest, thou, and slip
Into my bosom and be lost in me.

LORD TENNYSON

MY LOVE IS LIKE A RED RED ROSE

My love is like a red red rose
  That's newly sprung in June:
My love is like the melodie
  That's sweetly play'd in tune.

So fair art thou, my bonnie lass,
    So deep in love am I:
And I will love thee still, my dear,
    Till a' the seas gang dry.

Till a' the seas gang dry, my dear,
    And the rocks melt wi' the sun:
And I will love thee still, my dear,
    While the sands o' life shall run.

And fare thee weel, my only love,
    And fare thee weel awhile!
And I will come again, my love,
    Tho' it were ten thousand mile.

ROBERT BURNS

LOVE BADE ME WELCOME

Love bade me welcome; yet my soul drew back,
    Guilty of dust and sin.
But quick-eyed Love, observing me grow slack
    From my first entrance in,
Drew nearer to me, sweetly questioning
    If I lack'd anything.

'A guest,' I answered, 'worthy to be here':
    Love said, 'You shall be he.'
'I, the unkind, ungrateful? Ah, my dear,
    I cannot look on Thee.'
Love took my hand and smiling did reply,
    'Who made the eyes but I?'

'Truth, Lord; but I have marr'd them: let my shame
    Go where it doth deserve.'
'And know you not,' says Love, 'who bore the blame?'
    'My dear, then I will serve.'
'You must sit down,' says Love, 'and taste my meat.'
    So I did sit and eat.

GEORGE HERBERT

UPON JULIA'S CLOTHES

Whenas in silks my Julia goes,
Then, then, methinks, how sweetly flows
The liquefaction of her clothes!

Next, when I cast mine eyes and see
That brave vibration each way free,
—O how that glittering taketh me!

ROBERT HERRICK

CUPID AND THE NYMPH

It chanced of late a shepherd's swain,
That went to seek a strayed sheep,
Within a thicket on the plain
Espied a dainty nymph asleep.

Her golden hair o'erspread her face,
Her careless arms abroad were cast,
Her quiver had her pillow's place,
Her breast lay bare to every blast.

The shepherd stood and gazed his fill,
Nought durst he do, nought durst he say,
When chance, or else perhaps his will,
Did guide the God of Love that way.

The crafty boy that sees her sleep,
Whom if she waked he durst not see,
Behind her closely seeks to creep,
Before her nap should ended be.

There come, he steals her shafts away,
And puts his own into their place;
Ne dares he any longer stay,
But ere she wakes, hies hence apace.

Scarce was he gone when she awakes,
And spies the shepherd standing by;
Her bended bow in haste she takes,
And at the simple swain let fly.

Forth flew the shaft and pierced his heart,
That to the ground he fell with pain;
Yet up again forthwith he starts,
And to the nymph he ran amain.

Amazed to see so strange a sight,
She shot, and shot, but all in vain;
The more his wounds, the more his might;
Love yieldeth strength in midst of pain.

Her angry eyes are great with tears,
She blames her hands, she blames her skill;
The bluntness of her shafts she fears,
And try them on herself she will.

Take heed, sweet nymph, try not the shaft,
Each little touch will prick thy heart;
Alas! thou knowest not Cupid's craft,
Revenge is joy, the end is smart.

Yet try she will, and prick some bare;
Her hands were gloved, and next to hand
Was that fair breast, that breast so rare,
That made the shepherd senseless stand.

That breast she prick'd, and through that breast
Love finds an entry to her heart;
At feeling of this new-come guest,
Lord, how the gentle nymph doth start.

She runs not now, she shoots no more;
Away she throws both shafts and bow;
She seeks for that she shunn'd before,
She thinks the shepherd's haste too slow.

Though mountains meet not, lovers may;
So others do, and so do they.
The God of Love sits on a tree,
And laughs that pleasant sight to see.

UNKNOWN

LOVE IS ENOUGH

Love is enough: though the World be a-waning,
And the woods have no voice but the voice of complaining,
  Though the sky be too dark for dim eyes to discover
The gold-cups and daisies fair blooming thereunder,
Though the hills be held shadows, and the sea a dark wonder,
  And this day draw a veil over all deeds pass'd over,
Yet their hands shall not tremble, their feet shall not falter;
The void shall not weary, the fear shall not alter
  These lips and these eyes of the loved and the lover.

WILLIAM MORRIS

Eat, Drink and be Merry

LET US DRINK AND BE MERRY

Let us drink and be merry, dance, joke, and rejoice,
With claret and sherry, theorbo and voice!
The changeable world to our joy is unjust,
    All treasure's uncertain,
    Then down with your dust!
In frolics dispose your pounds, shillings, and pence,
For we shall be nothing a hundred years hence.

We'll sport and be free with Moll, Betty, and Dolly,
Have oysters and lobsters to cure melancholy:
Fish-dinners will make a man spring like a flea,
    Dame Venus, love's lady,
    Was born of the sea;
With her and with Bacchus we'll tickle the sense,
For we shall be past it a hundred years hence.

Your most beautiful bride who with garlands is crown'd
And kills with each glance as she treads on the ground,
Whose lightness and brightness doth shine in such splendour
    That none but the stars
    Are thought fit to attend her,
Though now she be pleasant and sweet to the sense,
Will be damnable mouldy a hundred years hence.

Then why should we turmoil in cares and in fears,
Turn all our tranquill'ty to sighs and to tears?

Let's eat, drink, and play till the worms do corrupt us,
    'Tis certain, *Post mortem*
      Nulla voluptas.
For health, wealth and beauty, wit, learning and sense,
Must all come to nothing a hundred years hence.

THOMAS JORDAN

WEST SUSSEX DRINKING SONG

They sell good Beer at Haslemere
    And under Guildford Hill.
At Little Cowfold as I've been told
    A beggar may drink his fill:
There is a good brew in Amberley too,
    And by the bridge also;
But the swipes they take in at Washington Inn
    Is the very best Beer I know.

Chorus
With my here it goes, there it goes,
    All the fun's before us:
The Tipple's Aboard and the night is young,
The door's ajar and the Barrel is sprung,
I am singing the best song ever was sung
    And it has a rousing chorus.

If I were what I never can be,
    The master or the squire:
If you gave me the hundred from here to the sea,
    Which is more than I desire:
Then all my crops should be barley and hops,
    And did my harvest fail
I'd sell every rood of mine acres I would
    For a belly-full of good Ale.

Chorus

With my here it goes, there it goes,
  All the fun's before us:
The Tipple's aboard and the night is young,
The door's ajar and the Barrel is sprung,
I am singing the best song ever was sung
  And it has a rousing Chorus.

HILAIRE BELLOC

THE MERMAID TAVERN

Souls of poets dead and gone,
What Elysium have ye known—
Happy field or mossy cavern
Choicer than the Mermaid Tavern?
Have ye tippled drink more fine
Than mine host's Canary wine?
Or are fruits of Paradise
Sweeter than those dainty pies
Of venison? O generous food!
Drest as though bold Robin Hood
Would, with his Maid Marian,
Sup and bowse from horn and can.

  I have heard that on a day
Mine host's signboard flew away
Nobody knew whither, till
An astrologer's old quill
To a sheepskin gave the story,
Said he saw you in your glory
Underneath a new-old Sign
Sipping beverage divine,
And pledging with contented smack
The Mermaid in the Zodiac.

Souls of poets dead and gone,
What Elysium have ye known—
Happy field or mossy cavern
Choicer than the Mermaid Tavern?

JOHN KEATS

DRINKING

The thirsty earth soaks up the rain,
And drinks and gapes for drink again;
The plants suck in the earth, and are
With constant drinking fresh and fair;
The sea itself (which one would think
Should have but little need of drink)
Drinks twice ten thousand rivers up,
So fill'd that they o'erflow the cup.
The busy Sun (and one would guess
By 's drunken fiery face no less)
Drinks up the sea, and when he's done,
The Moon and Stars drink up the Sun:
They drink and dance by their own light,
They drink and revel all the night:
Nothing in Nature's sober found,
But an eternal health goes round.
Fill up the bowl, then, fill it high,
Fill all the glasses there—for why
Should every creature drink but I?
Why, man of morals, tell me why?

ABRAHAM COWLEY

IN PRAISE OF ALE

When as the chill Charoko blows,
  And Winter tells a heavy tale,
And pyes and daws and rooks and crows
Do sit and curse the frosts and snows;
    Then give me ale.

Ale in a Saxon rumkin then,
  Such as will make grim Malkin prate;
Bids valour burgeon in tall men,
Quickens the poet's wits and pen,
    Despises fate.

Ale, that the absent battle fights,
  And forms the march of Swedish drum,
Disputes the princes' laws, and rights,
What's past and done tells mortal wights,
    And what's to come.

Ale, that the plowman's heart up-keeps,
  And equals it to tyrant's thrones,
That wipes the eye that ever weeps,
And lulls in sweet and dainty sleeps
    Their very bones.

Grandchild of Ceres, Bacchus' daughter,
  Wine's emulous neighbour, though but stale,
Ennobling all the nymphs of water,
And filling each man's heart with laughter—
    Ha! Ha! give me ale!

UNKNOWN

THE BROWN JUG

Dear Tom, this brown jug that now foams with mild ale,
(In which I will drink to sweet Nan of the Vale),
Was once Toby Fillpot, a thirsty old soul
As e'er drank a bottle, or fathomed a bowl;
In boosing about 'twas his praise to excel,
And among jolly topers he bore off the bell.

It chanced as in dog-days he sat at his ease
In his flower-woven arbour as gay as you please,
With a friend and a pipe puffing sorrows away,
And with honest old stingo was soaking his clay,
His breath-doors of life on a sudden were shut,
And he died full as big as a Dorchester butt.

His body, when long in the ground it had lain,
And time into clay had resolved it again,
A potter found out in its covert so snug,
And with part of fat Toby he formed this brown jug,
Now sacred to friendship, and mirth, and mild ale;
So here's to my lovely sweet Nan of the Vale.

FRANCIS FAWKES

IF I DRINK WATER

If I drink water while this doth last,
May I never again drink wine:
For how can a man, in his life of a span,
Do anything better than dine?
We'll dine and drink, and say if we think
That anything better can be;
And when we have dined, wish all mankind
May dine as well as we.

And though a good wish will fill no dish,
And brim no cup with sack,
Yet thoughts will spring, as the glasses ring,
To illume our studious track.
On the brilliant dreams of our hopeful schemes
The light of the flask shall shine;
And we'll sit till day, but we'll find the way
To drench the world with wine.

THOMAS LOVE PEACOCK
From *Crotchet Castle*

O FOR A BOWL OF FAT CANARY

O for a bowl of fat canary,
Rich Aristippus, sparkling sherry!
Some nectar else from Juno's dairy;
O these draughts would make us merry!

O for a wench! I deal in faces,
And in other daintier things;
Tickled am I with her embraces;
Fine dancing in such fairy rings!

O for a plump, fat leg of mutton,
Veal, lamb, capon, pig, and coney!
None is happy but a glutton,
None an ass, but who wants money.

Wines indeed, and girls are good;
But brave victuals feast the blood;
For wenches, wine and lusty cheer,
Jove would come down to surfeit here.

THOMAS MIDDLETON
From *A Mad World, My Masters*

THE BALLAD OF BOUILLABAISSE

A street there is in Paris famous,
  For which no rhyme our language yields,
Rue Neuve des Petits Champs its name is—
  The New Street of the Little Fields.
And here's an inn, not rich and splendid,
  But still in comfortable case;
The which in youth I oft attended,
  To eat a bowl of Bouillabaisse.

This Bouillabaisse a noble dish is—
  A sort of soup, or broth, or brew,
Or hotchpotch of all sorts of fishes,
  That Greenwich never could outdo;
Green herbs, red peppers, mussels, saffron,
  Soles, onions, garlic, roach, and dace:
All these you eat at TERRÉ's tavern
  In that one dish of Bouillabaisse.

Indeed, a rich and savoury stew 'tis;
  And true philosophers, methinks,
Who love all sorts of natural beauties,
  Should love good victuals and good drinks.
And Cordelier or Benedictine
  Might gladly, sure, his lot embrace,
Nor find a fast-day too afflicting,
  Which served him up a Bouillabaisse.

I wonder if the house still there is?
  Yes, here the lamp is, as before;
The smiling red-cheeked *écaillère* is
  Still opening oysters at the door.
Is TERRÉ still alive and able?
  I recollect his droll grimace:
He'd come and sit before your table,
  And hope you like your Bouillabaisse.

We enter—nothing's changed or older.
 'How's Monsieur Terré, waiter, pray?'
The waiter stares and shrugs his shoulder—
 'Monsieur is dead this many a day.'
'It is the lot of saint and sinner,
 So honest Terré's run his race.'
'What will Monsieur require for dinner?'
 'Say, do you still cook Bouillabaisse?'

'Oh, oui, Monsieur,' 's the waiter's answer;
 'Quel vin Monsieur désire-t-il?'
'Tell me a good one,'—'That I can, Sir;
 The Chambertin with yellow seal.'
'So Terré's gone,' I say, and sink in
 My old accustomed corner-place;
'He's done with feasting and with drinking,
 With Burgundy and Bouillabaisse.'

My old accustomed corner here is,
 The table still is in the nook;
Ah! vanished many a busy year is
 This well-known chair since last I took.
When first I saw ye, *cari luoghi*,
 I'd scarce a beard upon my face,
And now a grizzled, grim old fogy,
 I sit and wait for Bouillabaisse.

Where are you, old companions trusty
 Of early days here met to dine?
Come, waiter! quick, a flagon crusty—
 I'll pledge them in the good old wine.
The kind old voices and old faces
 My memory can quick retrace;
Around the board they take their places,
 And share the wine and Bouillabaisse.

There's Jack has made a wondrous marriage;
  There's laughing Tom is laughing yet;
There's brave Augustus drives his carriage;
  There's poor old Fred in the *Gazette*;
On James's head the grass is growing;
  Good Lord! the world has wagged apace
Since here we set the claret flowing,
And drank, and ate the Bouillabaisse.

Ah me! how quick the days are flitting!
  I mind me of a time that's gone,
When here I'd sit, as now I'm sitting,
  In this same place—but not alone.
A fair young form was nestled near me,
  A dear, dear face looked fondly up,
And sweetly spoke and smiled to cheer me
  —There's no one now to share my cup.

I drink it as the Fates ordain it.
  Come, fill it, and have done with rhymes:
Fill up the lonely glass, and drain it
  In memory of dear old times.
Welcome the wine, whate'er the seal is;
  And sit you down, and say your grace
With thankful heart, whate'er the meal is.
  Here comes the smoking Bouillabaisse!

WILLIAM MAKEPEACE THACKERAY

START HER ON CHAMPAGNE, BOY . . .

Start her on champagne, boy, but break her in to hock—
That's the only rule of life that's steady as a rock.
I've seen so many promising entanglements decline
'Cos the lady weren't contented with a nice still wine.

Start her on champagne, boy, but break her into hock;
And the longer you leave it the bigger is the shock.
        I used to say to Liz,
        'Now, what about some fizz?
        Or shall we have a nice glass of hock?'
I told her the history, the mystery of hock,
I told her that hock would go sweetly with her frock,
How the felon at the block as a rule demanded hock,
        And other things with which I needn't trouble 'ee;
And 'Hock,' said she, 'would do very well for me';
And I said, 'Waitah! a bottle of 53!'
        And then, I don't know why—
        Was it something in her eye?—
In a minute I'd be ordering the bubbly.

If a lady chooses lobster when there's plaice at one-and-ten
It's a strain upon the passions of the tenderest of men.
Give her dinner *à la carte* when your romance has just begun,
But if love is to be lasting stick to *table d'hôte*, my son.

Start her in the stalls, boy, but train her to the pit;
Educate them up until they don't care where they sit.
        I have done with Lizzie, boy,
        For her tastes were too Savoy,
        And mine were more Soho, I must admit.
I told her of the cooking and the quaintness of Soho,
I told her to Soho all the clever people go,
I told her that Soho was the haunt of the beau
        And the beginning of innumerable marriages;
And 'Soho!' she'd declare, 'I'll be happy anywhere.'
And I'd say, 'Splendid! Well, a bus goes there';
        And then, I don't know why—
        Was it something in her eye?—
We'd be driving in a motor-cab to Claridge's.

A. P. HERBERT

THE EPICURE

Underneath this myrtle shade,
On flowery beds supinely laid,
With odorous oils my head o'erflowing,
And around it roses growing,
What should I do but drink away
The heat and troubles of the day?
In this more than kingly state
Love himself on me shall wait.
Fill to me, Love! nay, fill it up!
And mingled cast into the cup
Wit and mirth and noble fires,
Vigorous health and gay desires.
The wheel of life no less will stay
In a smooth than rugged way:
Since it equally doth flee,
Let the motion pleasant be.
Why do we precious ointments shower?—
Nobler wines why do we pour?—
Beauteous flowers why do we spread
Upon the monuments of the dead?
Nothing they but dust can show,
Or bones that hasten to be so.
Crown me with roses while I live,
Now your wines and ointments give:
After death I nothing crave,
Let me alive my pleasures have:
All are Stoics in the grave.

ABRAHAM COWLEY

LAUGHING SONG

When the green woods laugh with the voice of joy,
And the dimpling stream runs laughing by;
When the air does laugh with our merry wit,
And the green hill laughs with the noise of it;

When the meadows laugh with lively green,
And the grasshopper laughs in the merry scene;
When Mary, and Susan, and Emily
With their sweet round mouths sing, 'Ha, ha, he!'

When the painted birds laugh in the shade,
When our table with cherries and nuts is spread:
Come live, and be merry, and join with me,
To sing the sweet chorus of 'Ha, ha, he!'

WILLIAM BLAKE

WINE OF THE FAIRIES

I am drunk with the honey wine
Of the moon-unfolded eglantine,
Which fairies catch in hyacinth bowls.
The bats, the dormice, and the moles
Sleep in the walls or under the sward
Of the desolate castle yard;
And when 'tis split on the summer earth
Or its fumes arise among the dew,
Their jocund dreams are full of mirth,
They gibber their joy in sleep; for few
Of the fairies bear those bowls so new!

PERCY BYSSHE SHELLEY

TOAST

Here's to the maiden of bashful fifteen!
  Here's to the widow of fifty!
Here's to the flaunting extravagant quean;
  And here's to the housewife that's thrifty!
      Let the toast pass,
      Drink to the lass!
  I'll warrant she'll prove an excuse for the glass!

Here's to the charmer, whose dimples we prize!
  Now to the maid who has none, sir!
Here's to the girl with a pair of blue eyes;
  And here's to the nymph with but one, sir!
      Let the toast pass,
      Drink to the lass!
  I'll warrant she'll prove an excuse for the glass!

Here's to the maid with a bosom of snow!
  Now to her that's as brown as a berry!
Here's to the wife with a face full of woe,
  And now to the girl that is merry!
      Let the toast pass,
      Drink to the lass!
  I'll warrant she'll prove an excuse for the glass!

For let them be clumsy, or let them be slim,
  Young or ancient, I care not a feather!
So fill a pint bumper, quite up to the brim,
  And let us e'en toast them together!
      Let the toast pass,
      Drink to the lass!
  I'll warrant she'll prove an excuse for the glass!

RICHARD BRINSLEY SHERIDAN
From *The School for Scandal*

WINE AND WATER

Old Noah he had an ostrich farm and fowls on the largest scale,
He ate his egg with a ladle in an egg-cup big as a pail,
And the soup he took was Elephant Soup, and the fish he took
    was Whale,
But they all were small to the cellar he took when he set out to
    sail,
And Noah he often said to his wife when he sat down to dine,
'I don't care where the water goes if it doesn't get into the wine.'

The cataract of the cliff of heaven fell blinding off the brink
As if it would wash the stars away as suds go down a sink,
The seven heavens came roaring down for the throats of hell to
    drink,
And Noah he cocked his eye and said, 'It looks like rain, I think,
The water has drowned the Matterhorn as deep as a Mendip
    mine,
But I don't care where the water goes if it doesn't get into the
    wine.'

But Noah he sinned, and we have sinned; on tipsy feet we trod,
Till a great black teetotaller was sent to us for a rod,
And you can't get wine at a P.S.A., or chapel or Eisteddfod,
For the Curse of Water has come again because of the wrath of
    God,
And water is on the Bishop's board and the Higher Thinker's
    shrine,
But I don't care where the water goes if it doesn't get into the
    wine.

G. K. CHESTERTON

DRINK TO-DAY

Drink to-day, and drown all sorrow,
You shall perhaps not do't to-morrow.
Best while you have it use your breath;
There is no drinking after death.

Wine works the heart up, wakes the wit,
There is no cure 'gainst age but it.
It helps the head-ache, cough and phthisic,
And is for diseases physic.

Then let us swill, boys, for our health;
Who drinks well, loves the commonwealth.
And he that will to bed go sober,
Falls with the leaf, still in October.

JOHN FLETCHER
From *The Bloody Brother*

JOLLY GOOD ALE AND OLD

Back and side go bare, go bare,
    Both hand and foot go cold,
But belly, God send thee good ale enough
    Whether it be new or old!

But if that I may have truly
    Good ale my belly full,
I shall look like one, by sweet Saint John,
    Were shorn against the wool.
Though I go bare, take ye no care,
    I am nothing cold,
I stuff my skin so full within
    Of jolly good ale and old.

I cannot eat but little meat,
   My stomach is not good;
But sure I think that I could drink
   With him that weareth an hood.
Drink is my life; although my wife
   Some time do chide and scold,
Yet spare I not to ply the pot
   Of jolly good ale and old.

I love no roast but a brown toast,
   Or a crab in the fire;
A little bread shall do me stead;
   Much bread I never desire.
Nor frost, nor snow, nor wind I trow,
   Can hurt me if it wold,
I am so wrapped within and lapped
   With jolly good ale and old.

I care right nought, I take no thought
   For clothes to keep me warm;
Have I good drink, I surely think
   Nothing can do me harm.
For truly then I fear no man,
   Be he never so bold,
When I am armed and thoroughly warmed
   With jolly good ale and old.

But now and then I curse and ban,
   They make their ale so small;
God give them care and evil to fare!
   They stry the malt and all.
Such peevish pew, I tell you true,
   Nor for a crown of gold
There cometh one sip within my lip,
   Whether it be new or old.

Good ale and strong maketh me among
    Full jocund and full light,
That oft I sleep and take no keep
    From morning until night.
Then start I up and flee to the cup;
    The right way on I hold;
My thirst to staunch, I fill my paunch
    With jolly good ale and old.

And Kit, my wife, that as her life
    Loveth well good ale to seek,
Full of drinketh she, that ye may see
    The tears run down her cheek.
Then doth she troll to me the bowl,
    As a good malt-worm shold,
And say 'Sweet-heart, I have take my part
    Of jolly good ale and old.'

They that do drink till they nod and wink,
    Even as good fellows should do,
They shall not miss to have the bliss
    That good ale hath brought them to.
And all poor souls that scour black bowls,
    And them hath lustily trolled,
God save the lives of them and their wives,
    Whether they be young or old.

UNKNOWN

LAUGH AND BE MERRY

Laugh and be merry, remember, better the world with a song,
Better the world with a blow in the teeth of a wrong.
Laugh, for the time is brief, a thread the length of a span.
Laugh, and be proud to belong to the old proud pageant of man.

Laugh and be merry: remember, in olden time,
God made Heaven and Earth for joy He took in a rhyme,
Made them, and filled them full with the strong red wine of
  His mirth,
The splendid joy of the stars: the joy of the earth.

So we must laugh and drink from the deep blue cup of the sky,
Join the jubilant song of the great stars sweeping by,
Laugh, and battle, and work, and drink of the wine out-poured
In the dear green earth, the sign of the joy of the Lord.

Laugh and be merry together, like brothers akin,
Guesting awhile in the rooms of a beautiful inn,
Glad till the dancing stops, and the lilt of the music ends.
Laugh till the game is played; and be you merry, my friends.

JOHN MASEFIELD

THE MERRY MONTH OF MAY

O, the month of May, the merry month of May,
So frolic, so gay, and so green, so green, so green!
O, and then did I unto my true love say,
Sweet Peg, thou shalt be my Summer's Queen.

Now the nightingale, the pretty nightingale,
The sweetest singer in all the forest quire,
Entreats thee, sweet Peggy, to hear thy true love's tale:
Lo, yonder she sitteth, her breast against a brier.

But O, I spy the cuckoo, the cuckoo, the cuckoo;
See where she sitteth; come away, my joy:
Come away, I prithee, I do not like the cuckoo
Should sing where my Peggy and I kiss and toy.

O, the month of May, the merry month of May,
So frolic, so gay, and so green, so green, so green;
And then did I unto my true love say,
Sweet Peg, thou shalt be my Summer's Queen.

THOMAS DEKKER
From *The Shoemaker's Holiday*

COME, LANDLORD, FILL THE FLOWING BOWL

Come, landlord, fill the flowing bowl
   Until it doth run over;
For to-night we'll merry merry be,
   To-morrow we'll be sober.

The man who drinketh small beer
   And goes to bed quite sober
Fades as the leaves do fade
   That drop off in October.

But he who drinks just what he likes
   And getteth half-seas over,
Will live until he dies perhaps,
   And then lie down in clover.

The man who kisses a pretty girl
   And goes and tells his mother,
Ought to have his lips cut off,
   And never kiss another.

UNKNOWN

MONARCH OF THE VINE

Come, thou monarch of the vine,
Plumpy Bacchus with pink eyne!

302

In thy vats our cares be drown'd,
With thy grapes our hairs be crown'd:
Cup us, till the world go round,
Cup us, till the world go round!

WILLIAM SHAKESPEARE
From *Antony and Cleopatra*

ROAST BEEF

When mighty Roast Beef was the Englishman's Food,
It ennobled our Veins and enriched our Blood,
Our Soldiers were brave and our Courtiers were good.
  Oh The Roast Beef of Old England,
  And Old English Roast Beef.

But since we have learn'd from all-conquering France
To eat their Ragouts as well as to dance,
We are fed up with nothing but vain Complaisance.
  Oh the Roast Beef of Old England,
  And Old English Roast Beef.

Our Fathers of old were robust, stout, and strong,
And kept open House with good Cheer all Day long,
Which made their plump Tenants rejoice in this song,
  Oh the Roast Beef of Old England,
  And Old English Roast Beef.

But now we are dwindled, to what shall I name?
A sneaking poor Race, half begotten—and tame,
Who sully those Honours that once shone in Fame.
  Oh the Roast Beef of Old England,
  And Old English Roast Beef.

When good Queen Elizabeth was on the Throne,
E'er Coffee, or Tea, and such Slip Slops were known,
The World was in Terror, if e'er she did frown.
    Oh the Roast Beef of Old England,
    And Old English Roast Beef.

In those Days, if Fleets did presume on the Main,
They seldom or never return'd back again,
As witness the vaunting Armada of Spain.
    Oh the Roast Beef of Old England,
    And Old English Roast Beef.

Oh then they had Stomachs to eat and to fight,
And when Wrongs were a-cooking to do themselves right!
But now we're a—I cou'd—but good Night.
    Oh the Roast Beef of Old England,
    And Old English Roast Beef.

RICHARD LEVERIDGE

INVITING A FRIEND TO SUPPER

To-night, grave sir, both my poor house and I
    Do equally desire your company:
Not that we think us worthy such a guest,
    But that your worth will dignify our feast,
With those that come; whose grace may make that seem
    Something, which, else, could hope for no esteem.
It is the fair acceptance, Sir, creates
    The entertainment perfect: not the cates.
Yet shall you have, to rectify your palate,
    An olive, capers, or some better salad
Ushering the mutton; with a short-legged hen,
    If we can get her, full of eggs, and then,
Lemons, and wine for sauce: to these, a coney
    Is not to be despaired of, for our money;

And, though fowl, now, be scarce, yet there are clerks,
    The sky not falling, think we may have larks.
I'll tell you of more, and lie, so you will come:
    Of partridge, pheasant, wood-cock, of which some
May yet be there; and godwit, if we can:
    Knat, rail, and ruff too. How so e'er, my man
Shall read a piece of Virgil, Tacitus,
    Livy, or of some better book to us,
Of which we'll speak our minds, amidst our meat;
    And I'll profess no verses to repeat:
To this, if ought appear, which I know not of,
    That will the pastry, not my paper, show of.
Digestive cheese, and fruit there sure will be;
    But that, which most doth take my Muse, and me,
Is a pure cup of rich Canary-wine,
    Which is the Mermaid's, now, but shall be mine:
Of which had Horace, or Anacreon tasted,
    Their lives, as do their lines, till now had lasted.
Tobacco, Nectar, or the Thespian spring,
    Are all but Luther's beer, to this I sing.
Of this we will sup free, but moderately,
    And we will have no Pooly, or Parrot by;
Nor shall our cups make any guilty men;
    But, at our parting, we will be, as when
We innocently met. No simple word,
    That shall be uttered at our mirthful board,
Shall make us sad next morning: or affright
    The liberty, that we'll enjoy to-night.

BEN JONSON

COUNTRY GLEE

Haymakers, rakers, reapers and mowers,
    Wait on your Summer Queen;
Dress up with musk-rose her eglantine bowers,
    Daffodils strew the green.

Sing, dance and play,
'Tis holiday;
The sun does bravely shine
On our ears of corn
Rich as a pearl
Comes every girl;
This is mine, this is mine, this is mine;
Let us die, ere away they be borne.

Bow to the Sun, to our Queen, and that fair one
Come to behold our sports.
Each bonny lass here is counted a rare one,
As those in princes' courts.
These and we
With country glee
Will teach the woods to resound,
And the hills with Echo's hollow.
Skipping lambs
Their bleating dams
'Mongst kids shall trip it round;
For joy thus our wenches we follow.

Wind, jolly huntsmen, your neat bugles shrilly,
Hounds make a lusty cry;
Spring up, you falconers, the partridges freely,
Then let your brave hawks fly.
Horses amain,
Over ridge, over plain;
The dogs have the stag in chase.
'Tis a sport to content a king.
So ho ho! through the skies
How the proud bird flies,
And sousing kills with a grace!
Now the deer falls. Hark, how they ring!

THOMAS DEKKER

A DISSERTATION UPON ROAST PIG

Mankind, says a Chinese manuscript, which my friend M. was obliging enough to read and explain to me, for the first seventy thousand ages ate their meat raw, clawing or biting it from the living animal, just as they do in Abyssinia to this day. This period is not obscurely hinted at by their great Confucius in the second chapter of his Mundane Mutations, where he designates a kind of golden age by the term Cho-fang, literally the Cooks' holiday. The manuscript goes on to say, that the art of roasting, or rather broiling (which I take to be the elder brother) was accidentally discovered in the manner following. The swine-herd, Ho-ti, having gone out into the woods one morning, as his manner was, to collect mast for his hogs left his cottage in the care of his eldest son Bo-bo, a great lubberly boy, who being fond of playing with fire, as younkers of his age commonly are, let some sparks escape into a bundle of straw, which kindling quickly, spread the conflagration over every part of their poor mansion, till it was reduced to ashes. Together with the cottage (a sorry antediluvian make-shift of a building, you may think it), what was of much more importance, a fine litter of new-farrowed pigs, no less than nine in number perished. China pigs have been esteemed a luxury all over the East from the remotest periods that we read of. Bo-bo was in utmost consternation, as you may think, not so much for the sake of the tenement, which his father and he could easily build up again with a few dry branches, and the labour of an hour or two, at any time, as for the loss of the pigs. While he was thinking what he should say to his father, and wringing his hands over the smoking remnants of one of those untimely sufferers, an odour assailed his nostrils, unlike any scent which he had before experienced. What could it proceed from?—not from the burnt cottage—he had smelt that smell before—indeed this was by no means the first accident of the kind which had occurred through the negligence of this unlucky young fire-brand. Much less did it resemble that of any known herb, weed, or flower. A premonitory moistening at the same time over-flowed his nether lip. He knew not what to think. He next stooped down to feel the pig, if there were any signs of life in it. He burnt his fingers, and to cool them he applied them in his booby fashion to his mouth. Some of the crumbs of the scorched skin had come away with his fingers, and for the first time in his life (in the world's life indeed, for before him no man had known it) he tasted —crackling! Again he felt and fumbled at the pig. It did not burn him so much now, still he licked his fingers, from a sort of habit. The truth at length broke into his slow understanding, that it was the pig that smelt so, and the pig that tasted so delicious; and, surrendering himself up to the newborn pleasure, he fell to tearing up whole handfuls of the scorched skin with the flesh next it, and was cramming it down his throat in his beastly fashion, when his sire entered amid the smoking rafters, armed with retributory cudgel, and finding how affairs stood, began to rain blows upon the young rogue's shoulders, as thick as hailstones, which Bo-bo heeded not any more than if they had been flies. The tickling pleasure, which he experienced in his lower regions, had rendered him quite callous to any inconveniences he might feel in those remote quarters. His father might lay on, but he could not beat him from his pig, till he had fairly made an end of it, when, becoming a little more sensible of his situation, something like the following dialogue ensued.

'You graceless whelp, what have you got there devouring? Is it not enough that you have burnt me down three houses with your dog's tricks, and be hanged to you, but you must be eating fire, and I know not what—what have you got there, I say?'

'O, father, the pig, the pig, do come and taste how nice the burnt pig eats.'

The ears of Ho-ti tingled with horror. He cursed his son, and he cursed himself that ever he should beget a son that should eat burnt pig.

Bo-bo, whose scent was wonderfully sharpened since morning, soon raked out another pig, and fairly rending it asunder, thrust the lesser half by main force into the fists of Ho-ti, still shouting out 'Eat, eat, eat the burnt pig father, only taste—O Lord,' with such-like barbarous ejaculations, cramming all the while as if he would choke.

Ho-ti trembled every joint while he grasped the abominable thing, wavering whether he should not put his son to death for an unnatural young monster, when the crackling scorching his fingers, as it had done his son's, and applying the same remedy to them, he in his turn tasted some of its flavour, which, make what sour mouths he would for a pretence, proved not altogether displeasing to him. In conclusion (for the manuscript here is a little tedious) both father and son fairly sat down to the mess, and never left off till they had despatched all that remained of the litter.

Bo-bo was strictly enjoined not to let the secret escape, for the neighbours would certainly have stoned them for a couple of abominable wretches, who could think of improving upon the good meat which God had sent them. Nevertheless, strange stories got about. It was observed that Ho-ti's cottage was burnt down now more frequently than ever. Nothing but fires from this time forward. Some would break out in broad day, others in the night-time. As often as the sow farrowed, so sure was the house of Ho-ti to be in a blaze; and Ho-ti himself, which was the more remarkable, instead of chastising his son, seemed to grow more indulgent to him than ever. At length they were watched, the terrible mystery discovered, and father and son summoned to take their trial at Pekin then an inconsiderable assize town. Evidence was given, the obnoxious food itself produced in court, and verdict about to be pronounced, when the foreman of the jury begged that some of the burnt pig, of which the culprits stood accused, might be handed into the box. He handled it, and they all handled it, and burning their fingers, as Bo-bo and his father had done before them, and nature prompting to each of them the same remedy, against the face of all the facts, and the clearest charge which judge had ever given,—to the surprise of the whole court, towns-folk, strangers, reporters, and all present—without leaving the box, or any manner of consultation whatever, they brought in a simultaneous verdict of Not Guilty.

The judge, who was a shrewd fellow, winked at the manifest iniquity of the decision; and, when the court was dismissed went privily, and bought up all the pigs that could be had for love or money. In a few days his Lordship's town house was observed to be on fire. The thing took wing, and now there was nothing to be seen but fires in every direction. Fuel and pigs grew enormously dear all over the district. The insurance offices one and all shut up shop. People built slighter and slighter every day, until it was feared that the very science of architecture would in no long time be lost to the world. Thus this custom of firing houses continued, till in process of time, says my manuscript, a sage arose, like our Locke, who made a discovery that the flesh of swine, or indeed of any other animal, might be cooked (burnt, as they called it) without the necessity of consuming a whole house to dress it. Then first began the rude form of a gridiron. Roasting by the string, or spit, came in a century or two later, I forget in whose dynasty. By such slow degrees, concludes the manuscript, do the most useful and seemingly the most obvious arts, make their way among mankind. . . .

CHARLES LAMB

The Great Occasion

THE OXEN

Christmas Eve, and twelve of the clock.
  'Now they are all on their knees.'
An elder said as we sat in a flock
  By the embers in fireside ease.

We pictured the meek mild creatures where
  They dwelt in their strawy pen,
Nor did it occur to one of us there
  To doubt they were kneeling then.

So fair a fancy few would weave
  In these years! Yet, I feel,
If someone said on Christmas Eve.
  'Come; see the oxen kneel

'In the lonely barton by yonder coomb
  Our childhood used to know,'
I should go with him in the gloom,
  Hoping it might be so.

THOMAS HARDY

CAROL

It came upon the midnight clear,
  That glorious song of old,
From Angels bending near the earth
  To touch their harps of gold;

'Peace on the earth, good will to man
From Heaven's all gracious King.'
The world in solemn stillness lay
To hear the angels sing.

EDMUND HAMILTON SEARS

JOURNEY OF THE MAGI

'A cold coming we had of it,
Just the worst time of the year
For a journey, and such a long journey;
The ways deep and the weather sharp,
The very dead of winter.'
And the camels galled, sore-footed, refractory,
Lying down in the melting snow.
There were times we regretted
The summer palaces on slopes, the terraces,
And the silken girls bringing sherbet.
Then the camel men cursing and grumbling
And running away, and wanting their liquor and women,
And the night-fires going out, and the lack of shelters,
And the cities hostile and the towns unfriendly
And the villages dirty and charging high prices:
A hard time we had of it.
At the end we preferred to travel all night,
Sleeping in snatches,
With the voices singing in our ears, saying
That this was all folly.

Then at dawn we came down to a temperate valley,
Wet, below the snow line, smelling of vegetation;
With a running stream and a water-mill beating the darkness,
And three trees on the low sky,
And an old white horse galloped away in the meadow.

Then we came to a tavern with vine-leaves over the lintel,
Six hands at an open door dicing for pieces of silver,
And feet kicking the empty wine-skins.
But there was no information, and so we continued
And arrived at evening, not a moment too soon
Finding the place; it was (you may say) satisfactory.

All this was a long time ago, I remember,
And I would do it again, but set down
This set down
This: were we led all that way for
Birth or Death? There was a Birth, certainly,
We had evidence and no doubt. I had seen birth and death,
But had thought they were different; this Birth was
Hard and bitter agony for us, like Death, our death.
We returned to our places, these Kingdoms,
But no longer at ease here, in the old dispensation,
With an alien people clutching their gods.
I should be glad of another death.

T. S. ELIOT

Stanzas from
ODE ON THE MORNING OF
CHRIST'S NATIVITY

It was the winter wild
While the heaven-born Child
All meanly wrapt in the rude manger lies;
Nature in awe to Him
Had doffed her gaudy trim,
With her great Master so to sympathize:
It was no season then for her
To wanton with the sun, her lusty paramour.

313

Ring out, ye crystal spheres!
Once bless our human ears,
If ye have power to touch our senses so;
And let your silver chime
Move in melodious time;
And let the bass of heaven's deep organ blow;
And with your ninefold harmony
Make up full consort to the angelic symphony.

For if such holy song
Enwrap our fancy long,
Time will run back, and fetch the age of gold;
And speckled Vanity
Will sicken soon and die,
And leprous Sin will melt from earthly mould;
And Hell itself will pass away,
And leave her dolorous mansions to the peering day.

Yea, Truth and Justice then
Will down return to men,
Orbed in a rainbow; and, like glories wearing,
Mercy will sit between
Throned in celestial sheen,
With radiant feet the tissued clouds down steering;
And Heaven, as at some festival,
Will open wide the gates of her high palace-hall.

JOHN MILTON

THE CRATCHITS' CHRISTMAS DINNER

There never was such a goose. Bob said he didn't believe there ever was such a goose cooked. Its tenderness and flavour, size and cheapness, were the themes of universal admiration. Eked out by the apple sauce and mashed potatoes, it was a sufficient dinner for the whole family; indeed, as Mrs. Cratchit said with great delight (surveying one small atom of a bone upon the dish) they hadn't ate it all at last! Yet every one had had enough, and the youngest Cratchits in particular, were steeped in sage and onion to the eyebrows! But now, the plates being changed by Miss Belinda, Mrs. Cratchit left the room alone—too nervous to bear witnesses—to take the pudding up and bring it in.

Suppose it should not be done enough! Suppose it should break in turning out! Suppose somebody should have got over the wall of the back-yard, and stolen it, while they were merry with the goose—a supposition at which the two young Cratchits became livid! All sorts of horrors were supposed.

Hallo! A great deal of steam! The pudding was out of the copper. A smell like a washing day! That was the cloth. A smell like an eating-house and a pastrycook's next door to each other, with a laundress's next door to that! That was the pudding! In half a minute Mrs. Cratchit entered—flushed, but smiling proudly—with the pudding like a speckled cannon-ball so hard and firm blazing in half of half-a-quartern of ignited brandy, and bedight with Christmas holly stuck into the top.

Oh, a wonderful pudding! Bob Cratchit said, and calmly too, that he regarded it as the greatest success achieved by Mrs. Cratchit since their marriage. Mrs. Cratchit said that now the weight was off her mind, she would confess she had had her doubts about the quantity of flour. Everybody had something to say about it, but nobody said or thought it was at all a small pudding for a large family. It would have been flat heresy to do so. Any Cratchit would have blushed to hint at such a thing.

At last the dinner was all done, the cloth was cleared, the hearth swept, and the fire made up. The compound in the jug being tasted, and considered perfect, apples and oranges were put upon the table, and a shovel-full of chestnuts on the fire. Then all the Cratchit family drew round the hearth, in what Bob Cratchit called a circle, meaning half a one; and at Bob Cratchit's elbow stood the family display of glass. Two tumblers, and a custard-cup without a handle.

These held the hot stuff from the jug, however, as well as

golden goblets would have done; and Bob served it out with beaming looks, while the chestnuts on the fire sputtered and cracked noisily. Then Bob proposed:

'A Merry Christmas to us all, my dears. God bless us!'

Which all the family re-echoed.

CHARLES DICKENS
From *A Christmas Carol*

REFLECTIONS ON A NEW YEAR'S DAY

Yes, yes, it's very true, and very clear,
By way of compliment and common chat,
It's very well to wish me a New Year,
    But wish me a new hat!

Although not spent in luxury and ease,
In course a longer life I won't refuse;
But while you're wishing, wish me, if you please,
    A newer pair of shoes!

Nay, while new things and wishes are afloat,
I own to one that I should not rebut—
Instead of this old rent, to have a coat,
    With more of the New Cut!

O yes, 'tis very pleasant, though I'm poor,
To hear the steeple make that merry din;
Except I wish one bell was at the door,
    To ring new trousers in!

To be alive is very nice indeed,
Although another year at last departs;
Only with twelve new months, I rather need
    A dozen of new shirts.

Yes, yes, it's very true, and very clear,
By way of compliment and common chat,
It's very well to wish me a New Year,
      But wish me a new hat!

THOMAS HOOD

EASTER

Most glorious Lord of Life! that, on this day,
Didst make Thy triumph over death and sin;
And, having harrow'd hell, didst bring away
Captivity thence captive, us to win:
This joyous day, dear Lord, with joy begin;
And grant that we, for whom thou diddest die,
Being with Thy dear blood clear washt from sin,
May live for ever in felicity!
And that Thy love we weighing worthily,
May likewise love Thee for the same again;
And for Thy sake, that all lyke dear didst buy,
With love may one another entertain!
   So let us love, dear Love, like as we ought,
   —Love is the lesson which the Lord us taught.

EDMUND SPENSER

EASTER SONG

I got me flowers to straw Thy way,
   I got me boughs off many a tree;
But Thou wast up by break of day,
   And brought'st Thy sweets along with Thee.

Yet though my flowers be lost, they say
   A heart can never come too late;
Teach it to sing Thy praise this day,
   And then this day my life shall date.

GEORGE HERBERT
From *The Temple*

3¹7

WHEN MARY THRO' THE GARDEN WENT

When Mary thro' the garden went,
　　There was no sound of any bird,
And yet, because the night was spent,
　　The little grasses lightly stirred,
　　The flowers awoke, the lilies heard.

When Mary thro' the garden went,
　　The dew lay still on flower and grass,
The waving palms above her sent
　　Their fragrance out as she did pass,
　　No light upon the branches was.

When Mary thro' the garden went,
　　Her eyes, for weeping long, were dim.
The grass beneath her footsteps bent,
　　The solemn lilies, white and slim,
　　These also stood and wept for Him.

When Mary thro' the garden went,
　　She sought, within the garden ground,
One for Whom her heart was rent,
　　One Who for her sake was bound,
　　One Who sought and she was found.

MARY ELIZABETH COLERIDGE

A BIRTHDAY

My heart is like a singing bird
　　Whose nest is in a watered shoot;
My heart is like an apple-tree
　　Whose boughs are bent with thickset fruit;
My heart is like a rainbow shell
　　That paddles in a halcyon sea;
My heart is gladder than all these
　　Because my love is come to me.

Raise me a dais of silk and down;
    Hang it with vair and purple dyes;
Carve it in doves and pomegranates,
    And peacocks with a hundred eyes;
Work it in gold and silver grapes,
    In leaves and silver fleurs-de-lys;
Because the birthday of my life
    Is come, my love is come to me.

CHRISTINA GEORGINA ROSSETTI

A SHORT SONG OF CONGRATULATION

Long-expected one and twenty,
Ling'ring year, at last is flown;
Pomp and Pleasure, Pride and Plenty,
Great Sir John, are all your own.

Loosen'd from the Minor's tether,
Free to mortgage or to sell,
Wild as wind, and light as feather,
Bid the slaves of thrift farewel.

Call the Betty's, Kates, and Jennys,
Ev'ry name that laughs at Care,
Lavish of your Grandsire's guineas,
Show the Spirit of an heir.

All that prey on vice and folly
Joy to see their quarry fly,
Here the Gamester light and jolly,
There the Lender grave and sly.

Wealth, Sir John, was made to wander,
Let it wander as it will:
See the Jockey, see the Pander,
Bid them come, and take their fill.

When the bonny Blade carouses,
Pockets full, and Spirits high,
What are acres? What are houses?
Only dirt, or wet or dry.

If the Guardian or the Mother
Tell the woes of wilful waste,
Scorn their counsel and their pother,
You can hang or drown at last.

SAMUEL JOHNSON

SILVER JUBILEE

On Monday, May 6, 1935, King George and Queen Mary went to St. Paul's Cathedral to attend a Thanksgiving Service on the occasion of their Silver Jubilee:

> 'A never to be forgotten day,' the King wrote in his diary, 'when we celebrated our Silver Jubilee. It was a glorious summer's day: 75° in the shade. The greatest number of people in the streets that I have ever seen in my life. The enthusiasm was indeed most touching.'

Every night of that exacting week the King and Queen appeared upon the flood-lit balcony of Buckingham Palace and were cheered with rapture by crowds who had waited there all day. On Thursday, May 9, in Westminster Hall, they received addresses from both Houses of Parliament. 'The Members,' the King wrote in his diary, 'sang the National Anthem and then cheered; which moved me much.' On the following days, wearing Field-Marshal's uniform and drawn by four greys with postilions, the King, accompanied by Queen Mary, drove through the poorer quarters of London. Through Battersea, Kennington and Lambeth they drove; through Limehouse, Whitechapel and the dock area;

320

through the slums and tenements to the North and the South-west. In each street they were greeted by hordes of children shouting lustily and waving flags; the elder people grinned delightedly and clapped their hands. From house to house there hung little flags and streamers, and banners bearing messages, and swags of green. The King was fascinated by these decorations: 'all put up,' he wrote in his diary, 'by the poor.' His satisfaction was intense:

'His pleasure,' wrote Sister Catherine Black, 'at the wonderful evidence of the people's love and regard during the Jubilee was touching. I can remember him coming back from a drive through the East End, very tired but radiantly happy. "I'd no idea they felt like that about me," he said with his usual frankness. "I am beginning to think they must really like me for myself".'

HAROLD NICOLSON
From *King George the Fifth:
His Life and Reign*

Simple Things

SIMPLICITY

How happy is the little stone
That rambles in the road alone,
And doesn't care about careers,
And exigencies never fears;
Whose coat of elemental brown
A passing universe put on;
And independent as the sun,
Associates or glows alone,
Fulfilling absolute decree
In casual simplicity.

EMILY DICKINSON

ODE TO SIMPLICITY

O Thou by Nature taught,
  To breathe her genuine Thought,
In Numbers warmly pure, and sweetly strong:
  Who first on Mountains wild,
  In Fancy loveliest Child,
Thy Babe, or Pleasure's, nurs'd the Pow'rs of Song!

Thou, who with Hermit Heart
  Disdain'st the Wealth of Art,
And Gauds, and pageant Weeds, and trailing Pall:
  But com'st a decent Maid
  In Attic Robe array'd,
O chaste unboastful Nymph, to Thee I call!

By all the honey'd Store
On Hybla's Thymy Shore,
By all her Blooms, and mingled Murmurs dear,
By Her, whose Love-lorn Woe
In Ev'ning Musings slow
Sooth'd sweetly sad Electra's Poet's Ear!

By old Cephisus deep,
Who spread his wavy Sweep
In warbled Wand'rings round thy green Retreat,
On whose enamel'd Side
When holy Freedom died
No equal Haunt allur'd thy future Feet.

O Sister meek of Truth,
To my admiring Youth,
Thy sober Aid and native Charms infuse!
The Flow'rs that sweetest breathe,
Tho' Beauty cull'd the Wreath,
Still ask thy Hand to range their order'd Hues.

While Rome could none esteem
But Virtue's Patriot Theme,
You lov'd her Hills, and led her Laureate Band:
But staid to sing alone
To one distinguish'd Throne,
And turn'd thy Face, and fled her alter'd Land.

No more, in Hall or Bow'r,
The Passions own thy Pow'r,
Love, only Love her forceless Numbers mean:
For Thou hast left her Shrine,
Nor Olive more, nor Vine,
Shall gain thy Feet to bless the servile Scene.

324

Tho' Taste, tho' Genius bless,
　　To some divine Excess,
Faints the cold Work till Thou inspire the whole;
　　What each, what all supply,
　　May court, may charm, our Eye,
Thou, only Thou can'st raise the meeting Soul!

Of These let others ask,
　　To aid some mighty Task,
I only seek to find thy temp'rate Vale:
　　Where oft my Reed might sound
　　To Maids and Shepherds round,
And all thy Sons, O Nature, learn my Tale.

　　　　　　　　　　　　WILLIAM COLLINS

ON BLENHEIM HOUSE

See, Sir, here 's the grand approach,
This way is for his Grace's coach;
There lies the bridge, and here's the clock:
Observe the lion and the cock,
The spacious court, the colonnade,
And mark how wide the hall is made!
The chimneys are so well design'd,
They never smoke in any wind.
This gallery 's contriv'd for walking,
The windows to retire and talk in;
The council-chamber for debate,
And all the rest are rooms of state.
　　Thanks, Sir, cry'd I, 'tis very fine,
But where d' ye sleep, or where d' ye dine?
I find, by all you have been telling,
That 'tis a house, but not a dwelling.

　　　　　　　　　　　　ABEL EVANS

THE MEANS TO ATTAIN HAPPY LIFE

Martial, the things that do attain
The happy life, be these, I find:
The riches left, not got with pain;
The fruitful ground, the quiet mind:

The equal friend, no grudge, no strife;
No charge of rule, nor governance;
Without disease, the healthful life;
The household of continuance:

The mean diet, no delicate fare;
True wisdom join'd with simpleness;
The night discharged of all care,
Where wine the wit may not oppress:

The faithful wife, without debate;
Such sleeps as may beguile the night;
Contented with thine own estate;
Ne wish for Death, ne fear his might.

HENRY HOWARD, EARL OF SURREY

PIED BEAUTY

Glory be to God for dappled things—
　For skies of couple-colour as a brindled cow;
　　For rose-moles all in stipple upon trout that swim;
Fresh-firecoal chestnut-falls; finches' wings;
　Landscape plotted and pieced—fold, fallow, and plough;
　　And all trades, their gear and tackle and trim.

All things counter, original, spare, strange;
　Whatever is fickle, freckled (who knows how?)
　　With swift, slow; sweet, sour; adazzle, dim;
He fathers-forth whose beauty is past change:
　　　　Praise him.　　　GERARD MANLEY HOPKINS

SIMPLE FAITH

Yon cottager who weaves at her own door,
Pillow and bobbins all her little store,
Content though mean, and cheerful, if not gay,
Shuffling her threads about the live-long day,
Just earns a scanty pittance, and at night
Lies down secure, her heart and pocket light;
She, for her humble sphere by nature fit,
Has little understanding, and no wit,
Receives no praise, but (though her lot be such,
Toilsome and indigent) she renders much;
Just knows, and knows no more, her Bible true,
A truth the brilliant Frenchman never knew;
And in that charter reads, with sparkling eyes,
Her title to a treasure in the skies.
   Oh happy peasant! Oh unhappy bard!
His the mere tinsel, her's the rich reward;
He prais'd perhaps for ages yet to come,
She never heard of half a mile from home;
He lost in errors his vain heart prefers,
She safe in the simplicity of her's.

WILLIAM COWPER
From *Truth*

THE MILLER

In a plain pleasant cottage, conveniently neat,
With a mill and some meadows—a freehold estate,
A well-meaning miller by labour supplies
Those blessings that grandeur to great ones denies:

No passions to plague him, no cares to torment,
His constant companions are health and content;
Their lordships in lace may remark if they will,
He's honest tho' daub'd with the dust of his mill.

Ere the lark's early carrols salute the new day
He springs from his cottage as jocund as May;
He chearfully whistles, regardless of care,
Or sings the last ballad he bought at the fair:

While courtiers are toil'd in the cobwebs of state,
Or bribing elections in hopes to be great,
No fraud, or ambition his bosom does fill,
Contented he works, if there's grist for his mill.

On Sunday bedeck'd in his homespun array,
At church he's the loudest, to chaunt or to pray:
He sits to a dinner of plain English food,
Tho' simple the pudding, his appetite's good;

At night, when the priest and exciseman are gone,
He quaffs at the alehouse with Roger and John,
Then reels to his pillow, and dreams of no ill;
No monarch more blest than the man of the mill.

JOHN CUNNINGHAM

GLAD IN HEART

Who can live in heart so glad
As the merry country lad?
Who upon a fair green baulk
May at pleasure sit and walk;
And amidst the azure skies
See the morning sun arise,
While he hears in every spring
How the birds do chirp and sing;
Or, before the hounds in cry,
See the hare go stealing by;
Or along the shallow brook
Angling with a baited hook,

See the fishes leap and play
In a blessed sunny day;
Or to hear the partridge call
Till she have her covey all;
Or to see the subtle fox,
How the villain plays the box,
After feeding on his prey
How he closely sneaks away,
Through the hedge and down the furrow
Till he gets into his burrow;
Then the bee to gather honey,
And the little black-haired coney
On a bank for sunny place
With her fore-feet wash her face:
Are not these with thousands moe
Than the court of kings do know?

NICHOLAS BRETON
(End From *The Passionate Shepherd*)

A MIND CONTENT

Sweet are the thoughts that savour of content;
 The quiet mind is richer than a crown;
Sweet are the nights in careless slumber spent;
 The poor estate scorns fortune's angry frown:
Such sweet content, such minds, such sleep, such bliss,
Beggars enjoy, when princes oft do miss.

The homely house that harbours quiet rest;
 The cottage that affords no pride nor care;
The mean that 'grees with country music best;
 The sweet consort of mirth and music's fare;
Obscured life sets down a type of bliss:
A mind content both crown and kingdom is.

ROBERT GREENE

SONG

Still to be neat, still to be drest,
As you were going to a feast;
Still to be powder'd, still perfumed:
Lady, it is to be presumed,
Though art's hid causes are not found,
All is not sweet, all is not sound.

Give me a look, give me a face
That makes simplicity a grace;
Robes loosely flowing, hair as free:
Such sweet neglect more taketh me
Than all th' adulteries of art;
They strike mine eyes, but not my heart.

BEN JONSON

THE SHEPHERD'S WIFE'S SONG

Ah, what is love? It is a pretty thing,
As sweet unto a shepherd as a king,
      And sweeter too;
For kings have cares that wait upon a crown,
And cares can make the sweetest love to frown,
      Ah then, ah then,
If country loves such sweet desires gain,
What lady would not love a shepherd swain?

His flocks are folded, he comes home at night,
As merry as a king in his delight,
      And merrier too;
For kings bethink them what the state require,
Where shepherds careless carol by the fire.
      Ah then, ah then,
If country loves such sweet desires gain,
What lady would not love a shepherd swain?

He kisseth first, then sits as blithe to eat
His cream and curds, as doth the king his meat,
    And blither too;
For kings have often fears when they do sup,
Where shepherds dread no poison in their cup.
    Ah then, ah then,
If country loves such sweet desires gain,
What lady would not love a shepherd swain?

To bed he goes, as wanton then I ween,
As is a king in dalliance with a queen,
    More wanton too;
For kings have many griefs affects to move,
Where shepherds have no greater grief than love.
    Ah then, ah then,
If country loves such sweet desires gain,
What lady would not love a shepherd swain?

Upon his couch of straw he sleeps as sound,
As doth the king upon his bed of down,
    More sounder too;
For cares cause kings full oft their sleep to spill
Where weary shepherds lie and snort their fill.
    Ah then, ah then,
If country loves such sweet desires gain,
What lady would not love a shepherd swain?

Thus with his wife he spends the year as blithe
As doth the king at every tide or sithe,
    And blither too;
For kings have war and broils to take in hand,
Where shepherds laugh, and love upon the land.
    Ah then, ah then,
If country loves such sweet desires gain,
What lady would not love a shepherd swain?

ROBERT GREENE

ODE ON SOLITUDE

Happy the man whose wish and care
    A few paternal acres bound,
Content to breath his native air,
      In his own ground.

Whose herds with milk, whose fields with bread,
    Whose flocks supply him with attire,
Whose trees in summer yield him shade,
      In winter fire.

Blest, who can unconcern'dly find
    Hours, days, and years slide soft away,
In health of body, peace of mind,
      Quiet by day,

Sound sleep by night; study and ease,
    Together mixt; sweet recreation;
And Innocence, which most does please
      With meditation.

Thus let me live, unseen, unknown,
    Thus unlamented let me die,
Steal from the world, and not a stone
      Tell where I lie.

ALEXANDER POPE

IN EXILE

Now, my co-mates and brothers in exile,
Hath not old custom made this life more sweet
Than that of painted pomp? Are not these woods
More free from peril than the envious court?
Here feel we but the penalty of Adam,

The seasons' difference; as the icy fang
And churlish chiding of the winter's wind,
Which, when it bites and blows upon my body,
Even till I shrink with cold, I smile and say
'This is no flattery: these are counsellors
That feelingly persuade me what I am.'
Sweet are the uses of adversity,
Which like the toad, ugly and venomous,
Wears yet a precious jewel in his head;
And this our life, exempt from public haunt,
Finds tongues in trees, books in the running brooks,
Sermons in stones, and good in every thing.
I would not change it.

WILLIAM SHAKESPEARE
From *As You Like It*

SWEET CONTENT

Art thou poor, yet hast thou golden slumbers?
       O sweet content!
Art thou rich, yet is thy mind perplex'd?
       O punishment!
Dost thou laugh to see how fools are vex'd
To add to golden numbers golden numbers?
  O sweet content! O sweet, O sweet content!
Work apace, apace, apace, apace;
Honest labour bears a lovely face;
Then hey nonny nonny—hey nonny nonny!

Canst drink the waters of the crisped spring?
       O sweet content!
Swim'st thou in wealth, yet sink'st in thine own tears?
       O punishment!
Then he that patiently want's burden bears,
No burden bears, but is a king, a king!
  O sweet content! O sweet, O sweet content!

Work apace, apace, apace, apace;
Honest labour bears a lovely face;
Then hey nonny nonny—hey nonny nonny!

THOMAS DEKKER

UNDER THE GREENWOOD TREE

Under the greenwood tree
Who loves to lie with me,
And turn his merry note
Unto the sweet bird's throat,
Come hither, come hither, come hither:
Here shall he see
No enemy
But winter and rough weather.

Who doth ambition shun,
And loves to live i' the sun,
Seeking the food he eats,
And pleased with what he gets,
Come hither, come hither, come hither:
Here shall he see
No enemy
But winter and rough weather.

WILLIAM SHAKESPEARE
From As You Like It

JACK AND JOAN

Jack and Joan they think no ill,
But loving live, and merry still;
Do their week-day's work, and pray
Devoutly on the holy day:

Skip and trip it on the green,
And help to choose the Summer Queen;
Lash out, at a country feast,
Their silver penny with the best.

Well can they judge of nappy ale,
And tell at large a winter tale;
Climb up to the apple loft,
And turn the crabs till they be soft.
Tib is all the father's joy,
And little Tom the mother's boy.
All their pleasure is Content;
And care, to pay their yearly rent.

Joan can call by name her cows,
And deck her window with green boughs;
She can wreaths and tutties make,
And trim with plums a bridal cake.
Jack knows what brings gain or loss;
And his long flail can stoutly toss:
Makes the hedge, which others break;
And ever thinks what he doth speak.

Now, you courtly dames and knights,
That study only strange delights;
Though you scorn the homespun grey,
And revel in your rich array:
Though your tongues dissemble deep,
And can your heads from danger keep;
Yet, for all your pomp and train,
Securer lives the silly swain.

THOMAS CAMPION

THE VAGABOND

Give to me the life I love,
　Let the lave go by me,
Give the jolly heaven above
　And the byway nigh me.
Bed in the bush with stars to see,
　Bread I dip in the river—
There's the life for a man like me,
　There's the life for ever.

Let the blow fall soon or late,
　Let what will be o'er me;
Give the face of earth around
　And the road before me.
Wealth I seek not, hope nor love,
　Nor a friend to know me;
All I seek the heaven above
　And the road below me.

Or let autumn fall on me
　Where afield I linger,
Silencing the bird on tree,
　Biting the blue finger;
White as meal the frosty field—
　Warm the fireside haven—
Not to autumn will I yield,
　Not to winter even!

Let the blow fall soon or late,
　Let what will be o'er me;
Give the face of earth around,
　And the road before me.
Wealth I ask not, hope nor love,
　Nor a friend to know me;
All I ask the heaven above,
　And the road below me.

ROBERT LOUIS STEVENSON

UPON THE DOWNS

Upon the downs when shall I breathe at ease,
Have nothing else to do but what I please?
In a fresh cooling shade upon the brink
Of Arden's spring have time to read and think.
And stretch, and sleep, when all my care shall be
For health, and pleasure my philosophy?
When shall I rest from business, noise, and strife,
Lay down the soldier's and the courtier's life,
And in a little melancholy seat
Begin at last to live and to forget
The nonsense and the farce of what the fools call great?

SIR GEORGE ETHEREGE

DELIGHT IN DISORDER

A sweet disorder in the dress
Kindles in clothes a wantonness;
A lawn about the shoulders thrown
Into a fine distraction:
An erring lace, which here and there
Enthralls the crimson stomacher:
A cuff neglectful, and thereby
Ribbons to flow confusedly:
A winning wave (deserving note)
In the tempestuous petticoat:
A careless shoe-string, in whose tie
I see a wild civility:
Do more bewitch me, than when art
Is too precise in every part.

ROBERT HERRICK

A THANKSGIVING TO GOD, FOR
HIS HOUSE

Lord, Thou hast given me a cell
    Wherein to dwell,
A little house, whose humble roof
    Is weather-proof;
Under the spars of which I lie
    Both soft, and dry;
Where Thou my chamber for to ward
    Hast set a guard
Of harmless thoughts, to watch and keep
    Me, while I sleep.
Low is my porch, as is my fate,
    Both void of state;
And yet the threshold of my door
    Is worn by th' poor,
Who thither come, and freely get
    Good words, or meat:
Like as my parlour, so my hall
    And kitchen's small:
A little buttery, and therein
    A little bin,
Which keeps my little loaf of bread
    Unchipp'd, unflead:
Some brittle sticks of thorn or briar
    Make me a fire,
Close by whose living coal I sit,
    And glow like it.
Lord, I confess too, when I dine,
    The pulse is thine,
And all those other bits, that be
    There plac'd by thee;
The worts, the purslain, and the mess
    Of water-cress,

Which of Thy kindness Thou has sent;
    And my content
Makes those, and my beloved beet,
    To be more sweet.
'Tis Thou that crown'st my glittering hearth
    With guiltless mirth;
And giv'st me wassail bowls to drink,
    Spic'd to the brink.
Lord, 'tis Thy plenty-dropping hand,
    That soils my land;
And giv'st me, for my bushel sown,
    Twice ten for one:
Thou mak'st my teeming hen to lay
    Her egg each day:
Besides my healthful ewes to bear
    Me twins each year:
The while the conduits of my kine
    Run cream (for wine).
All these, and better Thou dost send
    Me, to this end,
That I should render, for my part,
    A thankful heart;
Which, fir'd with incense, I resign,
    As wholly Thine;
But the acceptance, that must be,
    My Christ, by Thee.

ROBERT HERRICK

THE SHELL

See what a lovely shell,
Small and pure as a pearl,
Lying close to my foot,
Frail, but a work divine,
Made so fairly well
With delicate spire and whorl,
How exquisitely minute,
A miracle of design!

What is it? a learned man
Could give it a clumsy name.
Let him name it who can,
The beauty would be the same.

The tiny cell is forlorn,
Void of the little living will
That made it stir on the shore.
Did he stand at the diamond door
Of his house in a rainbow frill?
Did he push, when he was uncurl'd,
A golden foot or fairy horn
Thro' his dim water-world?

Slight, to be crush'd with a tap
Of my finger-nail on the sand;
Small, but a work divine,
Frail, but of force to withstand,
Year upon year, the shock
Of cataract seas that snap
The three-decker's oaken spine
Athwart the ledges of rock,
Here on the Breton strand!

LORD TENNYSON

IMMANENCE

I come in the little things,
Saith the Lord:
Not borne on morning wings
Of majesty, but I have set My Feet
Amidst the delicate and bladed wheat
That springs triumphant in the furrowed sod.
There do I dwell, in weakness and in power;
Not broken or divided, saith our God!
In your strait garden plot I come to flower:
About your porch My Vine
Meek, fruitful, doth entwine;
Waits, at the threshold, Love's appointed hour.

I come in the little things,
Saith the Lord:
Yea! on the glancing wings
Of eager birds, the softly pattering feet
Of furred and gentle beasts, I come to meet
Your hard and wayward heart. In brown bright eyes
That peep from out the brake, I stand confest.
On every nest
Where feathery Patience is content to brood
And leaves her pleasure for the high emprize
Of motherhood—
There doth My Godhead rest.

I come in the little things,
Saith the Lord:
My starry wings
I do forsake,
Love's highway of humility to take:
Meekly I fit my stature to your need.
In beggar's part

About your gates I shall not cease to plead—
As man, to speak with man—
Till by such art
I shall achieve My Immemorial Plan,
Pass the low lintel of the human heart.

EVELYN UNDERHILL

HAPPY THOUGHT

The world is so full of a number of things,
I'm sure we should all be as happy as kings.

ROBERT LOUIS STEVENSON
From A Child's Garden of Verses

TO A DAISY

Slight as thou art, thou art enough to hide,
 Like all created things, secrets from me,
 And stand a barrier to eternity.
And I, how can I praise thee well and wide
From where I dwell—upon the hither side?
 Thou little veil for so great mystery,
 When shall I penetrate all things and thee,
And then look back? For this I must abide,

Till thou shalt grow and fold and be unfurled
Literally between me and the world.
 Then I shall drink from in beneath a spring,
And from a poet's side shall read his book.
O daisy mine, what will it be to look
 From God's side even on such a simple thing?

ALICE MEYNELL

THE CIGAR

Some sigh for this and that;
  My wishes don't go far;
The world may wag at will,
  So I have my cigar.

Some fret themselves to death
  With Whig and Tory jar,
I don't care which is in,
  So I have my cigar.

Sir John requests my vote,
  And so does Mr. Marr;
I don't care how it goes,
  So I have my cigar.

Some want a German row,
  Some wish a Russian war;
I care not—I'm at peace,
  So I have my cigar.

I never see the 'Post,'
  I seldom read the 'Star';
The 'Globe' I scarcely heed,
  So I have my cigar.

They tell me that Bank Stock
  Is sunk much under par;
It's all the same to me,
  So I have my cigar.

Honours have come to men
  My juniors at the Bar;
No matter—I can wait,
  So I have my cigar.

Ambition frets me not:
  A cab or glory's car
Are just the same to me,
  So I have my cigar.

I worship no vain gods,
  But serve the household Lar;
I'm sure to be at home,
  So I have my cigar.

I do not seek for fame,
  A General with a scar;
A private let me be,
  So I have my cigar.

To have my choice among
  The boys of life's bazaar,
The deuce may take them all,
  So I have my cigar.

Some minds are often tost
  By tempests like a tar;
I always seem in port,
  So I have my cigar.

The ardent flame of love
  My bosom cannot char,
I smoke, but do not burn,
  So I have my cigar.

THOMAS HOOD

THE GREAT LOVER

I have been so great a lover: filled my days
So proudly with the splendour of Love's praise,

The pain, the calm, and the astonishment,
Desire illimitable, and still content,
And all dear names men use, to cheat despair
For the perplexed and viewless streams that bear
Our hearts at random down the dark of life.
Now, ere the unthinking silence on that strife
Steals down, I would cheat drowsy Death so far,
My night shall be remembered for a star
That outshone all the suns of all men's days.
Shall I not crown them with immortal praise
Whom I have loved, who have given me, dared with me
High secrets, and in darkness knelt to see
The inenarrable godhead of delight?
Love is a flame:—we have beaconed the world's night.
A city:—and we have built, these and I.
An emperor:—we have taught the world to die.
So, for their sakes I loved, ere I go hence,
And the high cause of Love's magnificence,
And to keep loyalties young, I'll write those names
Golden for ever, eagles, crying flames,
And set them as a banner, that men may know,
To dare the generations, burn, and blow
Out on the wind of Time, shining and streaming . . .
These I have loved:

              White plates and cups, clean-gleaming,
Ringed with blue lines; and feathery, faery dust;
Wet roofs, beneath the lamp-light; the strong crust
Of friendly bread; and many-tasting food;
Rainbows; and the blue bitter smoke of wood;
And radiant raindrops couching in cool flowers;
And flowers themselves, that sway through sunny hours,
Dreaming of moths that drink them under the moon;
Then, the cool kindliness of sheets, that soon
Smooth away trouble; and the rough male kiss
Of blankets; grainy wood; live hair that is

Shining and free; blue-massing clouds; the keen
Unpassioned beauty of a great machine;
The benison of hot water; furs to touch;
The good smell of old clothes; and other such—
The comfortable smell of friendly fingers,
Hair's fragrance, and the musty reek that lingers
About dead leaves and last year's ferns . . .

        Dear names,
And thousand other throng to me! Royal flames;
Sweet water's dimpling laugh from tap or spring;
Holes in the ground; and voices that do sing;
Voices in laughter, too; and body's pain,
Soon turned to peace; and the deep-panting train;
Firm sands; the little dulling edge of foam
That browns and dwindles as the wave goes home;
And washen stones, gay for an hour; the cold
Graveness of iron; moist black earthen mould;
Sleep; and high places; footprints in the dew;
And oaks; and brown horse-chestnuts, glossy-new;
And new-peeled sticks; and shining pools on grass;—
All these have been my loves. And these shall pass,
Whatever passes not, in the great hour,
Nor all my passion, all my prayers, have power
To hold them with me through the gate of Death.
They'll play deserter, turn with the traitor breath,
Break the high bond we made, and sell Love's trust
And sacramented covenant to the dust.
—Oh, never a doubt but, somewhere, I shall wake,
And give what's left of love again, and make
New friends, now strangers. . . .

      But the best I've known,
Stays here, and changes, breaks, grows old, is blown
About the winds of the world, and fades from brains
Of living men, and dies.

    Nothing remains.

O dear my loves, O faithless, once again
This one last gift I give: that after men
Shall know, and later lovers, far-removed,
Praise you, 'All these were lovely'; say, 'He loved.'

RUPERT BROOKE

O GOD! METHINKS IT WERE A
HAPPY LIFE

O God! methinks it were a happy life,
To be no better than a homely swain;
To sit upon a hill, as I do now,
To carve out dials quaintly, point by point,
Thereby to see the minutes how they run,
How many make the hour full complete;
How many hours bring about the day;
How many days will finish up the year;
How many years a mortal man may live.
When this is known, then to divide the times:
So many hours must I tend my flock;
So many hours must I take my rest;
So many hours must I contemplate;
So many hours must I sport myself;
So many days my ewes have been with young;
So many weeks ere the poor fools will yean;
So many years ere I shall shear the fleece:
So minutes, hours, days, months, and years,
Pass'd over to the end they were created,
Would bring white hairs unto a quiet grave.
Ah! what a life were this; how sweet! how lovely!
Gives not the hawthorn-bush a sweeter shade
To shepherds looking on their silly sheep,
Than doth a rich embroider'd canopy
To kings that fear their subjects' treachery?
O yes! it doth; a thousand-fold it doth.

347

And to conclude, the shepherd's homely curds,
His cold thin drink out of his leather bottle,
His wonted sleep under a fresh tree's shade,
All which secure and sweetly he enjoys,
Is far beyond a prince's delicates,
His viands sparkling in a golden cup,
His body couched in a curious bed,
When care, mistrust, and treason waits on him.

WILLIAM SHAKESPEARE
From *The Third Part of King Henry the Sixth*

ECSTASY

I saw a frieze on whitest marble drawn
Of boys who sought for shells along the shore,
Their white feet shedding pallor in the sea,
The shallow sea, the spring-time sea of green
That faintly creamed against the cold, smooth pebbles.

The air was thin, their limbs were delicate,
The wind had graven their small eager hands
To feel the forests and the dark nights of Asia
Behind the purple bloom of the horizon,
Where sails would float and slowly melt away.

Their naked, pure, and grave unbroken silence
Filled the soft air as gleaming, limpid water
Fills a spring sky those days when rain is lying
In shattered bright pools on the wind-dried roads,
And their sweet bodies were wind-purified.

One held a shell unto his shell-like ear
And there was music carven in his face,
His eyes half-closed, his lips just breaking open

348

To catch the lulling, mazy, coralline roar
Of numberless caverns filled with singing seas,

And all of them were hearkening as to singing
Of far-off voices thin and delicate,
Voices too fine for any mortal wind
To blow into the whorls of mortal ears—
And yet those sounds flowed from their grave, sweet faces.

And as I looked I heard that delicate music,
And I became as grave, as calm, as still
As those carved boys. I stood upon that shore.
I felt the cool sea dream around my feet,
My eyes were staring at the far horizon:

And the wind came and purified my limbs,
And the stars came and set within my eyes,
And snowy clouds rested upon my shoulders,
And the blue sky shimmered deep within me,
And I sang like a carven pipe of music.

WALTER JAMES REDFERN TURNER

The Knowledge and Love of God

CHRIST

Christ is a path—if any be misled;
He is a robe—if any naked be;
If any chance to hunger—He is bread;
If any be a bondman—strong is He!

GILES FLETCHER

BATTER MY HEART

Batter my heart, three person'd God; for, you
As yet but knocke, breathe, shine, and seeke to mend;
That I may rise, and stand, o'erthrow mee, and bend
Your force, to breake, blowe, burn and make me new.
I, like an usurpt towne, to another due,
Labour to admit you, but Oh, to ne end,
Reason your viceroy in mee, mee should defend,
But is captiv'd, and proves weake or untrue.
Yet dearely I love you, and would be loved faine,
But am betroth'd unto your enemie:
Divorce mee, untie, or breake that knot againe,
Take mee to you, imprison mee, for I
Except you enthrall mee, never shall be free,
Nor ever chast, except you ravish mee.

JOHN DONNE

351

WHAT ART THOU, DEAREST LORD?

'What art Thou, dearest Lord, and what am I,
Vile worm and worthless dust?'
                                        He answered me.
On Holy Cross Day to my prayer there came
And Angel bearing in his rainbow wings
Nailed Hands and Feet, the Image of my Lord.
How can I tell it? The thing is sacred, dear,
O brothers mine, I give you all I can,
And yet I leave you but the husk of it,
The heart of it I selfish take away.
How can I tell? The thing is sacred, dear,—
Hands grew to hands, feet seemed to grow to feet,
His Hands to my hands, Feet of His to mine;
Exalted and extended on His cross,
I seemed in one great stab of eager pain
To feel His heart beating within my heart.

Brethren, this thing so sacred, and so dear,
I would that I could tell you, for it seems
Surely a sin to give God's poor my all,
And yet to keep Love's purest ingot back,
That fever-throb of His within my heart,
That moment's gold refined in sharpest fire,
And anguish of a crucifying world.

'What art Thou, dearest Lord, and what am I,
Vile worm and worthless servant?'
                                        Answer came,
I felt His Heart to beat within my heart.
It seemed He lent His Sacred Heart to me:
One moment did I know His wish, His work,
As if mine own they were, and knew with them
The worm-like weakness of my wasted life,

My service worthless to win back His world.
(Sharp Sister Faintness knits dark brows at me,
And o'er her shoulder looks sweet Sister Death,
Holding a glass my last hour's sands run down.)

I cannot tell the half of it, yet hear
What rush of feeling still comes back to me,
From that proud torture handing on His Cross,
From that gold rapture of His Heart in mine . . .

The thing is very sacred, very dear,
Sweet Jesu, help me tell them, how my heart
Swelled near to breaking with the Love of Thine,
That felt it all and Loved and Loved and Loved.
I felt the Sacred Heart within my own,
And knew one pulse therein of purest strength,
That drove a cry of passion to my lips,
'Father, forgive, they know not what they do.'
Could I but tell you how that cry seemed truth—
The truest prayer my lips had ever made—
I had told you almost all! It may not be.

O Heart of Jesus, Sacred, Passionate,
Anguish it was, yet anguish that was bliss,
To love them heart to heart, each selfish heart,
To clasp them close, and pray in utter truth—
'Father forgive, they know not what they do.'
One was the heart of him that ground the poor,
Poor weary heart, so blinded and misled!
One was the heart of her that reeked in shame,
Poor weary heart, so blinded and misled!
One was my heart that wasted half its years,
And knew so little how to use the rest
To God's sole glory, and the love of men,
Poor weary heart, so blinded and misled!

But O! that Sacred Heart rushed out to them
In veriest anguish and in veriest bliss,
Demanding, craving, in sure hope of them,
'Father, forgive, they know not what they do.'

And O! that Sacred Heart burnt up in Flame
Against that harsh misleader of our world,
And O! I felt an awful thrill of Love
As with one heart-beat of wild ecstasy
I set my heel upon that Serpent's head
In resolute anguish, watching how the fangs
Snapped at my heel, and gored it into blood,
My heel that yet shall grind his head to dust.
Was it I that did it? Nay, the Christ in me,
But when I woke His Prints were in my hands,
And in my feet, while in my side there showed
As it were the Heart-Wound from the soldier's lance.

ARTHUR SHEARLY CRIPPS
From *The Death of St. Francis*

HYMN

God moves in a mysterious way,
    His wonders to perform;
He plants his footsteps in the sea,
    And rides upon the storm.

Deep in unfathomable mines
    Of never failing skill,
He treasures up his bright designs,
    And works his sovereign will.

Ye fearful saints, fresh courage take.
    The clouds ye so much dread
Are big with mercy, and shall break
    In blessings on your head.

Judge not the Lord by feeble sense,
　　But trust him for his grace;
Behind a frowning providence,
　　He hides a smiling face.

His purposes will ripen fast,
　　Unfolding ev'ry hour;
The bud may have a bitter taste,
　　But sweet will be the flow'r.

Blind unbelief is sure to err,
　　And scan his work in vain;
God is his own interpreter,
　　And he will make it plain.

WILLIAM COWPER

ETERNALL GOD

Eternall God! O thou that onely art
　　The sacred Fountain of eternall light,
And blessed Loadstone of my better part,
　　O thou, my heart's desire, my soul's delight!
Reflect upon my soul, and touch my heart,
　　　　And then my heart shall prize no good above thee;
　　　　And then my soul shall know thee: knowing, love thee;
And then my trembling thoughts shall never start
　　From thy commands, or swerve the least degree,
Or once presume to move, but as they move in thee.

FRANCIS QUARLES
From The Unsettled Soul

SEE THE SOLE BLISS

See the sole bliss Heaven could on all bestow!
Which who but feels can taste, but thinks can know:

Yet poor with fortune, and with learning blind,
The bad must miss; the good, untaught, will find;
Slave to no sect, who takes no private road,
But looks through Nature up to Nature's God;
Pursues that chain which links the immense design,
Joins heaven and earth, and mortal and divine;
Sees, that no being any bliss can know,
But touches some above, and some below;
Learns from this union of the rising whole,
The first, last purpose of the human soul;
And knows where faith, law, morals, all began,
All end, in Love of God, and Love of Man.

ALEXANDER POPE
From *An Essay on Man*

THE HOUND OF HEAVEN

I fled Him, down the nights and down the days;
  I fled Him, down the arches of the years;
I fled Him, down the labyrinthine ways
  Of my own mind; and in the mist of tears
I hid from Him, and under running laughter.
      Up vistaed hopes I sped;
      And shot, precipitated,
Adown Titanic glooms of chasmed fears,
From those strong Feet that followed, followed after.
      But with unhurrying chase,
      And unperturbed pace,
      Deliberate speed, majestic instancy,
      They beat—and a Voice beat
      More instant than the Feet—
'All things betray thee, who betrayest Me.'

      I pleaded, outlaw-wise,
By many a hearted casement, curtained red,
  Trellised with intertwining charities

(For, though I knew His love Who followed,
      Yet was I sore adread
Lest, having Him, I must have naught beside);
But, if one little casement parted wide,
  The gust of His approach would clash it to.
Fear wist not to evade, as Love wist to pursue.
Across the margent of the world I fled,
   And troubled the gold gateways of the stars,
    Smiting for shelter on their changed bars;
        Fretted to dulcet jars
And silvern chatter the pale ports o' the moon.
I said to dawn, Be sudden; to eve, Be soon;
  With thy young skiey blossoms heap me over
      From this tremendous Lover!
Float thy vague veil about me, lest He see!
    I tempted all His servitors, but to find
My own betrayal in their constancy,
In faith to Him their fickleness to me,
  Their traitorous trueness, and their loyal deceit.
To all swift things for swiftness did I sue;
  Clung to the whistling mane of every wind,
    But whether they swept, smoothly fleet,
  The long savannahs of the blue;
    Or whether, thunder-driven,
They clanged his chariot 'thwart a heaven
Plashy with flying lightnings round the spurn o' their feet:—
  Fear wist not to evade as Love wist to pursue.
    Still with unhurrying chase,
    And unperturbed pace,
  Deliberate speed, majestic instancy,
   Came on the following Feet,
   And a Voice above their beat—
'Naught shelters thee, who wilt not shelter Me.'
    Spumed of the wild sea-snortings;
     All that's born or dies
    Rose and drooped with—made them shapers

Of mine own moods, or wailful or divine—
    With them joyed and was bereaven.
    I was heavy with the even,
    When she lit her glimmering tapers
    Round the day's dead sanctities.
    I laughed in the morning's eyes.
I triumphed and I saddened with all weather,
    Heaven and I wept together,
And its sweet tears were salt with mortal mine;
Against the red throb of its sunset-heart
    I laid my own to beat,
    And share commingling heat;
But not by that, by that, was eased my human smart.
In vain my tears were wet on Heaven's grey cheek.
For ah! we know not what each other says,
    These things and I; in sound I speak—
Their sound is but their stir, they speak by silences.
Nature, poor stepdame, cannot slake my drouth;
    Let her, if she would owe me,
Drop yon blue bosom-veil of sky, and show me
    The breasts o' her tenderness:
Never did any milk of hers once bless
    My thirsting mouth.
    Nigh and nigh draws the chase,
    With unperturbed pace,
I sought no more that after which I strayed
    In face of man or maid;
But still within the little children's eyes
    Seems something, something that replies;
They at least are for me, surely for me!
I turned me to them very wistfully;
But, just as their young eyes grew sudden fair
    With dawning answers there,
Their angel plucked them from me by the hair,
'Come then, ye other children, Nature's—share
With me' (said I) 'your delicate fellowship;

Let me greet you lip to lip,
Let me twine with you caresses,
 Wantoning
With our Lady-Mother's vagrant tresses,
 Banqueting
With her in her wind-walled palace,
Underneath her azured dais,
Quaffing, as your taintless way is,
 From a chalice
Lucent-weeping out of the dayspring.'
 So it was done:
I in their delicate fellowship was one—
Drew the bolt of Nature's secrecies,
I knew all the swift importings
 On the wilful face of skies;
 I knew how the clouds arise
Deliberate speed, majestic instancy;
 And past those noised Feet
 A voice comes yet more fleet—
'Lo! naught contents thee, who content'st not Me.'

Naked I wait Thy love's uplifted stroke!
My harness piece by piece Thou hast hewn from me,
 And smitten me to my knee;
 I am defenceless utterly.
 I slept, methinks, and woke,
And, slowly gazing, find me stripped in sleep.
In the rash lustihead of my young powers,
 I shook the pillaring hours
And pulled my life upon me; grimed with smears,
I stand amid the dust o' the mounded years—
My mangled youth lies dead beneath the heap.
My days have crackled and gone up in smoke,
Have puffed and burst as sun-starts on a stream.
 Yea, faileth now even dream
The dreamer, and the lute the lutanist;

Even the linked fantasies, in whose blossomy twist
I swung the earth a trinket at my wrist,
Are yielding; cords of all too weak account
For earth with heavy griefs so overplussed.
       Ah! is Thy love indeed
A weed, albeit an amaranthine weed,
Suffering no flowers except its own to mount?
        Ah! must—
        Designer infinite!—
Ah! must Thou char the wood ere Thou canst limn with
        it?
My freshness spent its wavering shower i' the dust;
And now my heart is as a broken fount,
Wherein tear-droppings stagnate, spilt down ever
      From the dank thoughts that shiver
Upon the sighful branches of my mind.
      Such is; what is to be?
The pulp so bitter, how shall taste the rind?
I dimly guess what Time in mists confounds;
Yet ever and anon a trumpet sounds
From the hid battlements of Eternity;
Those shaken mists a space unsettle, then
Round the half-glimpsed turrets slowly wash again.
      But not ere him who summoneth
      I first have seen, enwound
With glooming robes purpureal, cypress-crowned;
His name I know, and what his trumpet saith.
Whether man's heart or life it be which yields
      Thee harvest, must Thy harvest fields
      Be dunged with rotten death?
      Now of that long pursuit
      Comes on at hand the bruit;
That Voice is round me like a bursting sea:
      'And is thy earth so marred,
      Shattered in shard on shard?
Lo, all things fly thee, for thou fliest Me?

Strange, piteous, futile thing!
Wherefore should any set thee love apart?
Seeing none but I makes much of naught'
   (He said)
 'And human love needs human meriting:
   How hast thou merited—
Of all man's clotted clay the dingiest clot?
  Alack, thou knowest not
How little worthy of any love thou art!
Whom wilt thou find to love ignoble thee
  Save Me, save only Me?
All which I took from thee I did but take,
   Not for thy harms,
But just that thou might'st seek it in My arms.
  All which thy child's mistake
Fancies as lost, I have stored for thee at home;
  Rise, clasp My hand, and come!'

  Halts by me that footfall:
   Is my gloom, after all,
 Shade of His hand, outstretched caressingly?
  'Ah, fondest, blindest, weakest,
   I am He whom thou seekest!
Thou dravest love from thee, who dravest Me.'

FRANCIS THOMPSON

DESIRE

 The desire of love, Joy:
 The desire of life, Peace:
 The desire of the soul, Heaven:
 The desire of God . . . a flame-white secret for ever.

WILLIAM SHARP

THE SPIRIT OF CATHOLICISM

Therefore we love our Church in spite of, nay just because of, her poor outward appearance. The Catholic affirms the Church just as it is. For in its actual form the Church is to him the revelation of the divine Holiness, Justice and Goodness. The Catholic does not desire some ideal Church, a Church of the philosopher or the poet. Though his mother be travel stained with long journeying, though her countenance be furrowed with care and trouble—yet, she is his mother. In her heart burns the ancient love. Out of her eyes shines the ancient faith. From her hands flow ever the ancient blessings. What would heaven be without God? What would the earth be without the Church? I believe in one Holy Catholic and Apostolic Church.

KARL ADAM
The Spirit of Catholicism

COLLECT

Almighty God, unto whom all hearts be open, all desires known, and from whom no secrets are hid; Cleanse the thoughts of our hearts by the inspiration of thy Holy Spirit, that we may perfectly love thee, and worthily magnify thy Holy Name; through Christ our Lord. *Amen.*

The Book of Common Prayer

THANKSGIVING

Almighty God, Father of all mercies, we thine unworthy servants do give thee most humble and hearty thanks for all thy goodness and loving-kindness to us, and to all men. We bless thee for our creation, preservation, and all the blessings of this life; but above all, for thine inestimable love in the redemption of the world by our Lord Jesus Christ; for the means of grace, and for the hope of glory. And, we beseech thee, give us that due sense of all thy mercies, that our hearts may be unfeignedly thankful, and that we shew forth thy praise, not only with our lips, but in our lives; by giving up ourselves to thy service, and by walking before thee in holiness and righteousness all our days; through Jesus Christ our Lord, to whom with thee and the Holy Ghost be all honour and glory, world without end. *Amen.*

The Book of Common Prayer

INDEX OF AUTHORS

INDEX OF FIRST LINES

INDEX OF PROSE